D1491855

3 3012 00065 5104

Political Economies of Landscape Change

The GeoJournal Library

Volume 89

The titles published in this series are listed at the end of this volume.

Political Economies of Landscape Change

Places of Integrative Power

Edited by

JAMES L. WESCOAT, JR.
Department of Landscape Architecture,
University of Illinois at Urbana-Champaign,
Champaign, IL, U.S.A.

and

DOUGLAS M. JOHNSTON
Department of Landscape Architecture and
Department of Community and Regional Planning,
Iowa State University,
Ames, IA, U.S.A.

 Springer

A C.I.P. Catalogue record for this book is available from the Library of Congress.

ISBN 978-1-4020-5848-6 (HB)
ISBN 978-1-4020-5849-3 (e-book)

Published by Springer,
P.O. Box 17, 3300 AA Dordrecht, The Netherlands.

www.springer.com

Printed on acid-free paper

Acknowledgments

The Landscape Architecture Foundation
Brenton and Jean Wadsworth Endowment
Graham Foundation for Advanced Studies
in the Arts
Illinois Chapter of the American Society of
Landscape Architects
University of Illinois at Urbana-Champaign,
Department of Landscape Architecture

Preface

This volume contributes to the *Landscape Futures Initiative* conceived by the Landscape Architecture Foundation at the start of the 21st century. In this period of millennial exploration the *Landscape Futures Initiative* seeks a long-term perspective on driving forces of landscape change – forces that will determine the survival of many and the experience of all – in this case the forces of political economy.

We invited a diverse group of designers and scholars to think broadly about how political and economic processes shape the landscapes in which they occur, and on which they operate. We also charged this group to consider how processes of landscape change affect politics and economics from the local to global scales. The contributors responded with approaches that involved a dialectical examination of political economy and landscape change. They raised major pragmatic questions: What difference can design make, if any, in a globalizing world? Partially in response to that question, some asked what a socially just landscape could "look like". Others presented partial answers to both questions, which stimulated further questioning.

The broader *Landscape Futures Initiative* selected a mix of familiar and imaginative topics for investigation. An initial gathering at the University of Pennsylvania focused on processes of global urbanization that encompass half of the world's population and may add a billion more people in the coming decades. A symposium at the University of Virginia then explored linkages between technology and culture, from the microbiology of brownfield remediation to satellite-guided precision excavation. The symposium series proceeded to examine "connectivity," "global urban and environmental change," "demographic change," and "leadership" at the University of Texas, Arizona State University, the University of California–Davis, and Clemson University, respectively.

This volume focuses on political and economic driving forces of landscape change and associated "places of power." Before launching into the topic, we want to make a few points about the spirit that has guided this project and those who have supported it. From its beginning, the *Places of Integrative Power* project sought a dialogue among social scientists, environmental planners, and designers. We embraced a broad spectrum of topics – from real estate development to environmental economics, institutional analysis, and radical politics. We drew inspiration from international as well as US experience. We convened the "high theory" of landscape scholars with the "high practice" of landscape architects. The spirited dialogue among these contributors constitutes one of the most gratifying aspects of the project.

The overarching theme of places of integrative power comes from Kenneth Boulding's *Three Faces of Power*, which linked political power, economic power, and what he called integrative power – the power of love – of people, place, and planet. When we write about places of power, we draw inspiration from Boulding's hopeful spirit alongside those who courageously expose political and economic disasters. We acknowledge the debt to Kenneth and his wife Elise Boulding who wrote persuasively about integrative power as the hidden side of history that has enormous transformative potential. Geographer Gilbert F. White showed how integrative inquiry broadens the range of choice for harmonizing human–environment relations and coping with hazards. Landscape architecture professor Robert "Doc" Reich exemplifies these ideals in a life devoted to cultivating the progressive power of design in thousands of students, treating each one as a creative individual. We dedicate this volume to these four visionaries.

Each chapter involves authors who share their visionary perspectives on landscape change. Before introducing them, we want to thank those who brought this project to fruition. The Landscape Architecture Foundation provided substantial funding, and its executive director Susan Everett gave sustained encouragement. Support for the entire conference series came from the National Endowment for the Arts, the Hideo Sasaki Foundation, and EDAW, Inc. The Brenton and Jean Wadsworth Endowment in the Department of Landscape Architecture co-funded the *Places of Integrative Power* conference. Brent Wadsworth's commitment to landscape architectural research that makes a difference for social well-being has enhanced the landscape architecture program at Illinois. Kathleen Conlin, former dean of the College of Fine and Applied Arts at the University of Illinois at Urbana-Champaign, supported us in launching the project. The Graham Foundation for Advanced Study in the Arts in Chicago personally supported this publication, and we pay tribute to its late director Richard Jay Solomon who encouraged this work. The Illinois Chapter of the American Society of Landscape Architects and its former officers Jay Womack and Brian Hopkins gave institutional, financial, and personal support. We are grateful to leaders in the landscape architecture profession in Illinois such as Debra Mitchell of JJR, Inc.; William Quinlan of Landscape Forms, Inc.; and Richard Hitchcock of Hitchcock Design Group – all from metropolitan Chicago – for their personal and financial support.

Chicago constitutes one of the great laboratories of political economy and landscape change from its initial settlement by the Creole trader Jean-Baptiste Point du Sable in the 1770s at the outlet of the Chicago River into Lake Michigan, to the current renewed investment in public parks, urban landscape design, and ecosystem restoration. The chapters of this volume were delivered in conjunction with a series of walks and talks across downtown Chicago – our transect began at the University of Illinois at Chicago, a modern campus designed by Walter Knetsch and backed by former Mayor Richard J. Daley in the 1960s, which displaced part of an Italian–American neighborhood in the near west side. This neighborhood walk took the group through a rapidly gentrifying neighborhood, across the once-notoriously polluted south branch of the Chicago River through the downtown Loop with its architectural masterpieces and expanding complement of urban landscape design projects. On the second day of the conference the group reconvened in the Art Institute of Chicago, in Adler and Sullivan's reconstructed Stock Exchange Room, before concluding with a walk through the newly opened Millennium Park with its extraordinary combination of public and privately commissioned sculpture and environmental design.

We especially thank our authors who joined in spirited debate, striving to communicate across political as well as professional boundaries. Although not printed here, comments on chapters by discussants thoughtfully stimulated those debates. We take this opportunity to thank discussants Robert Bruegmann of the University of Illinois at Chicago, Frederick Steiner of the University of Texas at Austin, George Ranney of Metropolis 2020, Debra Mitchell of JJR, Inc., Paul Gobster of the US Forest Service, and Dianne Harris and Chris Silver of the University of Illinois at Urbana-Champaign.

Political economies of landscape change enabled this group of scholars and friends to gather in Chicago in the early 21st century, and inspired us to collaborate on this study across continents and oceans. We look forward toward future places of integrative power that will expand this friendly dialogue among people, places, and ecosystems of the world.

Champaign, IL, 2007   Jim Wescoat and Doug Johnston

Kenneth Boulding
[Kenneth Abbot/UC-B]

Elise Boulding
[Kenneth Abbot/UC-B]

Gilbert F. White
[Kenneth Abbot/UC-B]

Robert S. Reich
[Jim Zietz/LSU]

Contents

Contributors

Terry L. Babcock-Lumish is a Research Associate at the Oxford Centre for the Environment, an Associate Fellow at the Rothermere American Institute, a Wertheim Fellow in the Labor & Worklife Program at Harvard Law School, and a Visiting Scholar at the University of Arizona. Previously, Babcock-Lumish worked as a researcher for former Vice President Al Gore and as an economist in President Clinton's Council of Economic Advisers. She has also served in various capacities for the United States Department of Agriculture, the Department of the Treasury, and Indiana Governor O'Bannon's Children's Environmental Initiative. As President of Islay Consulting LLC, an economic, policy, and political consulting firm, she specializes in helping organizations make complex decisions under high degrees of risk and uncertainty.

Anthony J. Bebbington is Professor of Nature, Society, and Development at the Institute of Development Policy and Management at Manchester University, UK. His research focuses on: rural development and rural livelihoods; nongovernmental organizations; social movements and indigenous organizations; policy processes within development bureaucracies; the political ecology of extractive industries; and the World Bank. He has conducted field research in Peru, Bolivia, Ecuador, Colombia, Chile, Nicaragua, Guatemala, Costa Rica, Indonesia, Nepal, Uganda, Sierra Leone. He has held fellowships with the Centre for Advanced Studies in the Behavioral Sciences (Stanford) and the Food and Agricultural Organizations visiting positions at the World Bank and the Peruvian Centre for Social Studies (Lima), and is currently an Economic and Social Research Council Professorial Fellow. Among his many publications is a coedited issue of ECUMENE on *Transnational livelihoods and landscapes: political ecologies of globalization*.

John B. Braden is Professor of Environmental Economics at the University of Illinois at Urbana-Champaign, where he has been on the faculty for 25 years. His work emphasizes policy and management issues surrounding the protection and remediation of water quality, most recently studies of the downstream economic consequences of conservation design practices and of remediating contamination in the Great Lakes. He was educated at Miami University of Ohio and the University of Wisconsin.

Gordon L. Clark is Halford Mackinder Professor and Head of the Oxford University Centre for the Environment, and he has previously taught at Harvard University, the University of Chicago, and Carnegie Mellon University. Professor Clark's research has focused, in part upon pension fund investment in Australia, the UK, and the USA as it relates to urban and regional economic development. This work involved collaboration with a number of foundations, consulting firms, banks, and major pension fund managers about the prospects for private pension fund investment in public infrastructure. *Pension Fund Capitalism* (OUP 2000) was the result of this work; more recently, he has been involved in a long-term project funded by the Ford and Rockefeller foundations on US public sector pension fund investment strategies (with Tessa Hebb and Lisa Hagerman at Harvard Law School). His current research combines economic geography with global finance and includes corporate governance, finance markets, pensions and environmental regulation. While at the University of Chicago he published *Judges and the Cities* based in part on experience as an expert witness in land use and zoning cases in Chicago.

Susan E. Clarke is Professor of Political Science at the University of Colorado at Boulder, Colorado, USA. She is active in research, teaching, and governance roles in political science: in addition to numerous publications on local economic development, cross-border regionalism, and local politics, she recently coauthored *The Work of Cities* and *Multiethnic Moments: The Politics of Urban Education Reform* and currently is Editor of Urban Affairs Review. Her research has been supported by the National Science Foundation, the Carnegie Foundation, the Fulbright Foundation, the Canadian government, the Annie E. Casey Foundation, the National League of Cities, and others. In addition to her faculty responsibilities, she also serves as Director of the Center to Advance Research and Teaching in the Social Sciences (CARTSS), a campus-wide interdisciplinary program at CU.

Kurt Culbertson is Chairman and CEO of the landscape architecture/land planning firm Design Workshop. Kurt Culbertson has been instrumental in the company's success, nationally and internationally. His leadership role in the Master Planning process for Missoula Riverfront Triangle in Missoula, Montana, and the planning and design efforts for the Gates Redevelopment in Denver, Colorado, is redefining land use trends in the West. Culbertson has initiated the creation of a model "sustainable development", a community that promotes stability between both the physical and social systems. A strong proponent of the profession, Kurt has been published numerous times, spoken to organizations throughout the country, and participated in community activities.

Tom Evans codirects the Center for the Study of Institutions, Population and Environmental Change (CIPEC) and is an Associate Professor in the Department of Geography at Indiana University. His research focuses on household land-use decision-making and land cover change utilizing GIS, remote sensing and modeling methods. Previous project research (NSF SES008351) has employed agent-based models of land cover change to explore the dynamics of deforestation and forest regrowth in the Midwest USA and the Brazilian Amazon. His most recent research explores the interaction between households, NGOs and government actors in forest regrowth in Indiana (USA) and the state of Sao Paulo, Brazil.

Douglas M. Johnston is Professor and Chair of the Departments of Landscape Architecture and Community and Regional Planning at Iowa State University. Previously, he held multiple appointments as Professor in Landscape Architecture, Senior Research Scientist for the National Center for Supercomputing Applications as well as an Affiliate Professor with Urban and Regional Planning and Adjunct Professor with Geography at the University of Illinois at Urbana-Champaign, where he directed the Geographic Modeling Systems Lab. His research is in land resource planning, geographic information systems, environmental systems analysis, decision analysis, water resources management, and computer applications.

Don Mitchell is Distinguished Professor and Chair of the Geography Department in the Maxwell School at Syracuse University. After receiving his Ph.D. in Geography from Rutgers University in 1992, he taught at the University of Colorado before moving to Syracuse. He is the author of *The Lie of the Land: Migrant Workers and the California Landscape* (1996); *Cultural Geography: A Critical Introduction* (2000); and *The Right to the City: Social Justice and the Fight for Public Space* (2003) as well as numerous articles on the geography of homelessness, labor, urban public space, and contemporary theories of culture. With Lynn Staeheli he is the author of the forthcoming book, *The People's Property? Power, Politics and the Public*. Mitchell is a recipient of a MacArthur Fellowship and recently held a Fulbright Fellowship in the Institutt for Sociologi and Samfunnsgeografi at the Universitetet i Oslo. He is the founder and director of the People's Geography Project (www.peoplesgeography.org).

Joan Iverson Nassauer is Professor of Landscape Architecture in the School of Natural Resources and Environment at the University of Michigan. A Fellow of the American Society of Landscape Architects and a Distinguished Practitioner of Landscape Ecology, she specializes in the relationship between landscape ecology and public perceptions of ecological design and planning. Her work on design and planning to enhance water quality and biodiversity in agricultural and metropolitan landscapes has appeared in *Conservation Biology, Journal of Soil and Water Conservation, Landscape Ecology, Landscape Journal, Landscape and Urban Planning, Wetlands*, and other journals, and her book *From the Corn Belt to the Gulf: Environmental and Societal Implications of Alternative Agricultural Futures* (2007) examines the effects of American agricultural policy on rural landscapes.

Elinor Ostrom codirects the *Workshop in Political Theory and Policy Analysis* at Indiana University. She is interested in exploring how institutional rules affect the structure of action situations within which individuals face incentives, make choices, and jointly affect each other. Problems involving collective goods and common-pool resource systems, and how various types of institutions enhance or detract from the capabilities of individuals to achieve equitable, workable, efficient solutions are a central theoretical concern. In urban settings she has been interested in the problems of collective action where citizens face problems of crime, poor education, and deteriorating environmental conditions. She is also interested in the same problems as they relate to resource problems in the Third World, particularly problems of collective action related to forests, fisheries, grazing areas, agricultural lands, and water systems. A major study of institutions and forests is being initiated as part of an effort to study the interrelationships between local and global commons. Professor Ostrom is currently working with colleagues in several tropical countries to investigate the impacts of diverse institutional arrangements on forest conditions and on global environmental change.

Dirk Wascher is Senior Researcher at the Alterra Institute in Wageningen, The Netherlands. As coordinator of the research network LANDSCAPE EUROPE and of international projects on issues such multifunctional land use, landscape character assessment and sustainability impact assessment (SENSOR), he recently edited the reports *European Landscape Character Areas* (2005) and *The Face of Europe* (2000); He is also lead-author of the contribution on cultural heritage and landscapes for the Millennium Assessment (UNEP, WRI) and coeditor of the Journal for Nature Conservation, published by Elsevier. In 2006, Mr. Wascher taught "Landscape Analysis and Planning" at the University of Michigan.

James L. Wescoat Jr. is Professor and Head of the Department of Landscape Architecture, University of Illinois at Urbana-Champaign. He has published on waterworks of the Mughal gardens of South Asia, water resources in the USA and internationally, and the human dimensions of global environmental change. In addition to the USA, he has conducted research in India, Pakistan, Turkmenistan, Uzbekistan, and Bangladesh. He has received fellowships and grants from the American Academy in Rome, Dumbarton Oaks, National Science Foundation, Phi Beta Kappa Society, and Smithsonian Institution. He has recently coauthored *Water for Life: Water Management and Environmental Policy* (Cambridge 2003) with geographer Gilbert F. White.

Abigail York is Assistant Professor of Urban Administration in the Henry W. Bloch School of Business and Public Administration at the University of Missouri-Kansas City. Her previous research evaluated zoning's effect on peri-urban development, land cover fragmentation, and community politics using econometrics, institutional analysis, computational modeling, and game theory. York has worked on several projects with the Center for the Study of Institutions, Population and Environmental Change (CIPEC) at Indiana University including an agent-based model of land use, evaluation of federal, state, and nongovernment forestry policy, and analysis of the legal mechanisms for cooperative land management.

Introduction

Three Faces of Power in Landscape Change

James L. Wescoat, Jr.

This chapter presents a conceptual perspective on political economies of landscape change. It begins with vignettes from metropolitan Chicago, and shows how those examples rapidly spin out to linkages and comparisons with other regions of the world. The first section surveys academic fields related to political economies of landscape change. While each of these fields makes important contributions, their literatures reveal surprisingly few concrete connections between landscape inquiry and social research on politics and economics. Surprising, because landscape planners and designers deal with "politics" and "economics" every day on every project. The second section thus develops a conceptual approach for bridging these gaps by adapting futurist Kenneth Boulding's *Three Faces of Power*, which links political and economic power with a third face that Boulding calls integrative power – the enabling force of human respect, wisdom and love. The main thesis in this volume is that integrative power is the inherent aim of landscape inquiry, planning, and design. This conceptual framework seeks a deeper understanding of relationships between political economy and landscape change. Along with the chapters and case studies that follow, it reveals just how much needs to be done to attain the integrative power of landscape change in the 21st century. And finally, we introduce the substantive chapters, each of which sheds new light on political economies of landscape change and the prospects for progressive places of power.

A Metropolitan Landscape Prelude

At the turn of the present century, the City of Chicago completed an extraordinary phase of urban landscape design under the direction of Mayor Richard M. Daley. Daley's personal commitment to urban landscape design helped transform Chicago's streets, boulevards, parks, and lakefront. Like the medieval ruler of Baghdad, Harun al-Rashid (ca.764–809 CE) who reportedly traveled through the city in disguise to observe conditions and hear citizens' concerns, modern legend has it that Daley bicycles through Chicago to direct city workers' attention to neglected streets, parks, and playgrounds. Vibrant new plantings arose in medians, sidewalks, and highway rights-of-way in Chicago. At the same time, leaders in

J.L. Wescoat, Jr. and D.M. Johnston (eds.), *Political Economies of Landscape Change.*
© Springer 2008

modern Baghdad struggle to deal with civil strife and provide even the most basic economic needs of safe water, sanitation, shelter, and livelihoods. Early warnings of these hazards of war from activists like Chicagoan Kathy Kelly of Voices in the Wilderness went unheeded, and her civil disobedience was punished with a prison sentence in Illinois. What questions does the history of medieval and modern Baghdad raise for landscapes and landscape architects in US centers like Chicago decades or centuries in the future?

Like leaders past and present, Mayor Daley traveled abroad comparing Chicago with other cities, mainly in Europe, emulating their green roofs, parks, porous paving, and landscape architecture in ways that complement the city's renowned buildings. Daley helped organize a Council of Great Lakes Mayors to address common waterfront resources, problems, and development opportunities in the USA and Canada. These actions entailed a strong vision of what the City of Chicago could become, "the greenest city," and Daley has concentrated some of Chicago's political and economic power on that aim (Hudson 2006; Kamin 2001; Waldheim and Ray 2006).

This vision drew inspiration in part from Chicago's natural and environmental history (Greenberg 2002). Whereas previous generations had filled and drained the wet prairies, the new urban design movement disconnected downspouts, created rain gardens, and reconstructed wetlands. Whereas the elder Mayor Daley had proposed to build a new airport in Lake Michigan, his son tore out the old Meigs Airfield on the lakefront. On the night of March 30, 2003, the younger Mayor Daley ordered city bulldozers to tear up the runways, ending a decade-long delay in its redesign as an ecological park by political fiat, justified in part as a post-9/11 security precaution. Over the same decade, Daley has endorsed thousands of tree plantings, roof gardens, green buildings, permeable surface pavements, and protective measures for birds and their habitats with the aim of increasing air quality, water quality, energy savings, and urban beauty – and advancing Chicago's vision of becoming the "greenest" city in the USA. These initiatives involved creative staffing of the city departments of Environment, Planning and Development, as well as the Chicago Park District. They leveraged funds from private as well as federal, state, city, and park district coffers – amassing the largest portfolio of urban landscape design projects in Chicago's history.

Millennium Park stands as the jewel in this urban landscape crown. Initiated by the rediscovery of public development rights over the downtown terminus of the Illinois Central Railway, Millennium Park evolved from a conventional Beaux Arts upgrading of the existing Grant Park into an innovative assemblage of public sculpture, performance spaces, and contemporary garden design. The financing that ultimately produced Millennium Park likewise evolved from a limited public budget to redoubled private funding of personally and corporately branded artistic works and park spaces (Gilfoyle 2006).

Private capital has played a key role in Chicago's recent landscape change as it has in past eras (Bluestone 1992, Hudson 2006). As manufacturing jobs hemorrhaged from the industrial corridors of the city, new investment poured into thousands of upscale condominium and town house complexes that extended the central business district "Loop" 20 blocks south and west (Wille 1998). New homes on the notorious Bubbly Creek, named for its putrid stockyard heritage, had million dollar price tags. The "greening" of Chicago is thus as much or more a political-economic as it is a cultural and ecological phenomenon. Could these trends extend another 20 or 100 blocks, across existing African-American and Hispanic communities; and beyond the outer boundaries of the city into the suburbs and exurbs?

The answer in the early 2000s, it seemed, was yes. Nonprofit and private sectors helped fuel and shape Chicago's green building phase. Environmental advocacy groups flourished from the neighborhood to regional scales. Over 100 environmental organizations gathered under the institutional umbrella of *Chicago Wilderness*. Urban environmental histories were written and updated (Cronon 1991; Greenberg, 2002). The Chicago Christian Industrial League (2004) trained low income and homeless workers for new landscape maintenance positions.

Residential landscape design, especially in the affluent northern suburbs expanded with skyrocketing real estate prices. Landscape architecture firms of all types grew with the advent of professional licensing, the downsizing of public agency design departments, the real estate boom, and the increasing number of public commissions for schools, parks, and transportation systems.

Much was accomplished at the turn of the present century, but for many reasons, not the least of which was the national "War on Terror," public infrastructure funding began to wither. In addition to constructing steel-core security bollards and surveillance cameras, local governments faced increasing emergency preparedness costs. Ironically, while September 11 helped justify the destruction of Meigs airfield, the political economy of "security" overtook some of the city's sustainable design agenda (with some inspiring security plantings, as at the General Services Administration building). Fiscal deficits led to reduced capital budgets and early retirement of senior City and Chicago Park District staff. Enlistment of massive private financial support did more than rescue Millennium Park on Chicago's downtown lakefront – it redefined the direction of urban park design. Structural decline of public finance has continued at federal, state, and local levels, which raised questions about the prospects for public–private financing in other areas of urban need (e.g., public schools). Chicago sought to plug its fiscal deficit in part with gambling licenses while the State of Illinois deferred pension contributions and increased cigarette taxes. Regional planning and transportation agencies struggled over shrinking resources. Neither could hope to draw as they had in the 1990s on federal funds for transportation, environmental protection, and housing investments, as those funds went toward financing wars in Afghanistan and Iraq, tax cuts, and disaster relief at home.

Some business leaders began to make derisive comments about cosmetic investment in planter boxes, while community and social service groups cried out for budget reallocation to failing public schools. A severe drought in 2005 required a shift from urban tree planting to emergency water sprinkling to keep the city's existing tree plantings alive. Ironically, trucks, and waterworks intersected in other ways as Federal prosecutors penetrated city patronage networks, from bagmen to bosses. The city has bid for the Olympic Games, in part with a proposal to locate a huge temporary stadium in the middle of historic Washington Park. By late 2007, it seemed Chicago would have to work mightily to maintain its landscape heritage and innovations of previous decades.

This brilliant, yet tenuous, chapter in Chicago landscape architectural history inspires our volume on political economies of landscape change. Every street tree, park, and city scene has remarkable stories to tell about the financial and political forces that shaped them. Chicago's landscape embodies intense economic and political struggles, as witnessed in historic debates about the Columbian Exposition, lakefront protection, skyscraper construction, urban renewal, and privatization. The urban landscape has persistent anomalies, like the long-vacant Block 37 in the middle of the Loop central business district (Miller 2003). It has had political showdowns that include the multiple firings and rehiring of leading 20th century landscape architects such as Jens Jensen and Alfred Caldwell (Grese 1992; Domer 1997; cf. Cranz 1982).

But the literature on design politics has had little connection with the larger literatures on urban politics, economics and, more broadly, political economic research. Chicago for example has provided important yet largely separate laboratories for social inquiry and environmental design from the early 20th century to the present. There are many significant yet partial exceptions. From the early physical *Plan of Chicago* by Daniel Burnham to mid-20th century land-rent models of urban economic development and human ecological studies of *The Gold Coast* and *The Slum*, Chicago has been a place of innovative human-ecological research. It has influenced exurban parklands like the Indiana Dunes, which linked political and landscape design movements in opposition to corporate steel and port development

(Engel 1983). It has fueled and exploited its regional economic hinterlands for raw materials and manufactured goods (Cronon 1991).

Chicago Metropolis 2020 has carried Burnham's vision into the 21st century (Johnson 2001; Ranney 2004). Landscape architect Philip Lewis (1996) has envisioned even larger regional constellations of interurban road, rail, ecological, and cultural corridors to link Chicago with other Midwestern cities. The Regional Economic Applications Laboratory (REAL) at the University of Illinois at Urbana-Champaign has shown that regional trade and investment centered in Chicago is greater in magnitude than that between the USA and Mexico under the North American Free Trade Agreement (NAFTA) (Seo et al. 2004). Everyone knows Burnham's (1909 [1993]) famous quote associated with the *Plan of Chicago* to, "make no small plans; they lack the power to stir men's blood," but how much do we know about how the relationships between plans and powers stir the blood, and whose blood they stir?

Beyond Chicago

Chicago's stories about the political economy of landscape change have their counterparts and connections in many if not in most places around the world. A small sample of contemporary projects that link environment, politics, and landscape change in the USA, Europe, and other regions of the world follows.

Economic and environmental infrastructure. In Boston, the Central Artery – Third Harbor Tunnel – known as the "Big Dig" – is the largest and most contested transportation design project in the nation's history with an important landscape component (Ahern 1999, p. 21). Declining manufacturing in most US and European cities has resulted in abandoned, often toxic, industrial sites that in some exemplary cases are becoming the focus of environmental justice movements, and brownfield remediation projects (Kirkwood 2001). The industrial Ruhr Valley in Germany is undergoing a transformation in places such as the Emscher Park that includes an industrial-recreational park designed by Peter Latz at Duisberg-Nord.

Political commemoration in the landscape. In New York, the "Ground Zero site" of September 11, 2001 is transforming the landscape of lower Manhattan and creating new landscapes of security and fear in much of the USA and Europe – as well as in the landscapes of war in Afghanistan and Iraq (Goldberger 2004). Washington DC is receiving a seemingly endless series of political memorials and commemorative landscapes (Wolschke-Bulmahn 1997, 2001). Around the same time, landscape conservation of Independence Mall in downtown Philadelphia sponsored by the US National Park Service hit "foundation" problems related to security issues and discovery of slave quarters at the former site of the President's house (Ulam 2006).

Community-based design. Across town, the University of Pennsylvania's West Philadelphia Landscape Project is linking streetscape improvements, community gardens, neighborhood development, and floodplain restoration through studio design and education programs in low-income African-American neighborhoods (Spirn 1998, 2005). A comparable East St. Louis Action Research Project

(ESLARP) led by the University of Illinois at Urbana-Champaign has sustained two decades of neighborhood improvement projects in the face of structural impoverishment and governance problems (Lawson 2004). In the San Francisco Bay area, a decades-long commitment to community-based design has shaped public spaces and regional parks (Hester 2006; Hester and Kweskin 1999; Linn and Anthony 1988). Immigration from Latin America is transforming the labor force of state and national landscape construction industries.

International design practice. On a larger scale, political rapprochement with China is opening urban landscape design markets and Pacific Rim landscape studies that would have been unimaginable a decade earlier (Prentice 1998; Yu and Padua 2006). Global demand for structural steel and energy in China, Brazil, and the Middle East is driving up global construction costs and affecting design decisions worldwide. Some leading US design firms report that as much as a third of their current work is in China. Others are pursuing new landscape development and design markets in South America and the Middle East. At the same time, many regions of the world are "off the map" of contemporary landscape architecture. In 2007, the International Federation of Landscape Architects (IFLA) had only 58 member associations of over 190 nations in the world.

"Glocal" change. Globalization generates complex patterns of landscape change. Networks of international landscape resorts, spas, and tourist centers encircle the globe. Digital technologies export virtual landscapes and download nearly real time webcam imagery from around the world. Partially in reaction to these trends, real estate development projects market nostalgic, fortified, and atomized as well as communitarian places. Examples of these political and economic landscape transformations are legion, as are accounts of quiet economic stagnation, political devolution, and socio-environmental distress. Local responses to these processes of globalization and global environmental change, otherwise known as "glocal" processes, are increasingly interconnected (Smith 2007).

Landscape Architecture as if Political Economy Mattered

How can landscape scholars and designers make sense of these complex trends? Although we can draw upon vast scholarly literatures in politics, economics, and landscape change, precious little is available on the political economies of landscape change, and even less on relationships between political economy and landscape architecture. Here we briefly review what has and has not yet been accomplished, which sets the stage for the "Three Faces of Power" framework.

Landscape architecture magazines frequently report on issues of politics and economics. They track budget windfalls and shortfalls, give advice on project finance, and present cautionary sometimes titillating tales of political controversy. But they draw upon surprisingly little formal research on the politics or economics of landscape change, as compared with research on ecological, historical, and technological aspects of design. In its first two decades of circulation as the flagship publication of the field, *Landscape Journal* published only six articles that deal with politics and three with economics (Avery Index keyword search, conducted August 7, 2005; see, for example, Wolschke-Bulmahn 1992). *OCLC World Cat*, a premier digital library catalog for books in US libraries, lists only twelve books on ' "landscape architecture" and "politics" ' and fifteen on ' "landscape architecture" and "economics," ' most of which address these fields in peripheral ways (OCLC *World Cat* keyword-subject search; conducted August 7, 2005).

This paucity of publications comes as a surprise because practicing landscape architects wrestle with political and economic issues every day on every project. At least one landscape architecture firm, Design Workshop, Inc. includes economics as one of its four main determinants of design; while another, Community Development by Design, has a clear political economic vision. Scholars of contemporary landscape architecture seem in large measure to eschew these large and powerful fields.

Before seeking explanations for this apparent gap, it should be acknowledged that partial exceptions abound. Back in Chicago, the politics of downtown architecture and land development have drawn detailed analyses (e.g., Miller 2003; Wille 1991, 1998; and Willis 1995) – and even novels like the immensely informative and lurid *Devil in the White City: Murder, Magic, and Madness at the Fair that Changed America* (Larson 2003). Large literatures expose the dynamics of race, class, gender, and religion in the suburbs (e.g., Duncan and Duncan 2004; Hayden 2003). The politics of gardens has drawn attention from Israel (Aronson 1998) to India (Wescoat 1999). Landscape architectural historian Dianne Harris (2003) gives extensive treatment to material and symbolic accumulation in aristocratic 18th century gardens of Lombardy, while geographer Nicholas Blomley (2005) analyzes property rights issues embedded in ordinary 20th-century Canadian gardens. Other studies examine the politics of parks (Cranz 1982), urban gardens (Lawson 2005), homeless places (Morton and Balmori 1995), landscape ecology (Karasov 1997), landscape conservation (Martin and Warner 1997), public works (Caro 1974), environmentalism (Spirn 2002), design industries (Gertler and Vinodrai 2004), and regional economic development programs (Cutler 1985).

Biographies of leading landscape architects recount their political and economic struggles. In Chicago, the examples of Jens Jensen (Grese 1992) and his protégé Alfred Caldwell (Domer 1997) defying political corruption stand out – only to be followed a half-century later by heated debate about associations between Jensen's ideas about native plants and racial politics (Egan and Tischler 1999; Wolschke-Bulmahn 1997). To be sure, some landscape architects explicitly discuss the politics they encounter and strategies they adopt (e.g., Hester 2006; Steinitz et al. 2005a, b), while others note the role of feigned naïveté in design. Still others focus on political struggles from the local to international scales, e.g., Hester and Kweskin's (1999) conference on late 20th-century landscape architecture in the Pacific Rim, a theme carried forward by the Pacific Rim Community Design Network.

Curiously, fewer works analyze economic aspects of designed landscapes, notwithstanding the large planning literatures on regional economic growth and decline (e.g., Power 2002). For all of the political interpretations of Mughal gardens in South Asia, for example, only one paper has focused on their economic role (Habib 1996; cf. Wescoat 1999, 2007). Landscape scholar Michel Conan (2002) organized a symposium on "bourgeois and aristocratic encounters in landscape design," though it focused as much on cultural relations as on economic class.

These selective connections between landscape architecture and economics deserve comparison with earlier periods of historical practice in which garden designers and theorists such as John Claudius Loudon (1806, underlining added) referred to economics in their publications, with titles such as:

> A treatise on forming, improving, and managing country residences and on the choice of situations appropriate to every *class* of purchasers, in all which the object in view is to unite in a better manner than has hitherto been done, a taste founded in nature with *economy and utility*, in constructing or improving mansions, and other rural buildings, so as to combine architectural fitness with picturesque effect, and in forming gardens, orchards, farms, parks, pleasure grounds, shrubberies, all kinds of useful or decorative plantations, and every object of convenience or beauty peculiar to country seats, according to the extent, character, or style of situations, and the *rank, fortune, and expenditure of proprietors*, from the cottage to the palace...

Other theorists wrote about political tensions among these different classes of proprietors and their designers.

More recently, Johnston et al. (2005) have written scientific articles on economic valuation of the environmental benefits of landscape design alternatives, and there are large gray literatures that connect these subjects, sponsored by organizations like the US Environmental Protection Agency (www.epa.gov), the Center for Watershed Protection (www.cwp.org), the National Association of Home Builders Research Center (www.nahbrc.org), the Urban Land Institute (www.uli.org), and others (cf. also Coiner, Wu, and Polasky 2001).

These exceptions present a mélange of perspectives on the politics and economics of landscape change. They address such different types of landscapes and from such a varied range of political and economic approaches that they do not offer the kind of coordinated perspective on political economies of landscape change that we seek in this volume. One consequence is that while political and economic critique of landscape change grows in rigor, it has tenuous connections with design.

The chapters in this volume are likewise diverse, but their diversity can help us map out some of the relationships among related fields of politics, economics, and landscape inquiry. The next section of the chapter presents a conceptual framework that seeks to bridge these fields. By fostering a dialogue between political economy and landscape inquiry, this book strives to shed light on landscape experience and design practice.

The Three Faces of Power: A Conceptual Framework

The Landscape Architecture Foundation's (LAF) Futures Initiative focuses on driving forces of landscape change that will shape societies and environments in the decades ahead, and thus on future challenges for the profession. LAF rejected the first proposal for this project on political economy because it concentrated on implications for the landscape architecture profession rather than for landscape change more broadly defined. The original proposal surveyed political and economic forces that shape design practice, from real estate markets and community design politics to global design markets. Building on previous assessments of landscape architecture, such as the Fein Report (1972), we wanted to identify political and economic factors that have fueled landscape architectural growth in some regions, such as Boston and San Francisco through the mid-20th century, and constrained it in others such as Chicago and New York during the same period (cf. Treib 2002; Neckar 1997). We wanted to map the uneven global practice of landscape architecture at the start of the 21st century, including its dramatic growth in Europe, East Asia, and parts of the Middle East and South America – as well as its lesser visibility in other regions such as South Asia and Africa, and its erosion in areas of violent political conflict.

Although interested in these trends in landscape architecture, per se, the LAF Board envisioned a broader examination of environmental and social transformations at the landscape scale that societies might experience decades ahead, and that landscape architects might thus anticipate and prepare to address. To borrow a metaphor, this broader challenge increases the degree of difficulty for our authors, and for you as readers, because it requires communication across lines of inquiry and professional practice that up till now have had limited connection. For example, research on the political economy of landscape change links social research at the regional scale with ecosystem research at the landscape scale, both of which operate at levels of abstraction and aggregation larger than those of mainstream landscape architectural practice. It emphasizes collective action over individual design decisions, and social structures over human agency. Conversely, landscape architectural practice often involves localized actions that culminate in built work, and in aggregate physical changes that have implications for human experience and environmental quality. While "context-sensitive design" seeks conscious connections with regional geographic influences, e.g., in transportation corridor design, it and other regionalist design movements remain largely unknown among the social sciences. A search in *Social Science Citation Index*, for example, yielded one hit for the term "context sensitive design" (accessed 1 June 2007). Our challenge in this volume is thus to examine political economies of landscape change in ways that have potential significance for environmental design, as well as social research, and the next section outlines how we approach that challenge.

Key Concepts

We begin with three constructs – politics, economics, and landscape change – and outline what they denote for their respective academic communities. We then assemble these words in the phrase "politics and economics of landscape change," and ask what it encompasses. As it includes an enormous variety of phenomena, we further hone this phrase into the theme of "political economies of landscape change."

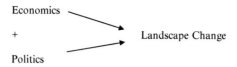

Figure 1 Economic and political driving forces of landscape change

Table 1 Types of landscape change (Johnston et al. (2000, 429–32); International Association for Landscape Ecology (www.landscape-ecology.org, checked 1 June 2007)
- Land cover – changes in the physical condition of forest, grassland, cropland, urbanized areas, etc., aggregated from the plot scale to larger regions
- Land use – human transformation of land cover for purposes of settlement, resource production, infrastructure, etc.
- Landscape technology – human means of modifying environments on a landscape scale including clearing, excavating, cultivating, building, planting, etc.
- Landscape ecology – relationships among physical, biotic, and human systems that occur at spatial scales of tens to hundreds of square kilometers
- Landscape morphology – spaces and forms established by combinations of land cover, land use, landscape ecology, and technology
- Landscape connectivity – physical, functional, and symbolic linkages among spaces and forms
- Landscape institutions – organizations and norms that regulate landscape change
- Landscape ideologies – belief systems that inspire, guide, and interpret those changes
- Landscape values – instrumental and inherent norms associated with places and regions
- Landscape experience – the life world of all of the above

To increase its salience for landscape architecture we employ futurist Kenneth Boulding's arguments about the three faces of power. This argument begins with an initial diagram of the three key concepts used in this project (Figure 1).

Landscape Change

Landscape change is often regarded as the outcome or dependent variable of political and economic forces. Although we challenge that presumption later in the chapter, it is useful to begin with the simple relations shown in Table 1, and work toward a more complex model. Landscape change refers to purposeful and inadvertent modifications of land use, land cover, and land experience (Table 1). Each type of landscape change affects many others, along with larger social and ecological systems. It encompasses manifold interactions and feedback relationships. Its historical and geographic context shapes the forms and meanings of landscape change. Research on landscape change looks backward in time to reconstruct historical geographies of land settlement and resource use, it undertakes synoptic appraisals of the contemporary moment, and it strives to envision more harmonious human-environment relations in the future. Thus, the dependent landscape variable to be explained in one study may become the independent variable that explains landscape change in other studies. Table 1 lists some of the major types of landscape change examined in different disciplines.

Each type of landscape change encompasses many phenomena, and the intersections among them constitute specialized fields of research. For example, research on the relationships between land-use and land-cover change is the subject of an interdisciplinary Land Use–Land Cover Change (LUCC) Program of the International Geosphere-Biosphere Project and International Human Dimensions Programme (Meyer and Turner 1995). Turner (1990) highlighted two main types of global land-use/land-cover change – those driven by global-scale processes of climate change such as greenhouse warming, and those that entail individual site-scale actions that aggregate in ways that have regional and ultimately global consequences. Both have relevance for landscape planning and design, as landscape design contributes to local aggregating changes, and largely responds to global-scale processes.

Economics

This volume is written at a time of increasing economic uncertainty for landscape architecture and broader processes of landscape change. Economically, the USA has witnessed a transition from booming economic growth, when the late Professor of Landscape Architecture Jot Carpenter (1999) stated that departments of landscape architecture could not produce enough graduates to meet immediate employment demand let alone long-term job growth, to mounting public deficits, private debt, and the prospect of recession that has worrisome implications for landscape architectural markets. Government deficits have eroded public budgets for landscape improvement; and volatile stock market prices have reduced some lines of commercial landscape design work while fueling real estate values that increased the pace of land development, followed by concerns about overbuilding.

The economic forces driving these trends range from microeconomic to macroeconomic processes that affect every scale of landscape change from household livelihoods to global trade. To illustrate this breadth, it may be noted that the American Economic Association identifies eighteen specialized fields of economic study (Table 2). Every one of these fields has many subspecialties. For example, one of the fields relevant for landscape inquiry – Urban, Rural, and Regional Economics – has its own 18 sub-specializations.

The point is that while this volume includes chapters on real estate, environmental and resource economics; economic development; and international finance, that is only a small sample of the economic phenomena and methods relevant for landscape change. What holds these fields together is a concern for what societies

Table 2 American Economic Association *EconLit* categories (From http://www.econlit.org/; accessed 1 June 2007)

A – General economics and teaching
B – Schools of economic thought and methodology
C – Mathematical and quantitative methods
D – Microeconomics
E – Macroeconomics and monetary economics
F – International economics
G – Financial economics
H – Public economics
I – Health, education, and welfare
J – Labor and demographic economics
K – Law and economics
L – Industrial organization
M – Business administration and business economics • Marketing
N – Economic history
O – Economic development, technological change, and growth
P – Economic systems
Q – Agricultural and natural resource economics
R – Urban, rural, and regional economics
R100 – General regional economics (includes regional data)
R110 – Regional economic activity: growth, development, and changes
R120 – Size and spatial distributions of regional economic activity
R130 – General equilibrium and welfare analysis of regional economies
R140 – Land use patterns
R150 – General regional economics: econometric and input–output models R190 – general
     regional economics: other
R200 – Household analysis: general
R210 – Urban, rural, and regional economics: housing demand
R230 – Regional migration; regional labor markets; population
R290 – Household analysis: other
R300 – Production analysis and firm location: general
R310 – Housing supply and markets
R320 – Other production and pricing analysis
R330 – Nonagricultural and nonresidential real estate markets
R340 – Production analysis and firm location: input demand analysis
R380 – Urban, rural, and regional economics: production analysis and firm
Location: Government policies; regulatory policies (rent control)
R390 – Production analysis and firm location: other

value, including their landscape values and valued landscapes, as well as how societies develop mechanisms for valuation they deem efficient and fair. Disputes about these economic principles, mechanisms, and values are sometimes colloquially attributed to "politics," but that field has its own expansive academic scope and relevance for landscape inquiry.

Politics

Landscape politics changed rapidly at the start of the 21st century. Political integration of Europe altered the interactions and in some cases the boundaries among nation states. In 2002, the USA shifted from political debates about domestic issues including environmental policy, to preoccupations with international terrorism, geopolitics, and war that had major implications for domestic and foreign landscapes, including those of landscape architectural practice. As noted above, however, public landscape planning face eroding budgets while markets for public landscape security and surveillance increase. Landscape design practice has expanded dramatically in East Asia, and to some extent the Middle East, which had rapid growth in landscape architecture in the late 20th century. Many public processes of landscape change continue, including capital budgeting for public works projects, planning and zoning decisions, public participation processes, patronage politics, and social movements, all of which shape designed landscapes (Orfield 2002; Smardon and Karp 1992; Tate 2001).

However, the scope of politics is much broader and more complex than the subfields that affect design practice. As in economics, political science ranges in scale from the person to the planet, and beyond that to outer space law. Consider the list of 38 specialized sections in the American Political Science Association below (Table 3).

This volume includes chapters that deal with urban politics, political institutions, political ecology, public policy, and comparative international relations. While these are only a small fraction of political inquiry, they point toward opportunities for deeper and broader investigation by other landscape researchers.

Table 3 American Political Science Association sections (From http://www.apsanet.org/section_300.cfm; accessed 1 June 2007)

1. Federalism & intergovernmental relations
2. Law and courts
3. Legislative studies
4. Public policy
5. Political organizations and parties
6. Public administration
7 Conflict processes
8 Representation and electoral systems
9. Presidency research
10. Political methodology
11. Religion and politics
12. Urban politics
13. Science, technology & environmental politics
14. Women and politics research
15. Foundations of political thought
16. Information technology and politics
17. International security and arms control

(continued)

Table 3 (continued)

18. Comparative politics
19. European politics and society
20. State politics and policy
21. Political communication
22. Politics and history
23. Political economy
24. Ecological & transformational politics
25. New political science
26. Political psychology
27. Undergraduate education
28. Politics and literature
29. Foreign policy
30. Elections, public opinion, and voting behavior
31. Race, ethnicity, and politics
32. International history and politics
33. Comparative democratization
34. Human rights
35. Qualitative methods
36. Sexuality and politics

Political Economy

To draw these threads together, our approach conjoins the driving forces of politics and economics under the heading of political economy, an 18th-century set of theories that sought to treat relationships among individual actions, economies, and political organizations in a unified way. Over the last two centuries, political economy has acquired a range of meanings that cut across theories of economic growth and governance and that guide to some degree the approaches employed in this volume, which are briefly introduced under the headings below:

- Neoclassical welfare economics and utilitarianism
- Social capital and development theory
- Marxian historical materialism
- Institutional economics and regulation theories
- Globalization theories

The line of political economy associated with neoclassical welfare economics combines quantitative analysis of markets with normative analysis of how individual choices can increase economic wealth. It has affinities with utilitarian philosophies that weigh choices based on their net benefits for individuals and society (i.e., by how much they increase well-being relative to current conditions). From this perspective, focusing on relative prices for land and environmental services and on how prices respond to design alternatives can help explain when, where, how, and in some measure why landscapes change. Douglas Johnston and John Braden's chapter six on "Green Economics" in this volume reflects the state of the art in applied welfare economics as it relates to landscape planning and environmental policy analysis.

Social capital theories also have a primary interest in human welfare. However, they give as much consideration to the equitable distribution of benefits and costs as to aggregate social gains – and even more attention to processes of human, economic, and political development that increase human capabilities for securing sustainable livelihoods through landscape change. Anthony Bebbington's chapter in this book on Andean landscapes examines the links between livelihoods and political strategies that, when taken together, have more or less sustainable landscape outcomes. In a related vein, Susan Clarke's chapter on the politics of landscape change examines the trend toward splintering urbanism, which allocates different levels of public infrastructure goods, including landscape improvements, to social groups based in part on their political capital, to which she responds with a call for more "democratic ecologies."

Marxian historical materialism, or radical political economy, also begins with a labor theory of value that goes further than social capital theories in assigning paramount importance to the "use value" of landscapes produced by labor, over the "exchange value" of landscapes defined by markets, which in capitalist systems privilege returns to capital and landed property over labor. Don Mitchell's chapter on "New Axioms for Reading the Landscape" develops this line of inquiry to argue for more socially just landscapes. Landscape architects in socialist and communist economies have pursued similar aims, though their work has received relatively little comparative analysis of its social benefits (cf. Blaikie and Brookfield 1987; Vergunov 1988).

Actors at every scale of landscape change work with institutions including markets, banks, regulatory bodies, laws, policies, and community norms. These institutions shape the landscapes in which they operate by regulating innovation, exchange, saving, development, and risk. Institutional approaches to political economy focus on how organizations, policies, laws, and informal rules affect land management. The formation of new public institutions during the progressive and New Deal eras ushered in new fields of landscape architectural practice in the 20th century (Cutler 1985), while private institutions have had a major influence on land development projects in the late 20th century. Landscape architects engage in institutional analysis when they interpret building ordinances, construction standards, and environmental policies for conservation design, watershed planning, brownfield reclamation, etc. (Abbey 2005; Kirkwood 2001). They navigate the twin pitfalls of "designing to the code," on the one hand, and failing to discern important design standards and liabilities, on the other. The chapter in this volume by Evans, York, and Ostrom offers a systematic treatment of resource management institutions in the USA, while Nassauer and Wascher compare landscape policies in Europe and the USA.

At the larger scale of global finance, which is a major arena of globalization, Babcock-Lumish and Clark's chapter on "Pricing the Economic Landscape" connects financial institutions with management of risk and innovation. They show

how finance capital invests and concentrates in some centers while divesting from others. Beyond that, they shed light on the necessary and supporting conditions for innovation management, which bear comparison with innovation networks in the globalizing practice of landscape design.

As these examples illustrate, this volume purposely ranges from capitalist to radical approaches in an effort to comprehend the *varieties* of political and economic driving forces of landscape change. That is why the volume has a plural title, political economies, and an ecumenical selection of authors. Our contributors vary widely in their approaches to political economy, and likewise in their perspectives on landscape change. They share a common interest, however, in exploring questions about the political economies of landscape change, and in understanding the power of landscape change.

The Power of Landscape Change

It is a mistake to regard political economy solely as a driving force of landscape change, when it is also shaped by landscapes that support or resist it. The mistake lies in treating driving forces as one-directional, stimulus-response relationships, in which economic and political stimuli lead to probabilistic, predictable, or innovative landscape responses. We must also consider the effects that landscape change and landscape architectural innovation have on politics and economics. To what extent, for example, did New Deal landscape design programs help attenuate effects of the 1930s depression? How has Chicago's lakefront park design amplified city and neighborhood economic development and urban political reform, as advocated by Frederick Law Olmsted, Jens Jensen, and others? Landscape change can operate as a driving force for certain kinds of political and economic change; it is more than a mere constraint or feedback loop (Figure 2). Landscapes set boundary conditions for political and economic activity that are influential, and malleable, subject to design in the broadest sense of the term.

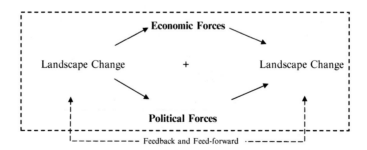

Landscape boundary conditions ················▶ *New landscape boundary conditions*

Figure 2 Political economies of landscape change

The expanded diagram in Figure 2 thus adds feed-forward as well feedback relationships, and boundary effects, to our working diagram. However, it does not yet convey the full "integrative power" envisioned by futurists such as Kenneth Boulding.

The Three Faces of Power in Landscape Change

Boulding's (1990) *Three Faces of Power* offers a novel thesis about relationships among political, economic, and what he calls integrative power. Boulding associates politics with the power of threat and coercion, economics with the power of production and exchange, and integration with the power of love, respect, and solidarity (Figure 3). While oversimplified in some respects, this threefold model presents a surprisingly hopeful view of how human beings can marshal their jointly political, economic, and integrative powers to improve social and environmental well-being.

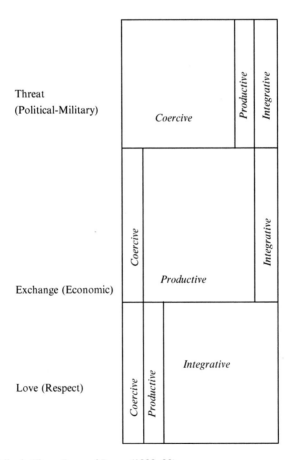

Figure 3 Boulding's *Three Faces of Power* (1990, 30)

By comparison, much of recent scholarly literature on the landscapes of power delves into what may be termed the dark side of landscape – its erasures, deceptions, illusions, and lies. W.J.T. Mitchell's *Landscape and Power* (2002) is a prominent example. Mitchell rejects art historian Kenneth Clark's view of landscape as a genre in which, "the human spirit once more attempted to create a harmony with its environment"(Mitchell 2002, 6). He compiles critical essays by humanists who expose historical exploitations of people and places as represented in landscapes of literature, art, and to a lesser extent design. Mitchell concludes that the power of landscape can only be understood if, "the harmony sought in landscape is read as a compensation for and screening off of the actual violence perpetrated there" (ibid. 7). Interestingly, by the time the second edition of *Landscape and Power* was issued, Mitchell came to regard landscape as such a weak form of power, relative to political economy, that he considered changing the focus from landscape to space, following the lead of geographers such as David Harvey and Henri Lefebvre. Much of the recent literature on landscape and power shares this view of political economy as coercive and exploitative. To the extent that this research considers landscape planning and design, it tends to implicate them as palliative at best and complicit at worst.

While not concerned with landscape, per se, Boulding offers a more optimistic perspective on political economy and power that has implications for landscape inquiry and design. He defines integrative power as:

[A]n elusive and multidimensional concept that is very hard to quantify, yet it has a strong claim to be, in the last analysis, the most significant of the three major categories of power. Without some source of legitimacy, which is an aspect of integrative power, neither threat power nor economic power can be realized in any large degree. (Boulding 1990, 109)

He reaches beyond the functional role of legitimacy when he writes about love and respect as central forms of integrative power. While the "power of love" is a cliché that has its own voluminous literature, it is rarely brought into alignment with politics and economics in any sustained way. Boulding argues that, "Integrative power often rests on the ability to create images of the future and to convince others that these images are valid... it enables people to carry themselves through bad times without collapse" (ibid. 122).

It strives to be both utopian and pragmatic (Light and Katz 1996). As a systems theorist and economist concerned to understand the connections between environmental and social change, and direct them toward the service of global needs, Boulding viewed environmental inquiry as a progressive enterprise. Although he did not use the term "landscape," he advocated the types of human-environmental harmony that W.J.T. Mitchell (2002) questions.

Kenneth and his wife, sociologist Elise Boulding, argued that these qualities of integrative power are real as well as desirable (i.e., "positive" as well as "normative"). Elise Boulding (2000) portrays them as the "hidden side of history," the everyday, extensive acts of social hope and kindness that, along with nonviolent struggles for social and environmental justice, make the world as good as it is and enable us to strive with some success to make it better than it is. These hopeful struggles face formidable opposition. Examine the US history section of most major bookstores. It is usually organized under the headings of successive wars from the Revolutionary war to the current Iraq war. Visit the Mall in Washington, DC, where memorials have been designed in memory of these wars and their participants. Why is the landscape of peacemaking far less commemorated? An inspiring exception occurs in a room of the FDR memorial designed by Lawrence Halprin that etches Roosevelt's words, "I hate war" in stone. Elise Boulding criticizes the disproportionate attention to violence in history and, in her closest reference to landscape and landscape architecture, she writes of a "peaceable garden culture" with roots in antiquity, expression in all present-day societies, and broader potential realization in the future (Boulding 2000, 22–24).

While the Bouldings do not make strong connections between integrative power, landscape inquiry, and landscape design, this volume does. It draws support and inspiration for this argument from several related lines of landscape architecture including:

- Affective human–environment relationships
- Progressive community-based design
- Public landscape design
- Place-based, context-sensitive, and bioregional design
- Sustainable design and green building movement

These themes build upon the *Eco-Revelatory Design Project* curated by Brown et al. (1998) to underscore the aspirations and accomplishments of contemporary designers.

These examples should be subjected to the same lines of critical inquiry that W. J. T. Mitchell (2002) and others direct toward the illusory harmony between humans and nature in picturesque tradition, and the purportedly self-evident character of Peirce Lewis's axioms for reading the landscape that Don Mitchell critiques in this volume. There is much that remains dark in landscape inquiry and design that must be illuminated to guide future landscape change.

Kenneth Boulding does discuss oppressive as well as liberating relationships among political, economic, and integrative power. He shows that integrative power can be destructive as well as constructive and that those processes are often related to one another in history. However, he believes the force of solidarity is more powerful than coercion, that there is a gift more powerful than exchange, and that harmonious relationships among political, economic, and integrative power can be forged through activities akin to landscape inquiry, planning, and design.

Organization of the Volume

The first major section introduces the themes of landscape struggle, possibility, and prosperity. In the opening chapter Don Mitchell calls for "reading" the history of political and economic injustice in the landscape. He focuses on the struggles of migratory laborers in rural California work camps, urban *colonia*s, and impoverished rural hinterlands of the US–Mexico borderlands, and in so doing he shows that there is no such thing as purely local places. Mitchell uses these examples to revise Peirce Lewis's classic, "Axioms for Reading the Landscape."

Further south in the Andean highlands, Anthony Bebbington explores the landscapes of struggle in a different context, and from the perspective of political and economic "possibilities" in three impoverished mountain districts of the Andean highlands that seek to become viable through jointly political and economic strategies. Bebbington distinguishes political strategies that lead to capital accumulation from those that aggravate poverty and oppression. He also draws intriguing comparisons between economic struggle in the Andes and the effects of globalization on out-migration from the hill country near his home in Britain to North America.

In chapter three, landscape architect Kurt Culbertson of Design Workshop, Inc., based in Aspen, Colorado, extends this comparative montane perspective to the USA where he examines unfolding processes of "amenity migration" to previously marginal and depressed areas of the Sierra and Appalachian mountains. He sheds light on the myths and realities of place-driven development, the quest for prosperity, and its consequences.

The discussion among these authors at the conference raised questions about what might constitute a politically and economically "just" landscape. Back in Chicago, whose affluent patrons helped establish premier ski areas in Colorado in the 20th century, blocks of deteriorating low-income high-rise public housing fell to the wrecking ball in the early 21st century, opening up large spaces for mixed-density combinations of subsidized and market housing, and relocating poor African-American residents across the state of Illinois. Urban public schools in Chicago left many if not most students behind, sparking innovative though as yet small-scale experiments in quasi-private charter schools that admit a fortunate few students by lottery.

Suburbs conceived as bourgeois utopias and yet blamed for urban disinvestment, racial segregation, sprawl, environmental degradation, and political fragmentation cry out for critical reexamination in the early 21st century. Some excavate the deep historical roots and aspirations of suburban development while others reexamine their modern reconstructions of class, gender, race, and interreligious relationships (Bruegmann 2005). Still others advocate "new urbanism" and "smart growth" movements that strive to mitigate impacts, bridge differences, and fill gaps in the expansive and in many respects dysfunctional metropolitan landscapes. Suburban poverty, traffic congestion, bankrupt schools, aggravated storm water flooding, and political corruption complicate simple narratives of metropolitan development.

As historian William Cronon (1991) argues in *Nature's Metropolis: Chicago and the Great West*, cities like Chicago drew upon expansive regional hinterlands for raw materials, finance capital, labor, retail markets, and regional trade from their very establishment. These cities continue to transform regional ecosystems at the landscape-scale of prairies, forests, and regional waterways while driving the growth and decline of ever-larger functional regions of trade, finance, communication, and concomitant political organization at macro-regional and global scales.

The chapters in Part II focus in on selected political and economic driving forces of landscape change. Susan Clarke introduces three political constructs that help explain current social change and its landscape consequences from the urban to global scales. The first of these constructs, "splintering urbanism" describes the increasing differentiation of premium, ordinary, and substandard urban infrastructure. It moves the analysis beyond simplistic oppositions between the so-called public and private sectors to more precise qualitative differentiation of uneven quasi-public and quasi-private spaces in contemporary urban landscapes (i.e., the spaces and work of contemporary urban landscape design). The "garrison state," a concept articulated by Harold Lasswell in the 1950s to highlight the consequences of political anxiety has renewed currency and landscape consequences in the "post-9/11 world." Our authors' walking transects across downtown Chicago noted increasing numbers of reinforced bollards, traffic barriers, and surveillance cameras surrounding government buildings. While society debates whether these new landscapes of security are excessive or not, Clarke points toward "political ecologies of democracy" or "democratic ecologies" as a promising theoretical framework for reconstructing the politics of landscape change.

A complementary approach in chapter five by the team of Evans, York, and Ostrom examines the difference that political institutions (i.e., laws, policies, and public organizations) make in natural and built environments from the USA to South America. Although politics exert manifold pressures on these political institutions, the institutions embody social norms that permit some political and economic forces while regulating others. This chapter demonstrates the importance of testing political assumptions and hypotheses, measuring the benefits and costs of institutional alternatives for the peoples and environments affected, and using that knowledge for both institutional and landscape design.

Estimating the benefits and costs of environmental change has a vast literature, but surprisingly little of that research measures the benefits of conservation design (e.g., ecological approaches to subdivision layout and storm water management). Johnston and Braden report on two research projects in northeastern Illinois. Their research in the Blackberry Creek watershed in the western suburbs of Chicago estimates the economic value of conservation design alternatives, while their second study estimates the aggregate urban economic benefits of cleaning up contaminated sediments in Waukegan Harbor through analysis of residential home values. These studies of downstream economic benefits offer insights into the economic potential, and justifications, for future landscape improvement.

Finance capital translates potential economic value into landscape change. Economists often call attention to the market distortions and uncertainties that divert financial flows from economically worthy to inefficient uses. In chapter seven, Babcock-Lumish and Clark offer a related perspective on the economic geography of financial markets. They show how the landscape of global finance revolves around the London, New York, and Tokyo markets – in which Chicago and other cities have decidedly lesser positions. Notwithstanding their globalizing structure and extent, these financial markets manage risk through two distinct strategies that bear comparison with the political chapters described earlier. For example, venture capital markets manage risk through communities of trust, comparable to close-knit political communities and design teams. By contrast, currency trading markets manage risk through regulation, comparable to broad political institutions and professional organizations. While the venture capital communities may direct investment into local landscape projects, currency markets direct large flows of funds toward some regions and away from others in ways that have large-scale landscape effects.

These political and economic driving forces of landscape change extend from the scale of detailed site design to cumulative global environmental change. Actions at each of these scales are linked with broad systems of political economy. Advances in landscape architecture during the 1990s forged linkages with distant metropolitan, ecosystem, and culture regions.

The third and final part of this book thus begins to explore these processes of "integrative landscape change." Landscape architects Joan Nassauer and Dirk Wascher compare land planning policies in the USA and Europe. They show how emerging European integration enables landscape planning for future land use, land cover, and habitat protection across national as well as local boundaries. Nassauer has previously worked in the contaminated wetlands of south Chicago where local activists draw inspiration from eco-industrial redevelopment projects in Duisborg-Nord, Germany, noted above, as well as from EPA brownfield projects in the USA.

Reflecting upon Nassauer and Wascher's vision of transnational landscape planning, and preceding chapters on political economies of landscape change, the final essay by Johnston and Wescoat reflects upon future avenues of landscape inquiry, planning, and design. By bringing these ideas back to design and designers it completes the circle of inquiry initiated by the Landscape Architecture Foundation in its Landscape Futures Initiative (ASLA 1999).

References

Ahern J (1999) *A Guide to the Landscape Architecture of Boston*. The Hubbard Educational Trust, Cambridge, MA

Aronson S (1998) *Making Peace with the Land: Designing Israel's Landscape*. Spacemaker Press, Washington, DC

American Society of Landscape Architects (ASLA) (1999) *ASLA/LAF Summit White Papers*. ASLA, Washington, DC

Blaikie P and Brookfield H (1987) *Land Degradation and Society*. Methuen, London

Blomley N (2005) The borrowed view: privacy, propriety, and the entanglements of property. *Law and Social Inquiry* 30: 617–662

Boulding E (2000) *Cultures of Peace: The Hidden Side of History*. Syracuse University Press, Syracuse, New York

Boulding KE (1990) *Three Faces of Power*. Sage, Newbury Park, CA

Brown B, Harkness T, and Johnston DM (eds) (1998) *Eco-Revelatory Design*. Special issue of *Landscape Journal*. University of Wisconsin Press, Madison, WI

Bruegmann R (2005) *Sprawl: A Compact History*. University of Chicago Press, Chicago, IL

Burnham D and Bennett E (1909 [1993 reprint]) *Plan of Chicago*. Princeton Architectural Press, New York

Caro RA (1974) *The Power Broker: Robert Moses and the Fall of New York*.Vintage, New York

Carpenter J (1999) Implosion or recession? *Landscape Architecture*, July, 129 ff.

Chicago Christian Industrial League (2004) *"City of Gardens" Tour Kicks Off Landscape Program 10-year Anniversary* 14(1): 1

Coiner C, Wu J, and Polasky, S (2001) Economic and environmental implications of alternative landscape designs in the Walnut Creek Watershed of Iowa. *Ecological Economics* 38: 119–121

Conan M (ed) (2002) *Bourgeois and Aristocratic Cultural Encounters in Garden Art, 1550–1850*. Dumbarton Oaks, Washington, DC

Cranz G (1982) *The Politics of Park Design: The History of Urban Parks in America.* MIT Press, Cambridge, MA

Cronon W (1991) *Nature's Metropolis: Chicago and the Great West.* W.W. Norton, New York

Cutler P (1985) *The Public Landscape of the New Deal.* Yale University Press, New Haven, CT

Domer DE (1997) *Alfred Caldwell: The Life and Work of a Prairie School Landscape Architect.* Johns Hopkins University Press, Baltimore, MD

Duncan J and Duncan NG (2004) *Landscapes of Privilege: The Politics of the Aesthetic in an American Suburb.*Routledge, London

Egan D and Tischler W (1999) Jens Jensen, native plants, and the concept of Nordic superiority. *Landscape Journal* 18: 11–29

Engel JR (1983) *Sacred Sands: The Struggle for Community in the Indiana Dunes.*Wesleyan University Press, Middletown, NJ

Fein A (1972) *Study of the Profession of Landscape Architecture.* ASLA Foundation, Alexandria, VA

Gertler M and Vinodrai T (2004) *Designing the Economy: Ontario's Design Workforce.* Design Industry Advisory Committee, Toronto

Gilfoyle TJ (2006) *Millennium Park: Creating a Chicago Landmark.*University of Chicago Press, Chicago, IL

Goldberger P (2004) *Up from Zero: Politics, Architecture, and the Rebuilding of New York.* Random House, New York

Greenberg J (2002) *A Natural History of the Chicago Region.* University of Chicago Press, Chicago, IL

Grese RE (1992) *Jens Jensen: Maker of Natural Parks and Gardens.* Johns Hopkins University Press, Baltimore, MD

Harris D (2003) *The Nature of Authority: Villa Culture, Landscape & Representation in Eighteenth-Century Lombardy.* Penn State Press, University Park, IL

Hester RT (2006) *Design for Ecological Democracy.* MIT Press, Cambridge, MA

Hester RT and Kweskin C (eds) (1999) *Democratic Design in the Pacific Rim – Japan, Taiwan and the United States.* Ridge Times Press, Mendocino, CA

Hudson JC (2006) *Chicago: A Geography of the City and Its Region.* University of Chicago Press, Chicago, IL

IGBP (International Geosphere-Biosphere Programme) (2005) Land Use Land Cover Change (LUCC) http://www.geo.ucl.ac.be/LUCC/lucc.html

Johnson EW (2001) *Chicago Metropolis 2020.* Commercial Club, Chicago, IL

Johnston RJ, Gregory D, Pratt G, and Watts M (eds) (2000) *The Dictionary of Human Geography,* 4th edition. Blackwell Publishers, Oxford

Johnston DM, Braden JB, and Price TH (2005) The downstream economic benefits from storm water management: a comparison of conservation and conventional development. *Journal of Water Resources Planning and Management, American Society of Civil Engineers* 130: 498–505

Kamin B (2001) *Why Architecture Matters: Lessons from Chicago.*University of Chicago Press, Chicago, IL

Karasov D (1997) Politics at the scale of nature. In Nassauer JI (ed) *Placing Nature: Culture and Landscape Ecology. Placing Nature: Culture and Landscape Ecology,* pp 123–138. Island Press, Washington, DC

Kirkwood N (2001) *Manufactured Sites: Rethinking the Post-Industrial Landscape.*Spon Press, New York

Larson E (2003) *The Devil in the White City: Murder, Magic, and Madness at the Fair that Changed America.* Vintage Books, New York

Lawson L (2004) The planner in the garden: a historical view of the relationship of planning to community garden programs. *Journal of Planning History* 3(2): 151–176

Lawson L (2005) *City Bountiful: A Century of Community Gardening in America.* University of California Press, Berkeley, CA

Lewis PH Jr (1996) *Tomorrow by Design: A Regional Design Process for Sustainability.* Wiley, New York

Light A and Katz E (1996) *Environmental Pragmatism*. Routledge, London

Linn K and Anthony C (1988) *Places of Peace; Working Papers*. Unpublished ms in the library of the Massachusetts College of Art, Boston, MA

Loudon JC (1806) *A Treatise on Forming, Improving, and Managing Country Residences and on the Choice of Situations Appropriate to Every Class of Purchasers, in all Which the Object in View is to Unite in a Better Manner than has Hitherto been done, a Taste Founded in Nature with Economy and Utility, in Constructing or Improving Mansions, and other Rural Buildings, so as to Combine Architectural Fitness with Picturesque Effect, and in Forming Gardens, Orchards, Farms, Parks, Pleasure Grounds, Shrubberies, all kinds of Useful or Decorative Plantations, and Every Object of Convenience or Beauty Peculiar to Country Seats, According to the Extent, Character, or Style of Situations, and the Rank, Fortune, and Expenditure of Proprietors, from the Cottage to the Palace: with an Appendix, Containing an Enquiry into the Utility and Merits of Mr. Repton's Mode of Shewing Effects by Slides and Sketches, and Strictures on his Opinions and Practice in Landscape Gardening*. Longman, London

Martin JA and Warner SB Jr (1997) Urban conservation: Sociable, green, and affordable. In Nassauer JI, *Placing Nature: Culture and Landscape Ecology*, pp 109–122. Island Press, Washington, DC

Meyer WB and Turner BL II (1995) *Land Use and Land Cover Change: A Global Perspective*. Cambridge University Press, Cambridge

Miller R (2003) *Here's the Deal: The Making and Breaking of an American City*. Northwestern University Press, Evanston, IL

Mitchell WJT (2002) *Landscape and Power*, 2nd edition. University of Chicago Press, Chicago, IL

Neckar LM (1997) Landscape architecture – recovery into prosperity 1950: an international inquiry into landscape design – and the social, political, and artistic forces that influenced it – from 1940–1960. *Landscape Journal* 16(2): 211–218

Orfield M (2002) *American Metropolitics: The New Suburban Reality*. Brookings Institution Press, Washington, DC

Power TM (2002) *Lost Landscapes and Failed Economies: The Search for a Value of Place*. Island Press, Washington, DC

Prentice HK (1998) *Suzhou: Shaping an Ancient City for the New China: An EDAW/Pei Workshop*. Spacemaker Press, Washington, DC

Ranney GA Jr (2004) *Chicago Metropolis 2020: An Example of Forces Driving Landscape Change*. Presentation at the Places of Power conference, September 11. Copy on file with author

Seo JY, Hewings GJD, and Sonis M (2004) *Vertical Connections in The Midwest Economies: The Role Of Internal And External Trade. REAL 04-T-10*. Regional Economics Applications Laboratory, Urbana, IL

Simo M (1999) *One Hundred Years of Landscape Architecture*. Spacemaker Press, Berkeley, CA

Smardon R and Karp JP (1993) *The Legal Landscape*. Van Nostrand Reinhold, New York

Smith CE (ed) (2007) *Designing for the Other 90%*. Cooper-Hewitt National Design Museum, New York

Spirn AW (1998) *The Language of Landscape*. Yale University Press, New Haven, CT

Spirn AW (2002) The authority of nature: conflict, confusion, and renewal in design, planning and ecology. In Johnson BR and Hill K (eds) *Ecology and Design: Frameworks for Learning*, pp 29–50. Island Press, Washington, DC

Spirn AW (2005) West Philadelphia Landscape Project http://web.mit.edu/4.243j/www/wplp/timeline.html

Steinitz C, Faris R, Flaxman M, Karish K, Mellinger AD, Canfield T, and Sucre L (2005) A delicate balance: conservation and development scenarios for panama's coiba national park. *Environment* 47(5): 24 ff.

Steinitz C, Faris R, Flaxman M, Vargas-Moreno JC, Canfield T. Arizpe O, Angeles M, Cariño M, Santiaqo F, Maddock T, Lambert, CD, Baird K, and Godínez L (2005) A sustainable path?: Deciding the future of La Paz. *Environment* 47(6): 24 ff.

Treib M (ed) (2002) *The Architecture of Landscape: 1940–1960*. University of Pennsylvania Press, Philadelphia, PA

Vergunov AP (1988) *Russkie sady i parki, Russian gardens and parks*. Nauka, Moscow

Waldheim C and Ray KR (eds) (2006) *Chicago Architecture: Histories, Revisions, Alternatives.* University of Chicago Press, Chicago

Wescoat JL Jr (1999) Mughal gardens: the re-emergence of comparative possibilities and the wavering of practical concerns. In Conan M (ed) *Perspectives on Garden Histories*, pp 107–126. Dumbarton Oaks, Washington, DC

Wescoat, JL Jr (2007) Questions about the Politics of Mughal waterworks. In Conan M (ed) *Middle Eastern Garden Traditions: Unity and Diversity.* Dumbarton Oaks, Washington, DC

Wille L (1991) *Forever Open, Clear and Free: The Struggle for Chicago's Lakefront.* University of Chicago Press, Chicago, IL

Wille L (1998) *At Home in the Loop: How Clout and Community Built Chicago's Dearborn Park.* Southern Illinois Press, Carbondale, IL

Willis C (1995) *Form Follows Finance: Skyscrapers and Skylines in New York and Chicago.* Princeton Architectural Press, New York

Wolschke-Bulmahn J (1992) From the war-garden to the victory garden: political aspects of garden culture in the United States during World War I. *Landscape Journal* Spring, 11(1): 51–57

Wolschke-Bulmahn J (ed) (1997) *Nature and Ideology: Natural Garden Design in the Twentieth Century.* Dumbarton Oaks, Washington, DC

Wolschke-Bulmahn J (ed) (2001) *Places of Commemoration: Search for Identity and Landscape Design.* Dumbarton Oaks, Washington, DC

Yu K and Pauda M (eds) (2006) *The Art of Survival: Recovering Landscape Architecture.* Images Publishing, Mulgrave, Australia

Part I
Landscapes of Struggle, Possibility and Prosperity

Top: Adandoned community center in the semiarid upper Colorado River basin. Bottom: Casino landscape downstream in arid Las Vegas, Nevada (Photos: jlw)

Chapter 1
New Axioms for Reading the Landscape: Paying Attention to Political Economy and Social Justice

Don Mitchell

Although the word is seldom so used, it is proper and important to think of cultural landscape as nearly everything that we can see when we go outdoors. Such common workaday landscape has very little to do with the skilled work of landscape architects, but it has a great deal to say about the United States as a country and Americans as a people.

— Geographer Peirce Lewis, 1979

I think the landscape is everything outside the building footprint. It is the moment you walk out of the house and enter the world.... The asphalt is our landscape. The streets are our landscape. The landscape is everything out there, and it looks like hell. The United States is getting uglier and uglier. We are sprawling out, and so little value is given to our landscape.

— Landscape Architect Martha Schwartz, 2004

It has been more than 25 years since Peirce Lewis (1979) laid out his "Axioms for Reading the Landscape: Some Guides to the American Scene." Lewis's axioms were designed to help us better see how, as he put it (complete with italics), *"all human landscape has cultural meaning,* no matter how ordinary that landscape might be" (p. 12). The axioms, Lewis suggested, "seem basic and self-evident," even if "what seems self-evident was not obvious to me a few years ago" (p. 15). By restating what he took to be obvious, Lewis's sought to provide a set of simple guidelines for understanding the meaning of the cultural landscape, and for using that meaning – gleaned from "reading" the landscape (that is, careful observation and inductive reasoning) – to come to some conclusions about American culture. For him, aesthetic judgments about the landscape were secondary. Primary was the question of why the landscape looked the way it did. What clues did the landscape itself present as to its own making?

To answer that question, Lewis suggested seven axioms:

- Landscape is a clue to culture. It "provides strong evidence of the kind of people we are, and were, and are in the process of becoming" (p. 15). By reading the landscape we could glean important insights into "who we are." As a corollary, Lewis argued, if landscapes looked different, it was because there were significantly different cultures at work. If they were growing more similar, it was because cultures were growing more similar. Moreover, both the diffusion of landscape items across space and local cultural "tastes" were central in giving landscape its particular look and feel.

J.L. Wescoat, Jr. and D.M. Johnston (eds.), *Political Economies of Landscape Change.*
© Springer 2008

- Nearly every item in the landscape "reflect[s] culture in some way" (p, 18). We need to pay attention even to what at first glance might seem commonplace, trivial, or just plain haphazard and ugly. At the same time we need to make judgments about when an item really just is the idiosyncratic whim of an individual and thus truly is unique.
- Landscapes are difficult to study "by conventional academic means" (p. 19). Rather, scholars need to turn to "nonacademic literature" (like trade journals, journalism, promotional literature, and advertisements). Most of all we need to train ourselves to "learn by looking" (as Lewis 1983, put it in a different piece): we need to train ourselves to pay attention to the visual evidence. (Lewis gives little idea of what constitutes "conventional academic means" but the sense is that it is limited to reading scholarly books).
- History matters to the structure and look of a landscape. We inherit a landscape which forms the basis for any changes or developments we subsequently make. Change itself is uneven (historically "lumpy" [p. 23]). Both technological and cultural change comes in great leaps forward, perhaps more so than as gradual evolution.
- Location matters too: "Elements of a cultural landscape make little cultural sense if they are studied outside their geographic (i.e., locational) context." Indeed, "[t]o a large degree cultures dictate that certain activities should occur in certain places, and only those places" (p. 24). Thus "context matters" (p. 25).
- So does physical environment, since "conquering geography' is often a very expensive business." Physical geography may not determine, but it does establish the limits of possibility and the costs of exceeding those limits.
- Finally, while all items in the landscape convey meaning, they do not do so readily: meaning can be obscure. Even so "chances are" any disagreement over meaning "can be cleared up by visual evidence" (p. 27).

How the visual evidence, which is "obscure" as to its meanings, can clear things up is never explained. Even so, Lewis's faith in "reading" has been infectious, attracting adherents not only in geography, but in landscape architecture and other fields as well. Following not only Lewis, but also landscape pioneers like J.B. Jackson, many were swayed by Lewis's argument that "One can … quite literally teach oneself how to see, and that is something that most Americans have not done and should do" (p. 27).

And yet, even as Lewis's axioms were being codified, their "self-evident" nature was being undermined by other trends in landscape studies,[1] trends that took a decidedly more critical – and historical – approach to understanding what the landscape was, and what it meant. Radical geographers like Denis Cosgrove (1984, 1985, 1993) and Stephen Daniels (1989, 1993; Cosgrove and Daniels 1988), inspired by developments in art history and incipient cultural studies, began to

---

[1] Even if, oddly, their rather chaotic and contradictory nature has rarely been criticized. It is amazing how little has been said about Lewis's odd notion that obscure meanings, if looked at hard enough, will reveal answers to even the thorniest scholastic questions.

explore not just how landscape had cultural meaning, but how it had *ideological* meaning (see also Duncan 1990). Even as early as 1962, geographers like Marvin Mikesell had warned that the history of the landscape idea in Western society was as important to understanding landscape form as was the physical evidence of the landscape itself. And by the mid-1980s, among critical historians, art historians, and geographers, a regular landscape industry developed, aiming at uncovering how landscape (both physical and representational) was central to maintaining and reproducing class relations and elite power (Barrell 1980; Bender 1993; Berger 1972; Bermingham 1984; Williams 1973). By the early 1990s a general consensus had developed, particularly in art history, about how landscape representation (including representation in the bricks and mortar of the built landscape) was a form of power: a power to determine what is and what is not seen. People often worked hard to make some aspects of the landscape "obscure" and others "obvious" (see, e.g., WJT Mitchell 1994c; Olwig 2003). "Visual evidence" was undoubtedly crucial, but such evidence did not so much explain (as Lewis would have it), but was itself in need of explanation. And, crucially, "culture" was too crude an explanation for much of anything, since any culture, as cultural studies was making it its business to show, was shot though with struggle, conflict, difference – in short the exercise of power (Duncan 1980; Eagleton 2000; Jackson 1989; D. Mitchell 1995; Williams 1958, 1977, 1980, 1982).

Such arguments were not only influential in art history and cultural studies – and were not limited to landscape representation. Geographers and others began to reconsider the basic suppositions that provided the foundation for Lewis's axioms about the built, physical landscape. Rooted in Carl Sauer's (1963 [1925]) reformulation of the German landscape morphology tradition, these suppositions argued that any morphological landscape was an expression of the local culture that made it. Change in landscape was attributed to the introduction of a new, "alien" culture (as Sauer put it) or the local adoption of some diffusing trait. The main assumption was one of cultural and morphological stability (even when made more complex by the adoption of something like an organic "life cycle" model that understood that cultures were born, developed and eventually died). The roots of reaction to this model, clear in the work of Cosgrove (1984), Kenneth Olwig (1984, 1993, 1996, 2003, 2005), and others (e.g., Duncan 1990; Jackson 1989; D. Mitchell 1996; Rose 1993) were complex, but revolved around what could be called a "modernization" of landscape theory – modernization in the sense that Sauer's emphasis on past, often archaic cultures allowed for rather simple arguments about the nature of culture and the stability of landscape that simply were not tenable in any contemporary (or even most historical) societies, even if these assumptions were often smuggled, without comment, into landscape theories like Lewis's (cf. Duncan 1980). A modern theory of *capitalist* landscape required a theory of culture, as well as a theory of morphology, that was at least as supple and complex as the world it wished to describe (Cosgrove 1984). The shape and structure – the morphology, the visual evidence – of manor houses built in early-capitalist England, for example, might say something important about English culture, but *only* when set within a theory, and especially a historical analysis, of changing property relations, new legal innovations (like vagrancy laws), transformations in the nature of political power, the growth of industrial towns and cities and the crucial role of colonialism (Cosgrove 1984; Daniels 1993; Helsinger 1994; Olwig 1996, 2003; Said 1993) – all things about which the local landscape, in fact, offered very little direct evidence. Indeed, evidence of such transformation that made the landscape possible had to be sought out by those "conventional academic means" that Lewis eschewed: careful archival research (see Holdsworth 1990), analysis of changing social structures and laws, ethnographic or other similar methods, and even "theory."

Or consider, as I have done, the production of the California agricultural land-scape (D. Mitchell 1996, 2001, 2003). Consider a photograph I have of a lone blue port-a-potty at the meeting point of four greenfields in the San Joaquin Delta (Figure 1). Taken from a levee, pear and peach orchards can be spied in the distance. The field at the time the picture was taken was empty: just new green shoots rising out of the flat earth and the toilet in the middle. This is as ordinary, as "common-place," a landscape as there is in California and the toilet is, seemingly, about as trivial a landscape "item" as can be imagined. But just looking at it tells us abso-lutely nothing about why it is there or in fact what it means. For it is mute about the more than 50 years of often violent social struggle that finally led, in 1914, to a new law governing sanitary conditions in agriculture, as well as to the subsequent six decades in which the law was almost never enforced (at least not without the inducement of violent strikes and walkouts), and to how once it was enforced, to some degree in the 1970s, agribusiness went back on the offensive against agricul-tural labor, finding allies in the governor's office all through the 1980s and 1990s so that by now such a toilet is in fact once again quite a rare site in the fields. The toilet in the field *in and of itself*, that is to say, provides very little evidence about the long history of struggle, often violent, between different factions of capital, between capital and the state, between capital and labor, and among laborers themselves, that give rise to the specific form of the landscape (and in which the landscape has always been such a crucial player), as well as specific items in the landscape. Nor, by the same token, do the cabins, washhouses, and pickup trucks in a contemporary county-run labor camp, or the dollar stores, fast-food joints, bars, and cheap apartments along Charter Way in Stockton, clearly say much at all about how they got there – and why.

There is, however, a huge amount of evidence to explain this toilet in the field (or the labor camps, bars, and apartments) and its history in archives, in government investigation records, in muckraking journalism, and in the remembrances and oral testimony of farm workers and activists, and, of course, in the scholarly books that have been written about California (e.g., Alamillo 2006; Daniel 1981; Galarza 1977; Garcia 2001; Henderson 1998; Majka and Majka 1983; McWilliams 1999 [1939]; Pincetl 1999; Stein 1973; Stoll 1998; Walker 2004).

To explain the morphology of the California landscape – the toilet in the field – no less than to explain the form of any other landscape, requires careful observation – learning to ask the right questions by looking in specific ways, as Lewis advocates – but it requires a lot more. As a capitalist agricultural landscape it requires theories of capital and labor circulation (Henderson 1998), attention to the ways capital and

Figure 1 San Joaquin Delta California, 1990 (dm)

labor flow *differently* in different eras (Walker 2004), and particularly close attention to what struggle in and over the landscape is *about*. It requires different means of analysis than those advocated by Lewis.

Perhaps it needs a different set of axioms.

Any new set of axioms for understanding – "reading" – the landscape will be anything but "self-evident." This is because, in fact, the landscape itself is anything but self-evident. In the generation since Lewis published his axioms, the explosion of critical landscape research, for all its diversity, has shown not that landscape exists in obscurity, but rather that landscape *obscures*. As W.J.T. Mitchell (1994a, 5) put it in one of his nine "Theses on Landscape:" "Like money, landscape is a social hieroglyph that conceals the actual basis of its value. It does so by naturalizing its conventions, and conventionalizing its nature." But this thesis does little more than name the problem. So, as Marx showed with his analysis of the real basis of value in capitalist society, if we are to make that which is never self-evident at least evident, if we are to begin to see *how* and *why* landscapes exist and to uncover their real basis, we need to turn from a focus on meaning and toward a focus on production. And, as with the analysis of capital, this focus on production needs to be set within a broader theory of circulation. The following new axioms of landscape are designed to codify a theoretical and methodological basis for doing so. But they are also designed to do something else: they are designed to form an analytical and normative basis, by providing a historical and materialist methodological foundation for what the land-scape *is* and *does*, and for what a more just landscape might *be*.[2]

---

[2] Though all the examples from the following are from the USA, designed to provide an empirical foundation to the Axioms, the Axioms themselves are conceptualized more broadly so as to be applicable to any landscape in the capitalist world (which is to say all of it).

Axiom 1: The landscape is produced; it is actively made: it is a physical intervention into the world and thus is not so much our "unwitting autobiography" (as Lewis put it) *as an act of will.* This will might be social more than individual will (it might indeed have little to do with "the skilled work of landscape architects"), and it might be shaped, transformed, even thwarted by any number of contrary social processes (zoning laws, the conventions of architectural or artistic language, riots, eminent domain, organized pressure groups, and so forth). But it is an act of will nonetheless. This is no less true of the built landscape – the landscape we live in – than it is of the painted or photographed landscape. The key issue at stake, therefore, is always the *relations* of production. If we are to understand what a landscape is, what is does, and why it looks the way it does, we need to pay attention to both the broad (societal) and the narrow (e.g., at a particular locality, within a particular firm, in the offices of a design studio) relations of production, relations that are, of course, always historically and technologically conditioned, and always and everywhere struggled over. The blue toilet in the California field, seen through the prism of relations of production, is both a *result* of struggle and a means to *end* struggle (Parker 1919): a result of struggle because people fought for the provision of toilets, clean water, and safer tools even as many farmers and agribusinesses fought actively against these (because of cost, because oppression was a means of labor control, because of racism, or some combination of these), and so the toilet in the field marks something of a victory, minor as it may seem and minor as it was; an end to struggle because state agencies required, with all the force of law and sometimes police power to back that up, that toilets be built precisely as a means of staving off labor unrest (D. Mitchell 1996).[3]

More generally, it matters deeply if the landscape (as a totality or as items in it) is produced as a commodity – if landscape production is commodity production, as it primarily is under capitalism – or through some other set of relations of production. Even within capitalism there remains room for community and collective state production, and, of course, individual or corporate property owners have a great deal of freedom in how they arrange landscapes, but these are never fully removed from the sphere of commodity production. What is possible and what is not – literally what can be produced in the landscape – is a function of what is produced elsewhere to be sold for profit. And, typically, what cannot be produced for profit fades out of existence. Relations of production, that is, run deep and are determinate. Social need, the context within which landscapes are produced, is vetted by the power of commodities – right down to the last bolt and washer. The analysis of the production of landscape, therefore, requires the analysis of networks of production (and the relations of production that sustain them).

---

[3] Of course the toilet in the field is produced in another way too: it is a *technical* achievement. In its early years the California Commission of Immigration and Housing produced several technical manuals on labor camp sanitation, complete with architectural drawings for toilets considered to be significant technical advances on previous models, and which were the result of years of research and experimentation (Mitchell 1993).

Axiom 2: *Any landscape is* (or was) *functional.* As produced spaces, landscapes have a role to play in social life: they exist for a reason (even if, as in Axiom 1, the explicit purposes for which a landscape is originally built are shaped, transformed, and sometimes thwarted by all manner of social forces and processes). In capitalist society, the first, if not always obviously foremost, function of landscape is either to directly realize value (make money), or to establish the conditions under which value can be realized. Besides the impact this has on relations of production, there are two additional aspects worth discussing.

First, landscape is a (highly complex) site of investment. The built landscape, as Harvey (1982, 233–234) has put it:

> [H]as to be regarded ... as a geographically ordered, complex, composite commodity. The production, ordering, maintenance, renewal and transformation of such a commodity pose serious dilemmas. The production of individual elements – houses, factories, shops, schools, roads, etc. – has to be coordinated, both in time and space, in such a way as to allow the composite commodity to assume an appropriate configuration. Land markets ... serve to allocate land to uses, but finance capital and the state (primarily through the agency of land use regulation and planning) also act as coordinators. Problems also arise because the different elements have different physical lifetimes and wear out at different rates. ... The built environment as a whole is part public good and part private, and markets for individual elements reflect the complex interactions between different kinds of markets.

All that is to say, landscape is produced through investment in it, investment that is coordinated through complex financial market arrangements and state intervention.[4] But because it is an investment in anticipation of future profits, no capital invested in the landscape is ever guaranteed. All landscape is speculative: it is a banking of capitalist value in bricks and mortar in hopes of creating the conditions for the realization of even more capitalist value. The first sense in which landscape is functional, then, is as (potential) *exchange value*. Fields, factories, roads, houses, offices, even parks, each perhaps possessed of differing use values, are nonetheless sites for the *realization* (if not always the direct production) of exchange value. Under capitalism, "all aspects of the production and use of the built environment are brought within the orbit of the circulation of capital" (Harvey 1982, 234).[5] Just as importantly, one of the important use values of the material landscape is not only that it is a *site* for the investment of circulating capital, but that it is also the *means* – the very physical conditions – for the circulation of capital. Capital – whether in the form of goods or electronic impulses – can circulate only if the physical infrastructure (roads, ports, satellite dishes, high-tension wires, offices full of cubicles and computers, routing stations, mobile telephone towers, shopping malls, factories, and so forth) is in place that allows for that circulation (Rosati 2005). In other words, capital can only freely

---

[4] See chapter 7 in this volume by Babcock-Lumish and Clark on financial institutions and decisions.

[5] For a brilliant discussion of the contradictions that arise from the relation between circulating capital and relatively fixed landscape, see Henderson (1998). Henderson's focus is on the peculiarities of the California agricultural landscape but his argument is easily generalizable to other settings.

circulate if some capital is frozen in place in the built landscape.[6] Therefore, as Harvey (1982, 233) suggests, "[a]t any one moment the built environment appears as a palimpsest of landscapes fashioned according to the dictates of different modes of production at different stages of their historical development."

The second way in which the landscape establishes the conditions necessary for the realization of value (the second way in which it is functional) resides in the fact that landscape is a *lived* space and thus is crucial to the reproduction of labor power. This is an aspect of landscape that has too often been overlooked, especially since it can only be understood to the degree that we understand the close relationship that must exist between landscape as a built space (as I have just been talking about it) and landscape as an ideologically represented space (as much contemporary landscape theory understands it) (see Mitchell D 2004). We all live in landscape, but we do not live in the same landscape. Landscape thus both expresses and naturalizes difference. Ideologically it is a means of saying: *this is how they live; this is what they need*. If the configuration of landscape requires motorized transport to get to work, then the cost of that has to be figured into the reproduction costs of labor. If, in the historical development of a place, piped in fresh-drinking water and a separate room for each family member are normal conditions of living, then these too must be accounted for in the cost of reproducing labor power.

Obviously labor power exists in differing qualities (difference of this sort is a sine qua non of capitalism) and these differing qualities, embodied as they are in differently positioned people, must be reproduced through differing levels of state and private investment (in, e.g., specialized training, advanced degrees, and so forth). High-value labor power – highly skilled or in-demand workers – can *command* landscapes commensurate with their status and needs; while easily reproducible (or interchangeable) labor power – low-skilled, often racially, or ethnically marginalized workers – are able to command far less. Even so, their needs must be met – a landscape must be produced for them too in which goods and services are made available. These days that is often a landscape of dollar stores, food pantries, low-overhead markets (with little fresh food), acres of parking, all on the edges of town (or in declining inner suburbs). Exactly the sort of landscapes that Martha Schwartz bemoans as ugly are also deeply functional for American capitalism.[7]

---

[6] As should be evident from this list, the necessary physical infrastructure for the circulation of capital is historically and socially variable, and is itself constructed *through* the investment of capital in particular places at particular times. This is what is meant by the slogan that in order for some capital to circulate freely other capital must be fixed in place. It is also the root of the contradiction of circulating capital, since capital is defined as "value in motion," and yet value can only be in motion if other value (other capital) is not. That value not in motion is always subject to obsolescence, depreciation, and so forth.

[7] They are functional in several ways: as a site for the reproduction of labor power, as a means of realizing at least some of the value wrapped up in commodities rejected in higher-end locales (the so-called secondary circulation of commodities), as a site for social services squeezed out of other sites, and, increasingly, as a ghettoization of low class functions as the upper and middle classes (who can command a landscape of reproduction of a very different sort) sequester themselves in gated communities, high-end malls, and gentrified city cores and wish to erase all evidence in the landscape of the classed nature of the society we live in.

To put that another way, one of the preeminent landscape struggles through which we all constantly live is the struggle over what is right and what is good for different classes of people.[8] It is not only racist to say, as did one California agriculturalist in the 1920s that "The Mexican likes the sunshine against an adobe wall and a few tortillas, and in the off time he drifts across the border where he may have these things" (quoted in McWilliams 1968, 190). It is not only racist to suggest, as did agricultural camp inspectors for the California Commission of Immigration and Housing in 1926, that cutting "the old Chinese B.H.'s [bunk houses] into about half" would assure that farmers "will have no Chinese there in the coming year" (quoted in D. Mitchell 1996, 99). And it is not only racist to make clear, as did advocates for federal government labor camps in the California fields in the wake of the dust bowl, that such camps were now appropriate because it was now destitute *white* workers populating the agricultural labor markets of the state (Mitchell D. 1996, 178). Rather, in each of these instances (and many more we could choose from other realms, like discussions of urban public housing, the *favela*s of Rio, or the sprawling suburban estates of the managers of the new economy) these were *normative* statements about what the *proper* landscape for a particular class of people was. That is to say, the form of the landscape (the long bunkhouses, the government camps, the 7,500 square foot McMansion) are presented as right and true indications of what is necessary for the reproduction of the class in question. Or to put that in different terms, one of the functions of landscape is to assure that Lewis's axiom that landscape is a clue to culture is taken to be literally true.[9]

That matters because it is part of the struggle over how labor power (of differing qualities) is to be reproduced and thus what the possibilities for realizing surplus value really are at any particular moment and in any particular place. People strive and struggle for better living and working conditions; under the conditions presented to them, they seek to make a better life, whether that "better" is defined in terms of access to bare necessities (like food and shelter), increased comfort, a faster powerboat (and a place to run it), or even opulent luxury (as with many in the managerial and professional classes). Simultaneously, since the value (and thus the cost) of labor power is the key determinant in how much surplus value can be produced in any economic process, it is in the interests of individual capitals to either directly drive down wages – that is, to lower standards of living (or keep them low) – or to displace the costs of social reproduction onto others. It is the interest of the capitalist *class*, however, to assure that the size of the market continues to grow and its power to purchase expands. Another function of the landscape – and of individual investors' and the state's involvement in it – is to mediate that contradiction, to find a *spatial* as well as a social solution to the constant differentiations within classes of both producers and consumers this contradiction requires.

---

[8] Quite obviously "class" in this sense necessarily incorporates differences of race, gender, nationality, and so forth. See, generally, Russo and Linkon (2005).

[9] I develop this argument more fully in D. Mitchell (2001; 2003).

Any lived-in and produced-in landscape, therefore, is a site of struggle. California farmers' long battle to retain the right to have their workers use the debilitating short-handled hoe, for example, was waged in part as a means of insuring control over labor (by beating it down) and thus reducing direct labor costs. Through the 1970s, the fields of California were continually *shaped* by this battle (Mitchell 2001; Jain 2006). Similarly, when the state of California has actively enforced labor camp laws, seeking to improve standards of living for both migratory and settled-out workers, growers have more often than not responded by simply closing the camps and letting workers fend for themselves (by sleeping in caves carved out of hillsides [Wells 1996] or in cardboard shanties in the arroyos [Langerweische 1998] or stacked 20 to a room in farm-town apartments [Rothenberg 1998]). Precisely this kind of class struggle shapes – gives form to – the landscape. The landscape that results is functional in the sense that it functions *within* the struggled over social relations of production and reproduction. The landscape serves a purpose.

But to leave matters there is, literally, myopic: it fails to see the true extent of the landscape, as I will argue in Axiom 3.

Axiom 3: *No landscape is local.* "Context matters," Lewis argues, and he is absolutely right. But the argument that landscapes "make little cultural sense if they are studied outside their geographic (i.e., locational) context" (p. 24) is incomplete. For it is also true that landscapes make little sense, culturally or otherwise, if they are *only* studied in relation to their nearby surroundings.

Tobler's First Law of Geography – that "everything is related to everything else, but near things are more related than distant things" – may or may not be true, but it hardly seems relevant to the complex processes, practices, and decisions that make a landscape. The fruit orchards of Brentwood, California in the 1930s, for example, were products of transient labor from China, Japan, the Northeast of the USA, the Philippines, and eventually Mexico (and thus a result of numerous major and minor events, decisions and disruptions to the landscapes of production and reproduction *there*). Much of the capital planted in the orchards was from Britain. The theories behind the development and management of labor camps came from Berkeley professors (at least one of whom was deeply influenced by Freud [Parker 1919]); the laws that governed laborers and camps were fought out in Sacramento and Washington. The suburban houses that are now replacing these orchards are likewise the products of transient labor (together with local construction workers), building materials from the world over, designs hashed out in contracting firms across the USA and diffused through trade journals, and capital that is global in scope (until the crises of the late 1990s, East Asian capital was quite evident). To understand any produced landscape thus requires tracing out these networks of capital, commodities, and labor, networks that have long extended across the globe. And when one makes such a tracing, starting in a place like agricultural California, there are some startling results.

For example, numerous studies have shown that prevailing wages, throughout the history of California agriculture, have actually been below the value of labor power (Fuller 1939; Wells 1996; Walker 2004):[10] the California agricultural land-scape simply does not support itself. The labor power necessary for the production of the landscape and the realization of profit from it simply cannot be reproduced in California. Instead, labor power is reproduced elsewhere, in other landscapes: China, Japan, Scandinavia, the Northeast USA, India, the Philippines, Mexico, and the Dust Bowl states in the early years; predominantly these days in Mexico and further south in Central America. For all the local struggles that go into shaping the land-scape, distant struggles are just as important. Mexican families, communities, and the Mexican state assume the cost of raising and educating children, of nurturing new workers, of providing the minimal level of health care and other necessities that prepares them for employment in the USA. Mexican society frequently assumes the cost of maintaining workers during slack periods (especially as the USA has tightened immigration and welfare laws), and of supporting them in their old age.[11] The California agricultural landscape is thus tied into a network of land-scapes and it is a reasonable proposition to suggest, for example, that the strawberry fields of Watsonville, California are more closely and directly connected to the landscape of Oaxaca and Chiapas than they are to the wealthy suburban landscapes of Orinda or Moraga, about a hundred miles up the coast (see D. Mitchell 2003).[12]

There is another way in which distant places can be determinative of the shape and nature of landscapes.[13] In a recent survey of vineyards in Sonoma and Napa Valleys more than a third of growers freely admitted to state agents that they paid below minimum wage (Furillo 2001b). Enforcement of labor laws in the fields of California are at an all time low (Furillo 2001a). Threats to the health and safety of workers are rife. Union density has dropped to levels below where it was when the UFW began campaigning against growers in the 1960s (Furillo 2001c). One reason for this – for the daily violence of the California landscape – can be found not directly in the landscape of fields, vineyards, and orchards itself, but elsewhere: at the border between the USA and Mexico. Since the introduction of Operation

---

[10] The value of labor power is defined in the same way the value of any commodity is defined: as the sum of the value of all the ingredients, including labor, that go into making that commodity. For labor power, these include the values of food, shelter, clothing, necessary entertainment, schooling or training, and so forth. It also includes the value of these for dependents. Value in this sense is social, not individual, and socially determined. And as Marx (1987, 168) put it: "In contra-distinction therefore to the case of other commodities, there enters into the determination of the value of labor-power a historical and moral element." That is, the value of labor power is a product of struggle and development.

[11] Of course the picture is much more complicated than this because remittances are such an impor-tant part of Mexican and Central American economies. But the point is that the processes of labor power reproduction that make one landscape (like the California agricultural landscape) possible, occur in another landscape (like a Zapatec village). Each is shaped by the other.

[12] Then again, in Moraga and Orinda, the lawns and foundation plantings are maintained, the toi-lets and stoves scrubbed, and even sometimes the children minded, by Mexican and Guatemalan immigrants and migrants. And so it might be that Orinda, Moraga, and Watsonville's landscapes are closely connected, but they are connected *through* the villages of Mexico and Guatemala.

[13] This paragraph reworks an analysis first presented in Mitchell (2002).

Gatekeeper in San Diego in 1994, a stepped up and militarized program of border enforcement and fence building in urban and suburban areas that pushed undocumented border crossers into the mountains and deserts to the east (and increasingly into Arizona), an average of more than one person a day has died making the attempt to enter the USA (Gross 1999; Smith 1999; Ellingwood 2004). As the lockdown on the border has been extended into the desert and especially into semi-urban areas of Arizona, the death toll has continued to increase. Short of death, border crossers are subject to threats of assault, rape, and abandonment by the "coyotes" they pay to shepherd them across the border or of dehydration, hypothermia, and other injuries of exposure, or of attack by vigilantes and bandits (Ellingwood 2004). The cost of crossing the border, in terms of physical safety, has skyrocketed. It has skyrocketed monetarily, too. Coyote-ing is now at least an $8 billion a year business. Once across the border, debt peonage is rampant; outright slavery is not unheard of (Langerwiesche 1998). Labor is utterly cheapened. Flowers, strawberries, and grapes are picked by workers receiving rock-bottom, below-minimum (and sometimes below survival) wages. Long capitalized on the assumption of cheap labor (Fuller 1939) the California landscape continues to rely on it. The border, and the way it is enforced, has a significant role to play in providing that labor. For workers, even if they escape death, injury, or bondage, remain here illegally and thus almost never report wage, housing, or work condition abuses. Many are even afraid to go to health clinics when injured or seriously ill, knowing that they cannot afford to cross the border again. Stepped up enforcement, while never designed to fully close down the border to economic migrants (Andreas 2000; Nevins 2001), drives down wages and helps maintain the agricultural landscape as a viable location for capital investment even in the face of encroaching suburbanization.[14]

To understand Watsonville or Orinda or Moraga – or (to take a different but related example) the landscape of trendy cuisine in Los Angeles, San Francisco or Berkeley[15] – requires looking not there, but south: south to the border, and south to the villages of Mexico and Central America. It requires looking to the University of California at Davis where new strawberries – and new labor management systems – are invented. And it requires looking east to Washington where border policies

---

[14] This was a point never explicitly raised, but certainly always behind, the debates over and eventual passing of a law by the US Congress in 2006 to add another 700 miles of fencing and fortification to the border. While Congress did its best to appear to be assuaging the anti-immigrant sentiment stirred up by the large-scale immigrant-rights protests of that year, it nonetheless was also making sure that it kept the interests of immigrant-using capital always in mind.

[15] As regional cuisine develops, for all that is good about it, too few questions are raised about the conditions under which "local" ingredients are produced. While there is little to fault, for example, in Chez Panisse's Alice Waters' sourcing of local ingredients, support for community farming, and investment in inner-city school gardening and nutrition programs, few restaurateurs, in what is in fact a highly corporatized and often low-margin business, are as scrupulous, nor (in purely economic terms) can they afford to be. More generally, as Guthman (1998, 2004) has shown, organic farming in California is not immune from the sorts of rapacious labor relations that mark the agricultural industry as a whole.

are determined, and to New York and London (and on to Tokyo) where capital markets are organized (cf. chapter 7 in this volume by Babcock-Lumish and Clark on global capital markets). No landscape is local.

Axiom 4: History does matter. Lewis is right. As alluded to above, California's agricultural landscape has always been capitalized on the assumption of ready supplies of cheap labor (as important as skilled labor might be to it at times [Fuller 1939; Walker 2004]). The size of farms, the intensity of production, the audacious variety of crops (audacious because it has required costly experimentation to figure out how many things can be grown profitably in California): all have, in essence, been subsidized by labor paid at or below its reproduction costs. The history of this capitalization is built into the ground: in patterns of landholdings (Liebman 1983); in the specific packing sheds and canneries of cooperatives and corporations; in the dozens of research buildings and experimental farms around the state run by the University of California; in the toilets and labor camps that sometimes sprout along with the crops in the fields; and in the refrigerated rail cars and trucks that haul produce east or to ports and airports along the coast. This landscape – this configuration of things on the land – at each moment in time provides the structure within or against which new investment must be made. To the degree that it is outmoded, or inefficient (however defined), or unprofitable, it must be destroyed (a costly business) and built anew (Harvey 1976, 1982, 2001, 2003; Walker 2004).

The landscape at any moment is shaped by the current state of technology and so (as Marx showed for capitalist production more generally) is always vulnerable to losing out to innovation as more modern production facilities capture more of the socially available relative surplus value. The invention of mechanized cotton reapers in the 1940s, for example, had a profound effect on the size and intensity of cotton farming in the southern San Joaquin Valley, and on local labor markets (Arax and Wartzman 2003). Among other results has been excessively high structural unemployment throughout the valley, and particularly in traditional cotton towns like Corcoran, California. Such towns, desperate for inward investment and for stable employment opportunities have increasingly sought out state investment in the form of prisons. Corcoran, once vibrant and streaked with a bloody history of class war in the fields is now, for all intents and purposes, a no-longer vibrant (but still bloody) neighborhood of South Central and East Los Angeles, warehousing unemployed black, Latino, and Asian men and providing jobs for (largely white) local guards (Gilmore 2002, 2007).

Both everyday history (the long grind of investment decisions, specific struggles over wages and living conditions, the myriad small and large events and practices of life) and extraordinary events (cataclysmic economic restructuring, wars, natural disasters, major technological innovations, etc.) shape the land, and shape the possibilities for the future. History is lumpy, as Lewis suggests, but it is also a sea of constant change, in which waves of investment, innovation, and struggle of varying periodicity and intensity wash back and forth. Within this sea it is sometimes hard to see that the landscape is not just flow – not just the constant transformation of social relations as some contemporary theory avers – but also stasis, a repository of a great deal of inertia, a storehouse of values that can only be destroyed at great human and economic cost. Capitalism may advance through the sort of creative destruction Schumpeter (1934) described (see also Berman 1984; Harvey 1989, 2001; Smith 1990), but we should never forget that as creative as this destruction may be, it is also the destruction of real places, real people, real communities, real landscapes. And none of these is easily destroyed; each is a storehouse of not just capitalist value molded into girders, linoleum, sheetrock, and the rest, but also valuable histories, histories people often fight to protect, to maintain, to stabilize. To understand landscape historically requires careful analysis of the dialect of change and stability, and the contradictions to which this dialectic gives rise.

This is a second way history matters. People fight over it and they fight for it. Landscape is a repository of memory, both individual and collective. It is a site of and for identity. Cartographers for Rand McNally or AAA may ignore the Ludlow Monument in Southern Colorado, for example, erasing any mention of it from their maps and atlases, but thousands of union members and labor activists nonetheless make pilgrimages there every year, to leave messages of solidarity and to survey the site of one of the most important labor battles in American history. And the history – the martyrdom – represented by the monument was powerful enough to induce someone to destroy it, to truly try to erase memory from the landscape a couple of years ago (Green 2004). In Youngstown, Ohio, almost all the steel mills that used to stretch 24 miles up and down the Mahoning River have been closed and torn down, the parts sold off and the buildings themselves cut up and sold for scrap, but their memory in the landscape is indelible. But since memory is indelible, the struggles to preserve the landscape that represents it are intense, for while memory may be indelible people are not, and whole traditions, whole ways of knowing and being in the world can fade with the generations (Bruno 1999; Linkon and Russo 2003).

Sometimes it is the *erasure* of history that matters the most.[16] In the 1980s in Johnstown, Pennsylvania, as the steel mills were closing, the city tried to capitalize on the city's history, especially the history of the great flood of 1889, to entice tourist and service economy investment. City leaders sought to mobilize the landscape as a symbol of the city's long history of triumph over adversity, encouraging tourists and potential investors to see in it a story of courage, determination, willing labor, and community. In the process they sought to erase from the landscape visible signs of the labor and racial conflict that was at least as much a part of the city's history. The struggle in Johnstown was one of whose history was to be represented in the landscape, with city officials arguing that allowing the history of strife to remain visible would undermine the city's chances for economic recovery. The city worked hard to mold memory in, and identification with, the landscape in specific ways and to specific ends. The landscape was *given* a specific historical role to play and, to the degree the vision of the economic planners was not countered, it was pushed along a specific historical trajectory (D. Mitchell 1992).

Or, for one final example, try to find anywhere, up and down the length of the state of California, direct, clearly memorialized evidence of the long history of agricultural

---

[16]Dolores Hayden's *The Power of Place* (1996) project is immensely important in this regard because it seeks to bring back to the landscape those struggles – by women, people of color, workers – that have been erased in the landscape.

martyrdom that has been so crucial to winning even the most minimal rights for farm workers. Try finding monuments to the workers killed at Wheatland, or Corcoran, or Arvin, or the Chinese burned out of their homes, and camps in the Delta and foothills. Try finding memorials to the Japanese who fought for a better life in California *before* they were incarcerated in concentration camps in World War II. Try finding, even, an accurate depiction of the violence arrayed against Cesár Chavez and the United Farm Workers. You cannot. That is a history that *made* the agricultural landscape, but is very hard to find *in* the California landscape.

All this is to say, the representation of history in landscape (and all that goes with it, including identity and identification, the politics of inclusion and exclusion, the production of "national" landscapes, memorialization, and so forth) is not somehow immanent in the landscape itself (in the bricks and mortar, lawns and shrubs); rather it is a product of struggles over meanings – the meanings that are attached to landscape and the ones that are made to stick (see, generally, Loewen 1999). History matters in this case because landscape as historical representation is obviously an expression of power, which is part of Axiom 5.

Axiom 5: *Landscape is power.* Landscape is power in many senses. It is an expression of power as argued in Axiom 4, an expression of who has the power to define the meanings that are to be read into and out of the landscape, and, of course, to determine just what will exist in (and as) the landscape. This power operates in many ways and many places, from corporate boardrooms to city halls, from kitchen tables to consultants' reports, and from the opinion mills of think tanks to streets marked by protest. Decisions about investment, or the setting of rents, or the setting aside of land for a memorial, or the selection of a final design, or, perhaps preeminently, the approval of a land-use plan and the granting of a building permit, all are acts of power that are incorporated in the form of the landscape; and all are acts of power that define the meaning of the landscape. These acts of power are accepted, negotiated, contested, and resisted, which is to say they are acts of *social* power. To read a landscape, in other words, requires fluency in the symbols and languages of social power. It requires close attention to how the landscape is an expression of power and in what ways that power is expressed. It also requires always keeping in mind that the preeminent power that landscape might express is the power to erase history, signs of opposition, alternative readings, and so forth.

Landscape is also power in the sense that it quite literally determines what can and cannot be done. This is a corollary of the argument that the preexisting form of the landscape matters. The landscape's very materiality shapes individual and social behavior, practices, and processes. The very fact of a building on a lot changes how we can interact on that lot. The construction of a freeway does not just express some sort of "automobile culture;" it quite literally helps to *produce* that culture by opening up some opportunities for travel, social life, commerce, and economic production and closing off others.[17] The shape of the land has the power to shape social life.

---

[17] In his wonderful historical geography of Second Empire Paris, Harvey (2003) makes much of the ways that changed "space relations" both foreclosed old and opened new possibilities for the circulation of capital, the power of the state, and the possibilities for revolutionary action.

As W.J.T. Mitchell makes clear in the introduction to *Landscape and Power* (W. Mitchell 1994b, 1), the important question for landscape analysis is one of what landscape *does*: "how it works as a cultural practice" (see also Matless 1998). Landscape, Mitchell (1994b, 1–2) writes, "does not merely signify power relations; it is an instrument of cultural power, perhaps even an agent of power that is (or frequently represents itself as) independent of human interactions." In particular, Mitchell avers, landscape has all the power of ideology. It has the power to naturalize and make seem inevitable what is really constructed and struggled over. But the key point is this: unlike ideology, which is as transient as words, landscape is solid, physical, the opposite of ephemeral. Landscape is thus ideology made solid: a produced space that does *more* than represent. It guides. So landscape is power in a further sense: it really is just what *is* and it is up to us to make something else of it.

Methodologically, the implications here are clear. It is *never* sufficient to assess landscape only in terms of meanings or identity, or even the kinds of cultural power W.J.T. Mitchell and his collaborators focus on. To understand landscape as power always requires a close attention to form, and (to come full circle) thus on relations of production. For it is these relations that are internalized in landscape.[18] Understanding landscape as power in this sense requires turning Peirce Lewis on his head. If, as Rich Schein (2003, 202) argues, we understand the landscape, with Lewis, to be "the *result* of human activity, material evidence that can be read to make any number of cultural observations," then we will leave "landscape itself out of social and cultural processing," too easily regarding it as "inert and exist[ing] as the detritus or spoor of cultural activity." All that has been argued here, about the production of landscape, about scale, about landscape functionality, and about history, suggest just the opposite. Landscape is active. Or as Alexander Wilson (1991) pithily put it, landscape is activity.

Finally, then, the power of landscape is aesthetic. As an activity, and as so many have made clear (Berger 1972; Cosgrove 1984, 1985; Olwig 1996, 2003; Rose 1993; Williams 1973), landscape is a structured way of seeing, a particular (and of course contested) way of viewing and therefore interacting with the land and built environment. But as a particular, structured way of seeing, landscape has historically been established as *the* way of seeing. Landscape is didactic in that it teaches us to look in certain ways and to value aesthetics (over any number of other ways of knowing) as a means toward understanding the nature, status, and meaning of a place. When Martha Schwartz, who defines landscape much as Peirce Lewis does, condemns the USA for its ugliness, questions concerning, for example, *relations of production, function, extra-local process, history*, and even to some degree *power* are pushed aside. To argue, as Schwartz (2004, 19) does that the blight of strip malls are a function of cheap land and "bottom-line" (that is nonaesthetic) thinking is no doubt correct, but it is also radically understated: strip malls are deeply functional in our current society. Among other things they make the reproduction of the working class *affordable*. Even more, they have been vital in reducing the *value* of labor

---

[18] For a methodological discussion of the importance of "internal relations" and processes of internalization within Marxian historical materialism (which is at the root of my arguments), see Ollman (1991).

power. Strip malls are a powerful intervention into the economy, a solution to problems a long time in the making. The aesthetic function of landscape, however, is to turn our gaze in different directions and to encourage us to ask different kinds of questions (for Schwartz's interviewer, the other kind of question was one of whether developing more stringent planning controls might make us "snobbish" like the Europeans: "But the price for their taste is snobbery"). This is not to say that aesthetics do not matter: they do, and deeply. But it is to say that aesthetics need to be understood within their social context, and that the functionality of aesthetics needs always to be raised (what, for example, would gentrification be without the strong ideological work of aesthetics that does so much to pave its way and justify its displacements). What are needed are questions about what different aesthetic movements, sensibilities, opportunities, and values do, Landscape is *powerful* activity.

Axiom 6: *Landscape is the spatial form that social justice takes*. As a concretization of social relations, and as a foundation for the further development of those relations, landscape literally marks out the spatial extent and limits of social justice. The spatial form of the landscape is both the result of and evidence for, the kind of society we live in. The true degree of spatial equality, environmental equity, affirmative (rather than destructive) possibilities for difference, degrees of autonomy – all these are simply *there* in the landscape. In the long economic boom of the 1990s, for example, inequality grew at as rapid a rate as it ever has. And the landscapes of every metropolitan area in the USA show this: massive tracks of McMansions in manicured lawns lining one new golf course after another sprawled out to the horizon, while inner-city neighborhoods decayed, places of employment were abandoned, houses crumbled, and storefront after storefront was boarded up, even those that used to house free health clinics and other evidence of the struggles for a more just society that marked an earlier generation. Inner-city churches devoted ever more space to soup kitchens and food pantries, in the hopes of providing at least some healthy food in neighborhoods with no near access to fresh fruit and vegetables. At the same time, the rise of community gardens on abandoned lots vied for community attention as means for combating neighborhood decline against more draconian "weed and seed" programs that populate the landscape with police masquerading as social workers. Meanwhile downtown streets bristle with security cameras, metal detectors, and defensive landscape designs geared toward always moving the homeless along by providing them no place to sit and rest, or just to hang out. No better evidence of the state – the on-going state – of social justice in America can be found. There is no truer foundation than this landscape for what social justice in the future possibly can be.

To take students – to take *ourselves* – on a transect of the urban landscape, from gentrified bar/warehouse district, to the black, Latino, and white neighborhoods of deep poverty, through the flatted mansions of the old elite neighborhoods, out into the early postwar suburbs, the extensive tract homes built to accommodate the baby boom, and on to the outer suburbs where those baby boomers now live in larger houses (with fewer kids) may say something about American culture and its changes, but it says even more about the nature of American justice and how we use space – distance as well as design – to separate ourselves from the poverty that our wealth so efficiently produces.

Or, to take another example, take a tour through the old mixed-farming and cattle-raising countryside north and west of Sioux Falls, South Dakota. Notice the abandoned farmsteads, the Wal-Mart in Aberdeen, which draws shoppers from 75 miles away as small-town stores and butcher-shops have closed (and provides low-wage work for these same shoppers). Notice how few feedlots there are, how few livestock auctions. This is a landscape radically and rapidly restructured over the last 30 years, one in which the very possibility of living and working is imperiled for more and more residents. School districts are consolidating or closing altogether, requiring children to endure hours-long commutes. Changes in the beef slaughtering industry, in global trade laws, in technology, and in the flows of capital through the countryside have all come together to create a landscape that simply cannot sustain communities of any size, even as they concentrate ever more people in select locations (like Kearney, Nebraska, or even Sioux Falls). A massively uneven and contradictory economic system has created a massively depopulated agricultural landscape (the second depopulation in just over a century, the first being the slaughter and removal of the Lakota). It's not so much that social and political processes and formations "conspire" to create such a landscape, and such conditions of and for social and spatial justice, but rather that social, economic, and political processes and formations *act* to create such landscapes, and that (unevenly and not without much tumult) landscapes are made to be functional within (to align with) changing social, economic, and political processes and formations (Breitbach 2006).

For this reason, George Henderson (2003, 180) urges us to focus our attention on "actually existing social and political formations" as a means of assessing possibilities for progressive social change. For him, such a focus requires close attention to the landscape because the landscape is produced through these social and political formations. And these formations are the antithesis of just. Or, as he puts it, "the study of landscape, that living thing that so often evokes the plane on which normal, everyday life is lived – precisely *because* of the premium it places on the everyday – must stand up to the facts of world in crisis, to the fact that everyday life is, for many people, the interruption or destruction of everyday life" (Henderson 2003, 196). The ugliness of the landscape, to put this in the aesthetic terms of Martha Schwartz, or the ordinariness of it, to put it in Peirce Lewis's terms, signifies something far greater than aesthetics or the banality of culture: it signals the shape and possibility of justice. Therefore, Henderson concludes, "what is … needed is a concept of landscape that helps point the way to those interventions that can bring about much greater social justice. And what landscape study needs even more is a concept of landscape that will assist the development of the very idea of social justice" (ibid. 196).

In other words, to understand landscape as the spatial form that social justice takes, and to understand that normatively as a means of finding ways to create a more progressively just landscape, requires that we return to landscape's origins – or at least one of them. As Ken Olwig (1996) has shown, one of the meanings of the continental terms that became the English "landscape" was of a place of justice. "A *landskab*," Olwig (1996, 633) writes, "was not just a region, it was a nexus of law and cultural identity" where people "had a greater right to self-determination and to participate in the judicial process and in government" (Olwig 1996, 631, quoting Trap 1864). That is, *landskab* was a place where justice was defined by its inhabitants and autonomy was a valued property. The history of landscape may since then be a history of progressive alienation and a greater distancing of authority; it may be a history of widening arcs of complexity and contradiction; but it is still the case that landscapes are made (if by other means than by "axe and plow") and so it must, in some senses still belong to "the people" who have made it (Olwig 1993, 311). The trick for us is to use our analysis, design, and other skills both to show how it does still belong to the people and to counter the heavy weight of alienation that is so much a part of the capitalist production of landscape.

But why landscape? Why put this weight of political economy and social justice on "landscape," both as a concept (limited as all concepts must be) and as a built form (particular as all built forms are). Landscape is important because it really is *everything* we see when we go outside. But it also is everything that we do not see. Landscape, in other words, is a way into, a foundation for the exploration of all that there is – the social totality within which we live. As a concretization of social relations, landscape properly understood provides a means to analyze – to make visible – the social relations that go into its making, even as one of the functions of landscape is precisely to make those social relations obscure. The fetishizing function of landscape should not be discounted. It really is not possible to directly "read" the landscape in any satisfying sense. But it is possible to analyze it: to search for how it is made, to explore its functions, to examine the other places that are foundational in its production and meaning, to understand its history and trajectory, to uncover how power works in and through it, and *therefore*, to learn what it says about the status of and possibility for a just world in the here and now. All this takes the work not just of looking, but also all those other scholarly tasks Lewis seemed so ready to jettison – archival research, theorizing, ethnographic analysis, and critically reading the scholarly literature. It also takes a commitment to a materialist analysis, for it is only by examining the landscape in its material form – as it really is, rather than as we wish it to be – and only by analyzing the social relations that go into its making, that we can begin to really learn (and learn from) what we are looking at.

In doing so, we ought to be able to learn how better to intervene into the landscape, to make better guesses about the reasons for and impacts of our designs, our solidarity work with activist groups, or just to do a better job of telling the landscape's story, and through that to gain a better purchase on how the totality of social relations operates in particular places and at particular times. Reading the landscape can raise important questions, but it can rarely answer them. To provide answers, which is always the first step in making change in the landscape, requires a different theory and methodology for understanding what the landscape is and how it operates. These new axioms, I hope, will provide a starting point for this methodology at least as fruitful as Peirce Lewis's once were.

References

Alamillo J (2006) *Making Lemonade Out of Lemons: Mexican-American Labor and Leisure in a California Town, 1880–1960*. University of Illinois Press, Urbana, IL

Andreas P (2000) *Border Games: Policing the US-Mexico Divide*. Cornell University Press, Ithaca, NY

Arax M and Wartzman, R. (2003) *The King of California: J.G. Boswell and the Making of a Secret American Empire*. Public Affairs Press, New York

Barrell J (1980) *The Dark Side of Landscape: The Rural Poor in English Painting, 1730–1840*. Cambridge University Press, Cambridge

Bender B (ed) (1993) *Landscape: Politics and Perspectives*. Berg, Oxford

Berger J (1972) *Ways of Seeing*. Penguin, London

Berman M (1984) *All that is Solid Melts into Air: The Experience of Modernity*. Simon & Schuster, New York

Bermingham A (1984) *Landscape and Ideology: The English Rustic Tradition, 1740–1840*. Thames & Hudson, London

Breitbach C (2006) Shifting landscapes of social reproduction in rural South Dakota. Unpublished Dissertation, Department of Geography, Syracuse University

Bruno R (1999) *Steelworker Alley: How Class Works in Youngstown*. Cornell University Press, Ithaca, NY

Cosgrove D (1984) *Social Formation and Symbolic Landscape*. Croom Helm, London

Cosgrove D (1985) Prospect, perspective and the evolution of the landscape idea. *Transactions of the Institute of British Geographers* 10: 45–62

Cosgrove D (1993) *The Palladian Landscape: Geographical Change and its Cultural Representation in Sixteenth-century Italy*. Pennsylvania State University Press, University Park, PA

Cosgrove D and Daniels S (eds) (1988) *The Iconography of Landscape: Essays on its Symbolic Representation, Design, and Use of Past Landscapes*. Cambridge University Press, Cambridge

Daniel C (1981) *Bitter Harvest: A History of California Farmworkers, 1870–1941*. Cornell University Press, Ithaca, NY

Daniels S (1989) Marxism, culture, and the duplicity of landscape. In Peet R and Thrift N (eds) *New Models in Geography*, vol. 2. Unwin Hyman, London, pp 196–220

Daniels S (1993) *Fields of Vision: Landscape Imagery and National Identity in England and the United States*. Princeton University Press, Princeton, NJ

Duncan J (1980) The super organic in American cultural geography. *Annals of the Association of American Geographers* 70: 181–198

Duncan J (1990) *The City as Text: The Politics of Landscape Interpretation in the Kandyan Kingdom*. Cambridge University Press, Cambridge

Eagleton D (2000) *The Idea of Culture*. Blackwell, Oxford

Ellingwood K (2004) *Hard Line: Life and Death on the U.S.–Mexico Border*. Pantheon, New York

Fuller V (1939) The supply of agricultural labor as a factor in the evolution of farm organization in California. United States Senate, Subcommittee of the Committee on Education and Labor, Hearings on S. Res. 266, Violations of free speech and the rights of labor (Part 54, Exhibit 8762-A). Government Printing Office, Washington DC, pp 19777–19898

Furillo A (2001a) Citation rare for violators: the state labor chief points to another approach – education. *Sacramento Bee* 20 May 2001

Furillo A (2001b) Toiling under abuse. *Sacramento Bee* 20 May 2001

Furillo A (2001c) With union in decline, farm workers are turning elsewhere. *Sacramento Bee* 22 May 2001

Galarza E (1977) *Farm-workers and Agribusiness in California*. University of Notre Dame Press, South Bend, IN

Garcia M (2001) *A World of its Own: Race, Labor, and Citrus in the Making of Greater Los Angeles, 1900–1970*. University of North Carolina Press, Chapel Hill, NC

Gilmore R (2002) Race and globalization. In Johnston RJ, Taylor P, and Watts M (eds) *Geographies of Global Change: Remapping the World*. Blackwell, Oxford, pp 261–274

Gilmore R (2007) *Golden Gulag: Prisons, Surplus, Crisis, and Opposition in California, 1982–2000*. University of California Press, Berkeley, CA

Green J (2004) Crime against memory at Ludlow. *Labor* 1: 9–16

Gross G (1999) 5-Year-Old Gatekeeper is praised, denounced. *San Diego Union* 31 October, B1

Guthman J (1998) Regulating meaning, appropriating nature: the codification of California organic agriculture. *Antipode* 30: 135–154

Guthman J (2004) *Agrarian Dreams: The Paradox of Organic Farming in California*. University of California Press, Berkeley, CA

Harvey D (1976) Labor, capital and class struggle around the built environment in advanced capitalist societies. *Politics and Society* 6: 265–295

Harvey D (1982) *The Limits to Capital*. University of Chicago Press, Chicago

Harvey D (1989) *The Condition of Postmodernity*. Blackwell, Oxford

Harvey D (2001) *Spaces of Capital*. Routledge, New York

Harvey D (2003) *Paris, the Capital of Modernity*. Routledge, New York

Hayden D (1996) *The Power of Place*. Yale University Press, New Haven, CT

Helsinger E (1994) Turner and the representation of England. In Mitchell WJT (ed) *Landscape and Power*. University of Chicago Press, Chicago, pp 103–125

Henderson G (1998) *California and the Fictions of Capital*. Oxford University Press, Oxford

Henderson, G. (2003) What (else) we talk about when we talk about landscape: for a return to the social imagination. In Wilson C and Groth P (eds) *Everyday America: Cultural Landscape Studies after J.B. Jackson*. University of California Press, Berkeley, CA, pp 178–198

Holdsworth D (1990) The landscape and the archives: texts for the analysis of the built environment. In Groth P (ed) *Vision, Culture, and Landscape*. Working Papers from the Berkeley Symposium on Cultural Landscape Interpretation, Department of Landscape Architecture, University of California, Berkeley, CA, pp 187–204

Jackson P (1989) *Maps of Meaning*. Unwin Hyman, London

Jain S (2006) *Injury*. Yale University Press, New Haven, CT

Langerweische W (1998) Invisible men. *New Yorker* 23 February–2 March, 141 ff.

Lewis P (1979) Axioms for reading the landscape: some guides to the American scene. In Meinig D (ed) *The Interpretation of Ordinary Landscape: Geographical Essays*. Oxford University Press, New York, pp 11–32

Lewis P (1983) Learning from looking: geographical and other writing about the American cultural landscape. *American Quarterly* 35: 242–261

Liebman E (1983) *California Farmland: A History of Large Agricultural Landholdings*. Rowman and Allenheld, Totowa, NJ

Linkon S and Russo J (2003) *Steeltown USA*. University of Kansas Press, Lawrence, KS

Loewen J (1999) *Lies Across America*. New Press, New York

Majka L and Majka T (1983) *Farmworkers, Agribusiness, and the State*. Temple University Press, Philadelphia, PA

Marx K (1987) *Capital*, vol. 1. International Publishers, New York

Matless D (1998) *Landscape and Englishness*. Reaction Books, London

McWilliams C (1968) *North from Mexico: The Spanish-speaking People of the United States*. Greenwood Press, Westport, CT

McWilliams C (1999 [1939]) *Factories in the Field: The Story of Migratory Farm Labor in California*. University of California Press, Berkeley, CA

Mitchell D (1992) Heritage, landscape, and the production of community: consensus history and its alternatives in Johnstown, Pennsylvania. *Pennsylvania History* 59: 233–255

Mitchell D (1993) State intervention in landscape production: The Wheatland riot and the California Commission of Immigration and Housing. *Antipode* 25: 91–113

Mitchell D (1995) There's no such thing as culture: towards a reconceptualization of the idea of culture in geography. *Transactions of the Institute of British Geographers* 20: 102–116

Mitchell D (1996) *The Lie of the Land: Migrant Workers and the California Landscape*. University of Minnesota Press, Minneapolis, MN

Mitchell D (2001) The devil's arm: points of passage, networks of violence, and the California agricultural landscape. *New Formations* 43: 44–60

Mitchell D (2002) The geography of injustice: borders and the continuing immiseration of California agricultural labor in an era of "free trade." *Richmond Journal of Global Law and Business* 2(2): 145–166

Mitchell D (2003) California living, California dying: dead labor and the political economy of landscape. In Anderson K, Pile S, and Thrift N (eds) *Handbook of Cultural Geography*. Sage, London, pp 233–248

Mitchell D (2004) Landscape. In Sibley D, Atkinson D, Jackson P, and Washbourne N (eds) *Cultural Geography: A Critical Dictionary of Key Ideas*. I.B. Taurus, London, pp 48–56

Mitchell WJT (1994a) Imperial landscape. In Mitchell WJT (ed) *Landscape and Power*. University of Chicago Press, Chicago, pp 5–34

Mitchell WJT (1994b) Introduction. In Mitchell WJT (ed) *Landscape and Power*. University of Chicago Press, Chicago, pp 1–4

Mitchell WJT (ed) (1994c) *Landscape and Power*. University of Chicago Press, Chicago

Nevins J (2001) *Operation Gatekeeper: The Rise of the "Illegal Alien" and the Remaking of the U.S.–Mexico Boundary*. Routledge, New York

Ollman B (1991) *Dialectical Investigations*. Routledge, New York

Olwig K (1984) *Nature's Ideological Landscape*. Allen & Unwin, London

Olwig K (1993) Sexual cosmology: nation and landscape at the conceptual interstices of nature and culture, or: what does landscape really mean? In Bender B (ed) *Landscape: Politics and Perspectives*. Berg, Oxford, pp 307–343

Olwig K (1996) Recovering the substantive nature of landscape. *Annals of the Association of American Geographers* 86: 630–653.

Olwig K (2003) *Landscape, Nature, and the Body Politic: from Britain's Renaissance to America's New World*. University of Wisconsin Press, Madison, WI

Olwig K (2005) Representation and alienation in the political land-scape. *Cultural Geographies* 12: 19–40

Parker C (1919) *The Casual Laborer and Other Essays*. Harcourt, Brace and Howe, New York

Pincetl S (1999) *Transforming California: A Political History of Land Use and Development*. Johns Hopkins University Press, Baltimore, MD

Rosati C (2005) The image factory: MTV, geography, and the industrial production of culture. Ph.D. dissertation, Department of Geography, Syracuse University

Rose G (1993) *Feminism and Geography: The Limits of Geographical Knowledge*. University of Minnesota Press, Minneapolis, MN

Russo J and Linkon S (eds) (2005) *The New Working Class Studies*. Cornell University Press, Ithaca, NY

Said E (1993) *Culture and Imperialism*. Knopf, New York

Sauer C (1963 [1925]) The morphology of landscape. In Leighly J (ed) *Land and Life: A Selection of the Writings of Carl Ortwin Sauer*. University of California Press, Berkeley, CA, pp 315–350.

Schein R (2003) Normative dimensions of landscape. In Wilson C and Groth P (eds) *Everyday America: Cultural Landscape Studies after J.B. Jackson*. University of California Press, Berkeley, CA, pp 199–219

Schumpeter J (1934) *The Theory of Economic Development*. Harvard University Press, Cambridge, MA

Schwartz M (2004) Can America go public? Interview with Deborah Solomon. *New York Times Magazine*, 16 May: 19

Smith N (1990) *Uneven Development: Nature, Capital and the Production of Space*, 2nd edition. Blackwell, Oxford

Smith C (1999) Condemning migrant job seekers to death. *San Diego Union*, 6 April 1999: B7

Stoll S (1998) *The Fruits of Natural Advantage: Making the Industrial Countryside in California*. University of California Press, Berkeley, CA

Trap JP (1864) *Statistik-topogrphisk beskrivlse af hertugdømmet Slevsig*. Gad, Copenhagen

Walker R (2004) *The Conquest of Bread*. New Press, New York

Wells M (1996) *Strawberry Fields: Politics, Class and Work in California Agriculture*. Cornell University Press, Ithaca, NY

Williams R (1958) *Culture and Society*. Chatto & Windus, London

Williams R (1973) *The Country and the City*. Oxford University Press, New York

Williams R (1977) *Marxism and Literature*. Oxford University Press, Oxford

Williams R (1980) *Problems in Materialism and Culture*. Verso, London

Williams R (1982) *The Sociology of Culture*. Schocken, New York

Wilson A (1991) *The Culture of Nature: From Disney to the Exxon Valdez*. Blackwell, Oxford

Chapter 2
Landscapes of Possibility?
Livelihood and Intervention in the Production
of Andean Landscapes

Anthony J. Bebbington

Landscapes of Constraint: The Challenge of Viable Livelihoods

"Is Bolivia viable?" The reply came without question. "It has to be viable." Later the question was recast: "Is the altiplano viable?" This time there was discussion and the eventual reply was more nuanced: "In some areas, yes."

(IDB 1996, my translation)

The altiplano is the high plain of the Andes, located at altitudes upward of 3,800 m above sea level (Figure 1). Though an important center of pre-Incaic peoples, in modern times it has become something of a conundrum for organizations seeking to foster economic growth and reduce poverty. Some have, indeed, come close to all but giving up and have been tempted to argue that the regional economies of such high-altitude areas, and the livelihoods of people residing there, are simply not economically sustainable under contemporary political–economic and sociocultural conditions.

The exchange noted above reflects such sentiments of frustration. It is drawn from the report of an Inter-American Development Bank team mandated to explore the possibilities for social and economic development in Bolivia. The statement can of course be easily derided. It could be written off as one more mistaken interpretation of external experts who, blinded by their technical and specialist knowledge fail to understand the landscapes and societies they encounter. It might also be viewed as a misreading of landscape driven by the underlying views of professionals inclined to denigrate what they view as backward forms of land and resource use (cf. Fairhead and Leach 1996). More perniciously still it could also be understood as a nefarious exercise of power in which the IDB team, informed by their neoliberal models of development and their economistic understandings of well-being, construct the notion of nonviability, constituting the *altiplano* as an object of future interventions that are likely only to foster further constraints on the livelihoods of people who call the high plains their home.

Such critiques – of a sort not hard to find in the literature – are not without foundation. They make the important point that no reading of landscape is innocent – all come with prior conceptions and are informed by the interests of their authors. They caution care in any effort to read the vast and (to outsiders) often inscrutable human landscapes of the high Andes, and even more care before drawing

Figure 1 An Andean landscape: Quispicanchi, Cusco, Peru (ajb)

policy conclusions (especially of the enormity of those that might be implied by the quotation). But at the same time such critiques can be made too easily. For they must also make sense of the decisions that so many residents of the Andes make each day to organize their lives in such a way as to help their children build their futures outside the countryside. They also have to sit beside striking convergences with processes underway in what would otherwise seem to be quite distinct regions of the world. A short while back, after I had presented a paper on rural livelihoods in Peru and Bolivia, the first hand to go up was that of a recently retired planner for one of the UK's national parks. He proceeded to identify all the ways in which the rural economy of the Peak District (on whose borders I live: Figure 2) was facing the same challenges as that of the Andes: out-migration, especially of youth; an aging farmer population; increasing dependence on globalized agri-food chains; and an agricultural economy in steady demise.[1] As if to embody such trends, not long after the talk, our mailman told us that in the face of limited opportunities on the edge of the Peaks, he and his partner had decided to migrate to Canada. Viability – at least the viability of a certain sort of rural economy and landscape – is not merely a discursive construct for him.

  Not that all locations in Canada will necessarily resolve his livelihood concerns – for North American landscapes and their residents face not dissimilar challenges.

---

[1] UK national parks differ from those of the USA in that people reside within park boundaries. Indeed, UK parks are more about conserving landscape than protecting wilderness. Thus farming and other economic activities continue, though there are stringent planning controls on what is and is not possible in park areas.

Figure 2   The Peak District and its borders, Derbyshire, England (ajb)

As just one example, Don Mitchell (2008, in this collection) refers to "the old mixed-farming and cattle-raising countryside north and west of Sioux Falls, South Dakota." He asks us to "[n]otice the abandoned farmsteads, the Wal-Mart in Aberdeen which draws shoppers from 75 miles away as small-town stores and butcher-shops have closed" and also to "[n]otice how few feedlots there are, how few livestock auctions." "This", he says, "is a landscape radically and rapidly restructured over the past thirty years, one in which the very possibility of living and working is imperiled for more and more residents." Some of the landscape transforming processes at play in Sioux Falls resemble those at work in the Andes and the Peak District. Here is Mitchell again: "[c]hanges in the beef slaughtering industry, in global trade laws, in technology, and in the flows of capital through the countryside have all come together to create a landscape that simply cannot sustain communities of any size," Livelihood viability and landscape form go hand in hand.

Of course, the challenge to build viable livelihoods in these rural landscapes is more severe for some than for others. As young adults in the highlands of Bolivia and Peru make their ways to Lima, La Paz, and other urban centers, so employees of mining companies and tour operators find new ways of living from, occupying, and moving through the high Andean landscape. And more constrained than any of us, in the Peaks and the altiplano alike, there are many who are too old, too poor, or too stubborn either to leave or to begin producing new landscapes. Closer to home, as our mailman plans his escape from the Peak District so we have just arrived, maintained by our university and NGO salaries, and inspired by loose ideas for how we would like to live in the countryside. The developers who now own the old cotton mill in our village, most recently a home to light industrial workshops, have commissioned architects to redesign and relandscape it for homes that would certainly not be affordable for our mailman, nor for most of the village's long-standing residents many of who have struggled against such a change in land use, and want to resist the incursion of so many new people into the village.[2] "Amenity migration" along with the landscape changes, social tensions and design dilemmas to which it gives rise are as real in the UK as they are in the USA discussed by Culbertson et al. in this book (chapter 3).

These movements – our movements – reflect the shifting possibilities and constraints delivered by contemporary patterns of economic development. They also reflect the varying desires of people living in these landscapes, their abilities to resist and rework these processes of economic development, and their diverse responses to the varying allures of modernity. And finally they reflect the degree to which organized interventions – of the Peak District National Park, of Bolivian nongovernmental development organizations or of citizen's movements in La Paz and Derbyshire – change what people *want*, and are *able*, to do and be in these landscapes. The net effect is that the composition of *landscape producers* changes as does the balance among different life, economic, and political projects being sought through these landscapes (Figure 3).

Figure 3 Abandoned mill site to be redeveloped into apartments and houses, Derbyshire, England (ajb)

---

[2] This struggle was apparently lost in the period between the submission of this paper and the final signing of the book contract. As of July 2006 small bulldozers were clearing out-buildings on the site.

Put simply, I want to suggest that while the high Andean region may be distinct in many ways, its processes of landscape and livelihood change are not absolutely different from those occurring in other, ostensibly more developed, rural parts of the world. With that said, the comparison with the Peak District now goes on hold and the remainder of this paper is concerned with the relationships among livelihoods, interventions, and political economy in the production of high Andean landscapes. The paper first lays out its conceptual building blocks, and then moves to discuss landscape, livelihood, and institutional changes that have occurred over the last four decades in three parts of the high Andes. It uses these cases to explore the conditions under which social justice oriented interventions might help broaden livelihood possibilities and foster fairer landscapes. The conclusions draw out implications for design efforts.

Livelihoods and Landscapes

The concept of livelihood, though not especially new in development studies, has enjoyed a small boom in recent years. It draws attention to people's agency,[3] while also emphasizing the material basis of that agency. In particular, livelihoods approaches explore the asset bases upon which people construct their lives, the ways in which people seek access to and control over different assets, and the effects of different asset mixes on livelihood possibilities. Figure 4 offers a simple schema for conceptualizing livelihoods. Livelihoods are understood as that process through which people transform their existing ecological, human, financial, social, and physical asset base into material well-being, meaning, power, and their future asset base.

The everyday, cumulative production of landscapes derives in large measure from these livelihoods. Indeed, some – perhaps many – large-scale, distinctive, and apparently defining features of landscape can be understood as the products of such quotidian actions. Geographer William Doolittle (1984) has shown how extensive, semi-terraced water management features in Mexican drylands resulted from countless, everyday acts of environmental manipulation by farmers as they organize their fields. The late anthropologist Robert Netting – though primarily concerned with understanding the dynamics of smallholder production systems – has also illuminated the ways in which the mosaics of smallholder landscapes in the Swiss Alps can also be explained in terms of the cumulative effects of families' rural livelihood decisions;

---

[3] "Agency" is a complicated notion in social theory (Giddens 1979). In its simplest sense, though, the concept is intended to emphasize people's role in reproducing and changing social structures – and to make clear that these structures cannot exist, or change, without the (intentional and unintentional) action of people. Many using the term are also concerned to highlight: the centrality of human action in social life (and thus in any design intervention); the fact that such action is meaningful to people; and the capacity that people have to transform and rework existing social arrangements.

and geographer Simon Batterbury has suggested much the same for rural landscapes in Niger (Batterbury 2001: see also Doolittle 1984; Netting 1993).

As Figure 4 also suggests, though, such everyday decisions are not made in a vacuum – social and political economic relationships and institutions structure incentives and aspirations. Whether, for instance, people will seek to invest in the natural capital they already control and build a livelihood from agriculture, or instead invest in their human capital with a view to building a more urbanized livelihood will depend on these wider incentives and aspirations. Indeed, while the practice of everyday life is central to landscape production, when villagers recount local histories their narratives tend to revolve around high magnitude, low-frequency events of a type that are equally determinant of landscape.[4] In these narratives, local histories are frequently organized around livelihood and landscape-defining events such as roads constructed, mines opened, schools built, mass protests, or extreme climatic events.[5] Many of these events are also part of more sustained programs of public and private organizations each intervening in these rural areas in pursuit of their own goals – goals which can range from state formation, to social justice, to business expansion. These goals each come with their (often implicit) visions of landscape. While sometimes convergent, more often than not these visions of landscape are in fact quite distinct – certainly envisioned landscapes of social justice generally look very different from those of neoliberal forms of capitalism.[6]

The following cases explore several such interfaces between everyday processes of landscape production and external interventions in these landscapes, interfaces at which meanings are negotiated and at which both collaboration and conflict occur, not infrequently at the same time. Each case is of an area with predominantly indigenous populations (Aymara [La Paz], Quechua [Ayacucho], and Quichua [Chimborazo]), with concentrations of severe and often chronic poverty, and occupying adversely incorporated and marginal positions within their national economies.[7] Each is therefore an area in which, some would say, many livelihoods are simply untenable in the medium and long terms. Yet, these areas have each experienced significant interventions by agencies seeking to create the conditions for more viable livelihoods and to promote more socially just ways of organizing society. They have also experienced important, if discontinuous, interventions of a state concerned to increase its presence and – inter alia – to avert social unrest. That said

---

[4] The implied analogy with theories of discontinuity and change in ecological systems (Holling 1986) is deliberate here.

[5] The role of such events in organizing local accounts of history in the Andes has been clear in both our and others' research (e.g., Bebbington et al. 2002; Bury 2004; VMPPFM 1998; Muñoz et al. 2000).

[6] Neoliberalism is another slippery term (Larner 2000; Peck 2004). Here it is used as an adjective to refer to those ways of governing capitalism that privilege the use of market reason to allocate resources of all types (productive, social, natural, financial …).

[7] For discussions of the concept of chronic poverty see CPRC (2004) and Hulme and Shepherd (2003) – on adverse incorporation see du Toit (2004).

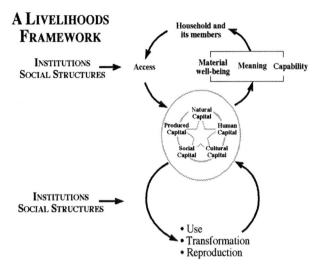

Figure 4 An assets-and-institutions-based livelihoods framework (Bebbington 2004)

each of these areas has seen significant social protest over the last two decades. Conversely, organized capitalist intervention in these areas has been far less significant, with the exception of La Paz where livelihoods and landscape dynamics have been affected by the recent privatization of dairy processing industry. While this relative absence of large-scale forms of capital investment makes these areas typical of most of the Andes, it also means that these examples do not include the types of transformation associated with extractive industries that have occurred throughout the history of the Andes, and taken on new impetus in the neoliberal period.[8]

Livelihoods, Interventions, and High Andean Landscapes: Three Cases

This caveat notwithstanding, the relative abandonment by both private and public sectors of large parts of the Andes might be viewed as the flip side of the neoliberal coin, structurally related to the sorts of geographically targeted, massive investments in natural resource extraction that have been apparent in certain localities in the Andean countries. Indeed, it might reasonably be argued that – seen from the

---

[8] This is a significant gap in the paper. The extraction of minerals and hydrocarbons has assumed a very important position within national development strategies in the neoliberal period, and the livelihood and landscape issues at stake have generated much political debate, social mobilization and violent protest (Bebbington et al. 2006). Such phenomena point, of course, to a further similarity with North America – especially the US west, but also Inuit and other native American areas of Canada. For further discussion see, for instance, Bury (2004), Ross (2001), and Bridge (2004).

perspective of national economic planners and Ministries of Finance – the relevance of the high Andes to national strategies of growth and economic development has been as a source of primary materials and little else. There are, as always, exceptions: the characterization is most pertinent for Peru, and least so for Ecuador; in both Peru and Ecuador there has been central government interest in the role of nontraditional agricultural exports in some parts of the highlands; and in each of Peru, Ecuador, and Bolivia, at certain historical moments, some elites have given peasant agriculture a role in national development (particularly during the periods when land reform and integrated rural development were in vogue). But by and large, the paucity of public and private investment in both social and physical infrastructure in much of the Andes has been – in social justice terms at least – appalling.

This section discusses livelihood–landscape relationships in three areas that come to a greater or lesser extent from this flip side of the coin. These are the province of Chimborazo in Ecuador (specifically the county of Guamote); the highlands of Ayacucho in Peru; and the department of La Paz in Bolivia (specifically the province of Los Andes). Each has a primarily agrarian landscape, though off-farm is important in livelihood strategies. Their relative remoteness varies, with Ayacucho being the most patently isolated region, and La Paz being the most articulated with major urban centers.

Guamote, Chimborazo: Landscapes of Power and Poverty[9]

Guamote is one of the poorest *cantones* (counties) of Ecuador, with a population close to 30,000 of whom 90% are rural and indigenous Quichua people. Located in the central highland province of Chimborazo, its altitudes vary from 3,000 to over 4,000 m above sea level. Precipitation is low, and many areas are effectively semiarid.

The canton was one of the last bastions of the traditional *hacienda* in Ecuador: large rural estates characterized by a system of tied Quichua labor, technical backwardness, and abusive labor relationships between owners/managers and the local Quichua population (Korovkin 1997). In 1954, just nine haciendas owned over 61% of the land in Guamote, and even by 1974 properties under 20 hectares constituted only 13% of the land. Organizationally and politically, Guamote was dominated by the hacienda through its control of labor and the local state (Casagrande and Piper 1969). The distribution of rights of access to natural resources and the income streams that might flow from their use was highly skewed against the Quichua population.

These social relationships were manifest not only in a landscape dotted with large, tile-roof hacienda buildings and miniature, thatched single-room homes of Quichua laborers – but also in the landscape of extensive agro-pastoralism pockmarked with

---

[9] See Bebbington and Perreault (1999) for more detail – the descriptive material presented here draws on this source.

small, more intensively farmed agricultural lots. The latter were the small plots that Quichuas received in return for their labor, the former reflected a hacienda land use strategy in which land was dedicated primarily to livestock rearing and profits were invested in consumption goods rather than land use intensification.

In a period of four decades, this situation has changed remarkably. Today no haciendas remain; a far wider population has rights of access to natural resources and social services; hacienda buildings are in disrepair while Quichua people have replaced many of their thatched, adobe homes with cinder-block, metallic-roofed houses; and the agricultural landscape is a quilt of intensively farmed, though frequently eroding small plots.

This transformation – for transformation it is – is the effect of the ways in which Quichuas have changed their livelihood practices and strategies in the context of more structural changes in the relationships between national political economy, organized interventions, and demographic increase. The central driver of these structural changes has been social protest – both silent and quotidian, and loud and organized. In the 1960s and 1970s, silent protest took the form of slowdowns among Quichua laborers, and gradual encroachment on hacienda land. The louder protests involved organized land invasions. These acts, small and large, made haciendas progressively less governable and profitable. As a result some hacienda owners gave up trying to preserve a particular regime of resource and social control, and sold their land to Quichua people. Other owners continued to resist but were ultimately forced to give up their land by national land reform laws passed in 1964 and 1973. These laws were implemented with particular vigor in Guamote because national government feared that the degree of social protest in Chimborazo might presage a more general rise of militant left wing politics (Jordan 1989; Barsky 1984).

This wholesale transfer of landownership laid the seeds for profound landscape change. There were now many more landowners, and the agricultural frontier expanded quickly. As children came of age land was further subdivided and as population grew communities decided to expand farming into higher and higher elevations, opening up high-altitude grassland to the hoe, plough and (increasingly) tractor. A number of nongovernmental organizations (NGOs) supported this shift in environmental governance. So too did government interventions – in particular integrated rural development programs from the late 1970s to early 1990s.

These interventions provided support to agricultural production, as well as to human capital formation and the creation and strengthening of indigenous social movements. The effects of these latter interventions culminated in 1992 and 1996 when candidates from indigenous organizations took control of the local government, removing all but one nonindigenous councilor. While demographically and culturally Guamote was already an indigenous municipality, by the mid-1990s it had also became one administratively and politically. It has since experimented with means for more direct forms of Quichua participation in development planning, governmental auditing, and public budgeting. This has attracted further external support with the effect that Guamote's local government has had resources to invest. Rural areas have been prioritized in investments in local roads, fisheries, agriculture, forestry, and other activities.

Meanwhile Guamoteños continue living their lives and building their livelihoods. The changes of the 1960s and 1970s have given them far greater freedom in how they do this, while subsequent interventions have enhanced their agricultural and educational options, and also enhanced their mobility. For some families, agriculture has offered scope for some accumulation – the fruits of which have been invested in schooling their children, building new cinder-block homes and further agricultural investment. For many though, agriculture still offers little more than basic needs – crop prices remain low and input prices high, and there is little scope for adding much value to agricultural products within Guamote (or even within Chimborazo). In this context, for most families seasonal migration to work in coastal agroindustry and urban areas provides income for covering costs of education, health, and housing improvement.

The contemporary landscape of Guamote is one that reflects three decades of Quichua people's freedom from dependence on landed rural estates and the traditional (preliberation ecology) Roman Catholic church, and is beginning to reflect a decade's freedom from *mestizo* small-town control over local government.[10] It also reflects the very limited economic opportunities open to people who live in Guamote. While there is visible evidence of accumulation in the landscape – and residents perceive two-storey houses, trucks, and improved rooftops in just this way – this is still the accumulation of petty commodity capitalism and migrant labor. The landscape still, therefore, speaks of the adverse incorporation[11] of Guamote's population in Ecuadorian economy and society.

The freedoms that have been opened up for Guamote's Quichua population are the effect of synergies among the interventions of a range of actors. Many of these actors have hailed from outside Guamote: a peculiarly reformist government rural development project in the 1980s, a parish priest committed since the 1970s to liberation theology, and more recently a mix of both conservative and more radical NGOs and international agencies. Others have come from within: new leaders who have emerged partly as a result of what they have learnt in dealing with these external actors and partly because of their innate abilities; and ordinary Quichua citizens who have, at crucial moments, demanded more freedoms and then used them. Together they have transformed both the material form and the meaning of Guamote's landscape.

Ayacucho: Conflicted Landscapes

Ayacucho is one of the poorest regions of Peru (IGN 2004). Located in the highlands east of Lima it is also one of the most isolated parts of the country. It was also the

---

[10] To such an extent, in fact, that the 2004 municipal elections were characterized not by interethnic tensions so much as by fierce struggles *among* different groups within the Quichua population – groups differentiated by religion, party affiliation, and geography (Bebbington 2006).

[11] On adverse incorporation, see Wood (2003), Hulme and Shepherd (2003), du Toit (2004), and CPRC (2004).

region in which Peru's civil war – waged from 1980 to 2000[12] - was most concentrated and most brutal (Figure 5). Of the estimated 70,000 people killed in that war,[13] some 26,259 were killed in Ayacucho (CVR 2004: 17) – roughly one in twenty of the region's 538,591 residents (CTAR 2001:25). The very great majority of those killed were Quechua people at the hands of the Shining Path (the Communist Party of Peru - *Sendero Luminoso*) but also of the Peruvian Armed Forces. The Peruvian Truth and Reconciliation Commission suggests that deeply sedimented racisms underlay both this targeting of violence, *and* the inadequate, careless responses of government and national elites[14] during the early years of violence, until they realized that it constituted a national crisis as opposed to merely a problem for isolated, rural indigenous people (CVR 2004: 10–12).

Figure 5 Memorial to the killed, inset in the paving of the main square of Ayacucho. The inscription reads: "To those Peruvian men and women who were victims of the longest and most painful period of violence that our country has suffered. May the process that we have initiated bring us closer to justice and a lasting peace," and is signed by the Truth and Reconciliation Commission (ajb)

---

[12] The dates are those used by the Truth and Reconciliation Commission (CVR 2004); others might suggest the war ended in the mid-1990s.

[13] There is great debate over this estimate. Elites and interest groups linked to government, army and the ruling party have suggested the figure is much lower – others in the human rights world argue it is much higher.

[14] The other institution that failed miserably to respond to or speak out on these human rights abuses was the Catholic Church – which in Ayacucho was as conservative and elitist as Guamote's church was pro-indigenous (see Diez 2004).

The intensity of violence suggested by such figures led – not surprisingly – to large population movements as people left rural communities in fear of their lives. Other movements were forced, as Sendero Luminoso relocated villages. Violence and movement disarticulated rural economies and livelihoods, and led also to rapid growth of urban settlements in the region – settlements which, while also prone to violence, offered more scope to hide, and which elites and the state would be relatively more inclined to protect and police than remote and wholly indigenous communities.

Livelihood geographies and processes of landscape production changed massively in this period. The quotidian producers and maintainers of rural landscapes (Figure 6) declined dramatically in number with the effect that the (only ever partial) domestication of many landscapes began to unravel. At the same time urban landscapes reflected the displacement of rural populations and the increased claims on urban space and services (Figure 7).

The period of greatest violence in Ayacucho (from 1982 to 1993) was also one in which the only significant (albeit hugely significant) public intervention in rural parts of the department was a military one. Nongovernmental interventions were equally scarce – as NGOs were subject to intimidation and violence from both Sendero and the army. Indeed only a handful of NGOs continued work in rural areas during the violence – often in locations close to urban centers. As violence declined (following the capture of the core of Sendero's leadership) hopes were high in Ayacucho that there would be a step change in external investments, in order to reconstruct livelihoods, lives, and the economy.

Figure 6 Rural landscape of Ayacucho near the city of Huari ruins (ajb)

Figure 7 Urban migration pressures in the Ayacucho (ajb)

In the early 1990s, then, the challenge in Ayacucho was literally one of reconstruction and return. The government's primary instrument for this was called the Program to Support Repopulation (PAR), although in practice most "returns" were self organized.[15] More generally, the challenge was to create a landscape that would speak of reduced exclusion, increased livelihood opportunities, and indeed national reparation. Such reparation would be a recognition of the extent to which the region had suffered as a consequence of the nation's neglect of Ayacucho prior to 1980, the all but abandonment of public investment there during the 1980s and early 1990s, and – during counter-insurgency activities – the direct persecution of its residents (approximately 55% of all Peruvians killed during the war by employees of the state were from Ayacucho: CVR 2004: 60).[16] This would necessarily be a landscape that would speak of new opportunity for, and reparation to, indigenous populations – for indigenous people constituted some 70% of the region's population, and over 95% of people killed in Ayacucho during the violence (CVR 2004: 24).

---

[15] Some of these self-organized returns received support from nongovernmental organizations and others. It ought also be noted that the concept of one displacement followed by one return has been questioned by commentators who note that even during the violence there was more of a cycle of displacements (some local, some more long distance) and of returns (Coxshall 2004).

[16] The figure is the percentage of all killings that were directly reported to the Commission for Truth and Reconciliation.

A decade and a half later there appears to be a general sense that this has scarcely happened.[17] A comparison of poverty maps from 1993 to 2000 suggests that of the region's 11 provinces, only two have shown any reduction of poverty (CTAR 2001: 22). While small-scale social and infrastructural investments are visible in the landscape (Figures 8 and 9) – symbols of some increased state presence – larger investments that would have opened up livelihood possibilities (and, inter alia, encouraged a recolonization and intensified use of landscape) are absent. Here there were many options: significant increases in investment in small-scale irrigation systems throughout the region to reduce water constraints on peasant agriculture, the construction of arterial roads linking Ayacucho to other parts of Peru, the building of feeder roads to link communities to these larger arteries and the coordinated building of infrastructure to stimulate Ayacucho's evident tourist potential.[18] Of the two major public

Figure 8 Rural infrastructure projects (ajb)

[17] I refer to recent interviews conducted by myself and Denise Humphreys Bebbington in Ayacucho and Lima in August 2004, and by myself during 2006. Thanks to the Anne U. White Fund of the Association of American Geographers and the Global Poverty Research Group at Manchester for helping finance the interviews in 2004, and the British Academy for supporting the more recent research. Write up was supported by an Economic and Social Research Council Professorial Fellowship (RES-051-27-0191).

[18] Opportunities to link landscape architecture and livelihoods in this sense are legion – just thirty (curvy) minutes from Ayacucho is Peru's largest settlement dating from the pre-Incaic Huari culture; and four (painful) hours away is Vilcashuaman, an important Incaic settlement.

Figure 9 Microfinance banking projects (ajb)

infrastructure projects that were pursued, the asphalted road to Lima was completed, but the advance of the combined dam, water supply, and irrigation scheme on the Rio Cachi has been painfully slow, and surrounded by corruption, broken promises to communities and bureaucratic incompetence (Diez 2004; Muñoz and Nuñez 2006). Fifteen years since the end of the worst violence, the department's landscape conveys little by way of national reparation, social justice or recompense for what the memorial plaque in Ayacucho's Plaza de Armas (main square) calls "the longest and most painful period of violence that our country has suffered" (Figure 5).

Worse still, one of the few significant infrastructure investments that did occur – the recent[19] privately built pipeline carrying California bound gas from the lowlands of Cusco to the Peruvian port of Ica – passes right through Ayacucho. Yet the benefits to Ayacucho of the liquid gas piped through its territory are few, and certainly well short of any recompense for the years of violence. Meanwhile, because of malpractices in the hurried construction of the pipeline, it has been plagued by problems in its first years of operation, with a series of leaks and explosions, some of which have affected Ayacucho directly. The pipeline (and any future ones that might also be built) will all too easily come to symbolize the continuing exclusion of Ayacucho from any national project. Equally painful – given rural Ayacucho's excruciating need for water – is that one of the new large-scale water investments being considered proposes the damming of rivers in western Ayacucho in order to export irrigation water to the coast. Residents and authorities of affected communities

---

[19] Ceremonies for its formal opening were in August 2004.

have criticized the development, suggesting that this may become a standoff between local populations and the private interests underwriting the project, with the Peruvian government arbitrating this standoff. Without significant changes, the landscapes that will be produced by these public and private projects and the visions of "development" that underlie them will speak of exclusion and elite neglect, in much the same way as did the pre-violence landscape of the 1970s – landscapes that spoke to Sendero (and others)[20] of the need for radical change, while suggesting to those elites who first ignored this violence, and then sought to repress it in ways that ignored all human rights, that Ayacucho was "another country".[21]

Meanwhile, as ever, people in Ayacucho aim to get on with their lives, and rebuild their livelihoods. Some have returned to their old communities to bring lands back into production though many have not – whether because the pain is too great, their families too destroyed, or their children (or themselves) now too acculturated to urban life. In most locations – distant from markets – accumulation possibilities are very few, and landscapes speak of subsistence agriculture and at best petty commodity production (cf. Smith 1989). In villages that are closer to urban centers there are somewhat more economic possibilities, though still limited – and these lie not in agriculture but other activities. Interviews in NGO-sponsored village banks – which have shown some vibrancy in such areas (Humphreys Bebbington and Gomez 2005) – suggest that participants are mostly interested in using income to fund their children's education and de-agrarianization. The implication is that – unless there is significant change in patterns of public investment – the rural landscape will continue to reflect constrained economic opportunities, and continuing depopulation. Meanwhile the urban landscape will reflect continuing in-migration and pressure on services – and the design challenges will be the familiar ones of integrating new populations, expanding service provision, accommodating sociocultural difference and alleviating the sense of urban exclusion.

Los Andes, La Paz: Commodity Chains and the Search for Social Justice

The *altiplano* (high plain) of Bolivia is one of the more stunning yet – for those concerned with development – perplexing landscapes in Bolivia. A one-time centre of pre-Hispanic empires and landscape modifications that allowed relatively intensive

---

[20] It was not only Sendero that sought radical change. Other groups – in the university, civil society, and elsewhere – also felt the need for thoroughgoing transformation, though they pursued distinct and nonviolent avenues (and again often fell foul of both Sendero and the army for this reason).

[21] The Truth and Reconciliation Commission comments that in their thousands of interviews and testimonies, it was "common to encounter phrases that spoke of the sense of exclusion and indifference experienced by those people and communities who were the main victims of the conflict" many of whom "sensed that for the rest of the country, especially for the main centers of political and economic power, what was happening in their villages, houses and families was going on in "another country" (CVR 2004: 20).

forms of agriculture, since the latter 20th century, it has presented a series of agrarian conundrums both to its residents and external agencies. At altitudes of 3,800 m above sea level and higher, it is subject to significant diurnal temperature changes, frosts, and drought. Village level research suggests that people feel precipitation unpredictability and overall dryness have become more serious problems over time (VMPPFM 1998) and, therefore, that the risks to agriculture have also increased.

As in Ecuador, haciendas controlled much of this landscape until the mid-1950s when land reform programs redistributed land to indigenous peasants. This in itself led to important landscape changes, reflecting the new structure of ownership, but further interventions also sought to refashion the altiplano landscape by seeking to increase the productivity of peasant agriculture and animal husbandry.

Early on in this modern history of intervention, the Corporación Boliviana de Fomento (Bolivian Development Corporation) sought to promote the dairy sector as an opportunity for the altiplano. This was followed by a series of internationally funded government programs that together built a publicly owned milk processing plant in La Paz, fostered herd and animal management improvements in communities, and elaborated a system for collecting, transporting, processing, and marketing dairy products.

Meanwhile a growing number of social justice-oriented NGOs sought alternative development paths. Initially these emphasized agricultural intensification and group economic activity. Consistently disappointing experiences with agriculture led to a change of strategy among a number of these NGOs – in particular the larger ones – who themselves turned to livestock production as a preferable alternative. These interventions sought to help poorer producers participate in the emerging dairy economy by providing them with the initial capital and technical assistance, and fostering the forms of social organization required to organize the marketing of milk to the processing plant in La Paz.

At both aggregate and local scales, as the dairy sector grew the landscape reflected this change. In the province of Los Andes, patches of alfalfa became more numerous, Holstein cattle dotted the fields, and feed stalls went up beside houses. Not all families pursued this option, however. Many could not – the initial investment costs were too great, and unless they were fortunate enough to be a beneficiary of NGO programs subsidizing this start-up they pursued other options. Some – who had the necessary access to water – specialized in producing alfalfa to sell to milk producers; others stuck with their agriculture and traditional livestock and engaged in artisanal cheese production; yet others pursued off-farm livelihoods – in many instances commuting on a daily or weekly basis to the expanding metropolitan area of La Paz and its neighboring city El Alto, that, as it grew, was coming ever closer to Los Andes.

Each of these activities – which tended to be distributed by socioeconomic class with relatively wealthier families more likely to specialize in dairy production – brought their own landscape modifications, and reflected the different ways in which residents of La Paz were hooked into economic networks in Bolivia. By the same token the stability of livelihoods – and the landscape features they supported – depended on processes in those parts of these networks over which residents of

La Paz had no control. This was most notably the case for the dairy farmers selling to the milk processing plant. When, as part of a broader liberalizing macroeconomic platform the government sold its shares in the dairy processing plant in La Paz, the plant was purchased by a Peruvian subsidiary of a transnational company. At that point, dairy producers' organizations found it more difficult to negotiate prices and other conditions than had been the case when they dealt with the Bolivian state. The situation became more severe when ownership of the plant passed to another transnational which then decided to close the plant as part of a rationalization of its sourcing operations in the Andes (notably this was the same transnational corporation whose shifts in sourcing strategy have caused problems for Peak District farmers in Derbyshire). This left producers with the option of selling their milk at the roadside in the frigid early hours of the morning to trucks heading for a processing plant on the Peruvian coast. With time a number of producers have progressively lost interest. Quite what the longer-term landscape implications of this change will be are hard to tell at this early stage but it may well mean that the landscape patches of intensification associated with circuits of capital and consumption linked to the dairy sector will reduce in size, and feeding stalls will be converted to other uses – one more artifact of what has been described on the Peruvian side of the altiplano as the "archaeology of development," built forms in the landscape whose abandonment speaks of failed ideas about what the Andes might possibly be, and how their landscapes and resources might possibly be managed.

Design and the Production of Possibility

I called this paper "Landscapes of possibility" to reflect that notion of "development" as an expansion of "freedoms" (Sen 1999). The idea that many people's livelihoods in the Andes are – under contemporary forms of capitalism – not viable, flies in the face of any such sense of expanded freedom. Indeed, it implies that these people will no longer have the freedom to pursue their lives in rural areas. Rural landscapes with these people in them would be different from those landscapes in which they are no longer present. In this sense it is not just that different landscapes hold open different possibility sets – it is that some landscapes hold possibilities for more people than do others. Some landscapes are more obviously landscapes of freedoms than are others – they are more socially just.

That said, while each of the landscapes discussed here holds more possibilities for proportionately more of their residents than they did in the middle of the 20th century (primarily because of land reform programs and social mobilization), they all still reflect the continuing existence of many constraints on people's livelihoods and on their freedoms – they reflect the extent to which many livelihoods face very real pressure on their viability under present circumstances. This raises a range of questions, but in the spirit of being speculative the paper closes with reflections on three questions:

1. What is likely to be the future of these landscapes?
2. What might a more socially just future for these landscapes possibly look like?

3. Under what conditions – if any – could design interventions help usher in these more socially just futures?

Probable Landscapes

Even if mainstream neoliberal thinking is beginning to shift, and once again is recognizing that the state has a role in steering development, Andean states are going to suffer chronic financial and/or capacity constraints for the foreseeable future (on the concept of "steering resources" see chapter 4 in this volume by Susan Clarke). None of these regions will be of particular interest to commercial capital, and their economies will remain relatively stagnant. There will be basic state social investment – primarily in education and (less so) health – and the state is likely to invest in the maintenance and possibly improvement of the principal trunk roads that run through each area. Of the three regions Guamote will see the least new investment in economic activity, and what there is will come from its residents reinvesting their income in petty activities that will generate few jobs (most of which will be assumed by family members). Ayacucho will see some expansion of tourist activity, and there may even be some investment in homes by "new age" northerners and possibly Limeños seeking alternative lifestyles – though on a far smaller scale than is likely to happen in Cusco, closer to the heart of the old Incan empire.[22] Los Andes will see somewhat greater real estate investment as the city of El Alto continues to grow rapidly in the face of a continuing influx of rural migrants to the La Paz–El Alto metropolitan area. Indeed Los Andes will in time become a commuter municipality for El Alto, with some land use tensions between agriculture and small town growth, especially over water rights.

In this context, Ayacucho and Guamote will see a slow out-migration of their population, though – given the overall employment constraints in their respective national economies – much of this will not be permanent and circular migration will continue. Some farms will thus further subdivide, and natural resource degradation will continue. NGOs will continue to invest in these areas, though less so than in the past as Latin America becomes less and less important for European development agencies. The scale of such investment will do little to offset pressures on natural resources. The dynamic in Los Andes will be somewhat different largely because of the proximity to La Paz and El Alto. Here there will be less out-migration, but instead an increase in daily commuting as proportionately more people assume day jobs in the city. Family livelihoods in Los Andes will increasingly combine agriculture and off-farm employment. Some of this agriculture – among families with more money – will become intensive producing value added products for the urban market

---

[22] Again the parallel is with Culbertson's contribution to this collection. While amenity migration may be at its zenith (or nadir, depending on how you see it) in the USA, it is also a phenomenon in countries such as Peru, and with time will become more significant.

(milk derivatives, honey, prepared foods, etc.); much of it will remain semi-subsistence in orientation. The result will be a patchy agrarian landscape.

It is also probable that each region will continue to be politically unstable. Ayacucho in particular will continue to host armed columns of terrorists using the label of *Sendero Luminoso* though mostly resourced by and linked to the drug production economy on the borders of the region[23] (an economy that has its own, very particular local landscapes). The other two regions will be less violent, though mobilizations seem likely to recur as indigenous groups protest against generic forms of racism and exclusion, as well as broadly neoliberal government policy. Such instability will further deter significant capital investment though may pull in some public investment in infrastructure and social services.

"Stagnant" is perhaps the first adjective to spring to mind when thinking of these likely landscapes. They will *be* stagnant – little will change, new investment will be limited – and they will *speak of* stagnation. In countries such as these, however, riven by racism and characterized by social relations and geographies of exclusion, such stagnation will also take on more politically significant meanings and it is conceivable that such landscapes will be read by their residents in ways that incite further protest. The one possible exception to this trend will be if significant and commercially viable mineral deposits are encountered in these areas (perhaps most likely in Ayacucho, 17.44 percent of whose surface area is already under mining claims: INACC 2006).[24] Such discovery may stimulate targeted investment in extractive industry. While the immediate physical landscape implications of this are evident, the symbolic implications are less clear. If this extraction generates few local multiplier effects, it will suggest that after centuries of national indifference to Ayacucho's highlands, state and capital only become interested in the region when the opportunity arises to extract its subsoil resources. As has occurred elsewhere in Peru, under such conditions this landscape will be a stage for social conflict. However, *if* resources from extraction are shared and invested in ways that enhance local livelihoods and freedoms, then other types of physical and symbolic landscapes will be produced. Experience to date in Peru suggests, however, that social conflict seems to have to occur first if this second "future" to become possible.

Possible Landscapes

Rural social movements in Ecuador and Bolivia are relatively strong (though far less so in Peru). While their mobilizations still tend to be more sporadic than sustained, and their ability to articulate alternative views of development are far weaker than their ability to protest against current policies, they have the potential

---

[23] This economy is concentrated in the lower valleys of the "VRAE", the Valley of the Rivers Apurimac and Ene, though some of the transport of coca derivatives passes through the highlands.
[24] I owe this data to Jeffrey Bury.

to further transform the political landscapes of each country and to pull state and other institutions into the countryside. Possible – more socially just – landscapes will emerge when elites are willing to allow alternatives to emerge from these mobilizations, and governments (and thus elites again) are willing to channel resources to support the building of such alternatives. In the language of Kenneth Boulding, and as discussed by Wescoat (2007) in the introductory chapter to this volume, these socially just future landscapes will only be fashioned and sustainable through the exercise of integrative power in which elites and social movements are able to work together in pursuit of enhanced justice (cf. Boulding 1990). This is one of the positive lessons of Guamote.

Putting incredulity on one side to create space for the mental exercise, what might such landscapes look like?

(a) While certainly not autonomous nor autarkic, they will enjoy significant levels of self-governance.
(b) They will show signs of significant public investment in collective assets conceived and positioned in ways that benefit historically excluded and disadvantaged social groups. Such public works will include roads, water management systems, and health and secondary education provision. These will be indicators – symbols in the landscape – of the willingness of the state to offset historical patterns of inequity, and will be read as such by landscape residents.
(c) In this sense these landscapes will not erase history. They will recognize the ills of the past and this recognition will reflect the extent to which national society has itself acknowledged its complicity in such ills, and is prepared to begin repairing some of them.
(d) They will show signs of significant household investment. As well as being an indicator of accumulation, this investment will also be an indicator that households feel there is sufficient opportunity for them to continue pursuing their futures in such landscapes. In part they will come to this estimation because the provision of public investment is such as to allow them to gain access to the range of assets they and their children need to control in order to build more viable livelihoods.
(e) They will be landscapes in which a diversity of income generation strategies are possible and this diversity will also be visible in the landscape. Agriculture alone will never sustain many viable livelihoods in these regions.
(f) They will be landscapes that speak of reduced isolation – not only in the form of roads, but a range of other communication possibilities.

Producing the Possible

No single actor will bring such possible landscapes into being. Indeed, this is one thing that can be learned from the landscapes already produced. In a case like Guamote, the politically (if not economically) most self-governed and autonomous of the three landscapes discussed here, the emergence of patchwork landscapes governed primarily by Quichua community assemblies and county government is evidently a result of state–society synergies of the type that Peter Evans (1996) and others have shown can play such a role in fostering more socially just forms of development: synergies that would seem to be vehicles for the exercise of Boulding's integrative power. In Guamote, the central state, the Catholic Church, Ecuadorian NGOs, European and North American Foundations, and even the World Bank have played roles in the emergence and subsequent protagonism of the strong local and national Quichua social movements that have changed the shape of politics there. The contemporary landscape is a composite effect of massive social protest, redistributive land reform, targeted social and productive investment, and myriad individual and family decisions. It is also the effect of boom-bust potato markets, and the new market for building materials in Ecuador one of whose effects has been the steady replacement of the adobe/thatch built landscapes of Quichua space with prefabricated brick and zinc roof landscapes (albeit ones still composed with a distinctly Quichua architectural aesthetic).

But plenty of other parts of the Andes have had their state interventions, NGOs, reformist and radical priests, and international solidarity funders. So why did Guamote get its Indigenous Parliament, indigenous municipality, and thorough land reforms while other areas did not? Why did Guamote come to *mean* something in Ecuador that few other municipalities mean?[25] Much of this explanation is historically specific,[26] but central to this story must be *protest*. Land reform was particularly thoroughgoing in Guamote because of the degree of Quichua protest and the concerns that this might become further radicalized; the integrated rural development program in Guamote was pro-poor partly because of its early director, but also because communities demanded that it be so; and the strength of mobilization in Guamote during the national indigenous uprising in 1990 was an important factor in pulling state and nongovernmental agencies and investment resources into the county.

That said, another factor that has made Guamote possible is that it is *marginal* to the interests of capital. This was not an oil, gas, mineral, or agro-export rich county – had it been, capital would have insisted that these activities be defended at all costs from movements attempting to foster more socially just landscapes. It was, perhaps, easier to begin producing such landscapes precisely because there was less elite resistance to such a project (cf. Bebbington 2006).

The picture is, though, more complicated. Ayacucho is also at the margins. Yet when protest took the form that it did there, the elite did become interested – albeit slowly and only when this regional protest began to raise issues of national security. The result crowded out not only any hopes of alternatives, but also the chance of any basic public investment in producing more socially just landscapes. Rural Ayacucho

---

[25] Even if the sheen of some of this meaning has been lost, given the conflicts that have emerged within Guamote's indigenous civil society (Bebbington 2006).

[26] As I have explored elsewhere (Bebbington 2000).

was denied any real public investment for over a decade. Only certain forms of protest will inspire positive, pro-poor, pro-justice public, and elite responses.[27]

These observations may have implications for design interventions. They do not mean that interventions in pursuit of alternatives are only possible in areas that at once exhibit already fermenting social protest and mobilization and also exist at the margins of capital. Far less do they mean that they are always possible in such spaces. But they may suggest that such spaces can open up special opportunities for design interventions. It may also be that such interventions are more likely to be effective in building alternatives when they work from the demand side. In this instance, demand originates not in purchasing power, but in protest, i.e., in demands for different ways of producing and controlling landscapes and livelihoods. Eliciting that protest – for much of it will be silent, hidden, and unorganized (Scott 1985; 1990) – is never easy and arguably requires close ethnographic encounters between design professionals and communities of the excluded as a precursor to imagining alternatives. Indeed, the general point may be that for those design professionals committed to fostering social justice through design, then the only place to start is from the vocal and silent protests of those on the receiving end of injustice. The design process would elicit new elements of landscape implicit in those protests and then move out from there, incorporating material resources and (just as crucially) elite and technocratic support in order to make possible the realization of those designs. Design would be part of the process of building forms of integrative power. Of course, pursuing this through the for-profit private sector will be difficult (if not impossible). The call, perhaps, is for more publicly funded, publicly motivated forms of design.

Second, as noted earlier, the state has to be able, and at least partly willing, to finance some constructive response to protest (and here is one of the links to the notion of publicly funded, public interest design). Yet here is the irony (or tragedy?) – the Ecuadorian state invested in places like Guamote partly on the back of government income from hydrocarbon development. In other words, there is a relationship – not direct, not simple, but nonetheless real – between Guamote's landscape transformations and the far less felicitous ones that have occurred in the oil producing territories of Ecuador's Amazonian indigenous peoples. If Ayacucho is to see any significant state investment in the next decade, this too will be on the back of a similar irony – for such investment, if it ever materializes, will be funded from government income deriving from natural resource extraction. Above all it will be financed by central government royalties generated by gas from the Camisea field located east of the Andes and mineral development in the highlands.[28] The development

---

[27] Comparative study of this example is needed. For example, some low-income areas of Chicago burned during the riots of 1968 have suffered multi-decadal out-migration and public disinvestment.

[28] Indeed, during August of 2006, Peru's newly elected government began to discuss the possibility that, given the extraordinary profits that mining companies were making in a context of high mineral prices, they ought to make voluntary contributions to public investment (additional to tax payments). One of several criteria for allocating these funds would be to attend to areas affected by the violence of the 1980s and 1990s.

of Camisea's gas, for instance, will likely sacrifice the livelihoods and landscapes of some of Peru's last noncontact peoples, at the same time as its export to the USA will involve significant landscape transformations in Baja California that will derive from the building of on or offshore LNG plants designed to receive gas from Camisea (as well as Indonesia and Bolivia). Mineral development elsewhere in the Andes will change (and possibly compromise) the livelihoods of those families whose land is acquired in order for mineral exploitation to proceed (cf. Bury 2004). And just to complete the picture, natural gas extraction in the East will be a principal source of income for the Bolivian government – and will thus underwrite any possible increase in public investment in Los Andes too.

In the language of economists (and pragmatists) these are trade-offs – high stakes trade-offs – that operate at far wider scales. Some landscapes are built through the destruction of other landscapes. All forms of intervention are, somewhere, at some point, caught up in these trade-offs even if in most cases we do not – or chose not to – realize this. In most cases the trade-off is one that is mediated by the market mechanism plus a few planning ordinances around the edges (here we are again back to the case of amenity migration). Those landscapes that are brought into being are those that people can pay for – and those that are lost are those whose defenders (and frequently residents) are unable to pay for. In the current political economy of capitalism (in which design certainly *is* implicated) this makes the prognosis for landscapes of enhanced social justice seem bleak.[29]

Or at least, the prognosis is bleak if the marginally regulated market, and government committed to enhancing the role of market reason, are the only the mechanisms through which trade-offs will be made. But other mechanisms for making choices about trade-offs and interrelations among landscape dynamics in different locations are possible. They would seem to revolve around finding ways of fostering public debate – perhaps through the public sector, but at the very least through the public sphere – about landscape design options at a macro, national scale. In some respects national parks systems – in some countries – reflect the outcome of such debates. In the face of increasingly mobile, extractive forms of capital, and of increasingly mobile, space, and natural resource consuming upper-middle classes, it is perhaps time to deepen those national – and increasingly transnational – public debates on landscape design. Such debates would be the vehicles through which far more powerful integrative forces might begin to be built.

---

[29] During the symposium at which these papers were first presented, the notion of socially just landscapes was challenged several times with the question: "what would a socially just landscape look like?" This question is a red herring. It is not so much that there are socially just landscapes, as that any (ANY) given landscape can become more or less socially just – and those who are best placed to comment on the direction of change are those on the receiving end of injustice.

References

Batterbury SPJ (2001) Landscapes of diversity: a local political ecology of livelihood diversification in south-western Niger. *Ecumene* 8(4): 437–464

Bebbington AJ (1999) Capitals and capabilities: a framework for analysing peasant viability, rural livelihoods and poverty. *World Development* 27(12): 2021–2044

Bebbington AJ (2000) Re-encountering development. Livelihood transitions and place transformations in the Andes. *Annals of the Association of American Geographers* 90(3): 495–520

Bebbington AJ (2004) Livelihood transitions, place transformations: grounding globalization and modernity. In Gwynne R and Kay C (eds) *Latin America Transformed. Globalization and Modernity*. Arnold, London

Bebbington AJ (2006) Los epacios públicos de concertación local y sus límites en uUn municipio indígena: Guamote, Ecuador. *Debate Agrario* 40/41: 381–404

Bebbington A and Perreault T (1999) Social capital, development and access to resources in highland Ecuador. *Economic Geography* 75(4): 395–418

Bebbington A, Hinojosa L, and Rojas R (2002) *Contributions of the Dutch Co-financing Program to rural development and rural livelihoods in the highlands of Peru and Bolivia*. Stuurgroep Evaluatie Medefinancierings-Programma, Ede

Bebbington A, Humphreys Bebbington D, Bury J, Lingan J, Muñoz JP, and Scurrah M (2006) Los movimientos sociales frente a la minería: disputando el desarrollo territorial andino In Bengoa J (ed) *Movimientos sociales y desarrollo territorial rural en América Latina*. Editorial Catalonia, Santiago

Boulding KE (1990) *Three Faces of Power*. Sage Publications, Newbury Park, CA

Bridge G (2004) Mapping the bonanza: geographies of mining investment in an era of neo-liberal reform. *Professional Geographer* 56(3): 406–421

Bury J (2004) Livelihoods in transition: transnational gold mining operations and local change in Cajamarca, Peru. *Geographical Journal* 170(1): 78–91

Casagrande JB and Piper AR (1969) La transformación estructural de una parroquía rural en las tierras altas del Ecuador. *América Indígena* XXIX(4)

Coxshall W (2004) Rebuilding disrupted relations: widowhood, Narrative and silence in a contemporary community in Ayacucho,Peru. Thesis submitted for the degree Ph.D. in the Faculty of Social Sciences and Law. Department of Social Anthropology, University of Manchester

CPRC (2004) *Chronic Poverty Report 2004–5*. Chronic Poverty Research Centre, Manchester and London

CTAR (2001) *Base para construir el futuro, 2011. Plan estrategico de desarrollo departamental Ayacucho*. Consejo Transitorio de Administración Regional, Ayacucho

Culbertson K et al. (2008) Moving to the mountains: amenity migration in the Sierra and Southern Appalachian Mountains. In Wescoat JL and Johnston DM (eds) *Places of Power: Political and Economic Driving Forces of Landscape Change*. Springer, Dordrecht, The Netherlands

CVR (2004) *Hatun Willanakuy. Versión abreviada del informe final de la Comisión de la Verdad y REconciliación, Perú*. Comisión de la Verdad y Reconciliación, Lima

Diez Hurtado A (2004) *Élites y poderes locales: sociedades regionales ante la descentralización*. Servicios Educativos Rurales and Department for Internacional Development, Lima, OH

Doolittle W (1984) Agricultural change as an incremental process. *Annals of the Association of American Geographers* 74:124–137

Du Toit A (2004) Social exclusion discourse and chronic poverty: a South African case study. *Development and Change* 35(5): 987–1010

Evans P (ed) (1996) *State-society Synergy: Government and Social Capital in Development*. Institute for International Studies, Berkeley,CA

Fairhead J and Leach M (1996) *Misreading the African Landscape*. Cambridge University Press, Cambridge

Giddens A (1979) *Central Problems in Social Theory*. Action, structure and contradiction in social analysis. MacMillan, London

Holling CS (1986) The resilience of terrestrial ecosystems; local surprise and global change. In Clark WC and Munn RE (eds) *Sustainable Development of the Biosphere*. Cambridge University Press, Cambridge, pp 292–317

Hulme D and Shepherd A (2003) Conceptualizing chronic poverty. *World Development* 31, 403–424

Humphreys Bebbington D and Gomez A (2005) Rebuilding social capital in post conflict regions. Womens village banking in Ayacucho, Peru and in highland Guatemala. In Fernando J (ed) *Microfinance: Perils and Prospects*. Routledge, London

IDB (1996) *Bolivia: desarrollo diferente para un pais de cambios. Salir del circulo vicioso de la riqueza empobrecedora. Informe final de la Misión Piloto sobre Reforma Socio-Economica en Bolivia*. Banco InterAmericano del Desarrollo, La Paz

IGN (2004) *Atlas digital del Peru*. Instituto Geografico Nacional, Lima, OH

INACC (2006) *Atlas Catastral Minero Regional*. Instituto Nacional de Concesiones y Catastro Minero, Lima, OH

Jordan F (1989) *El minifundio*. IICA, San Jose, CA

Korovkin T (1997) Indigenous peasant struggles and the capitalist modernization of agriculture: Chimborazo, 1964–1991. *Latin American Perspectives* 24(3): 25–49

Larner W (2000) Neo-liberalism: policy, ideology, governmentality. *Studies in Political Economy*. 63: 5–26

Mitchell D (2008) New axioms for reading the landscape: paying attention to political economy and social justice. In Wescoat JL and Johnston DM (eds) *Places of Power: Political and Economic Driving Forces of Landscape Change*. Springer, Dordrecht, The Netherlands

Muñoz D, con Espinar A, Canedo M, Bebbington A, and Croxton S (2000) *Los campesinos y las políticas públicas: encuentros y desencuentros*. D. Muñoz. Editorial Plural, La Paz.

Muñoz Ruiz U and Nuñez Espinoza O (2006) *Los Kanas de Quispillacta. Historia de un pueblo Quechua*. Territorio Kana, Ayacucho

Netting RMc (1993) *Smallholders, Householders: Farm Families and the Ecology of Intensive, Sustainable Agriculture*. Stanford University Press, Stanford, CA

Peck J (2004) Geography and public policy: constructions of neo-liberalism *Progress in Human Geography* 28(3): 392–405

Ross M (2001) *Extractive Sectors and the Poor*. Oxfam America, Boston, MA

Scott J (1990) (ed) *Domination and the Arts of Resistance: Hidden Transcripts*. Yale University Press, New Haven, CT

Scott J (1985) *Weapons of the Weak: Everyday Forms of Peasant Resistance*. Yale University Press, New Haven, CT

Sen A (1999) *Development as Freedom*. Alfred Knopf, New York

Smith G (1989) *Livelihood and Resistance*. University of California Press, Berkeley, CA

VMPPFM-Banco Mundial (1998) *Estudio de Productividad Rural y Manejo de Recursos Naturales: Informe Principal*. Vice Ministerio de Participacion Popular y Fortalecimiento Municipal, Lima, OH

Wescoat JL (2007 or 2008) Introduction: the three faces of power in landscape change. In Wescoat JL and Johnston DM (eds) *Places of Power: Political and Economic Driving Forces of Landscape Change*. Springer, Dordrecht, The Netherlands

Wood G (2003) Staying secure, staying poor: the faustian bargain. *World Development* 31(3): 455–471

Chapter 3
Moving to the Mountains: Amenity Migration in the Sierra and Southern Appalachian Mountains

Kurt Culbertson, Diedra Case, Drake Fowler, Heather Morgan, and Sue Schwellenbach

Two of the rural regions currently undergoing dramatic landscape change are the Sierra Nevadas, John Muir's "Range of Light," and the Blue Ridge Mountains, described by John Denver in his song "Take Me Home, Country Roads." These are mythical landscapes, the Sierras of television's "Bonanza" and the Blue Ridge Mountains of Mount Airy, North Carolina, television's "Mayberry." These are landscapes on opposite sites of the USA yet undergoing similar transformations.

The Sierra Nevada is a 400-mile-long stretch of extraordinary beauty and landscape diversity. Approximately two thirds of the bird and mammal species and one half of all the reptile and amphibian species in California are found here. The world's largest living plants, the Giant Sequoia, are found there, as is the tenth deepest freshwater lake in the world, Lake Tahoe. Almost two thirds of the range (12.6 million acres) is publicly owned and lies in three national parks – Yosemite, Sequoia, and Kings Canyon – nine national forests, and the lands of the Bureau of Land Management. The remaining one third is privately owned. These are some of the most heavily used public lands in the country. Yosemite National Park alone attracts 4 million visitors a year (The Wilderness Society 2004, 1).

Twenty-one counties comprise the Sierra Nevada region. It is estimated that 40 million people live within a half-day's drive of the Sierra Nevada. Between 1970 and 1998, the resident population in the Sierra nearly tripled, rising from 237,000 to 664,000. It is estimated that by 2020, more than 1 million people will call the Sierra home. Some estimate that the portion of landscape set aside for human settlement by the year 2040 will quadruple from today's measure (Steinicke and Hofmann 2004, 12). This counter-urbanization has been compared by Ernst Steinicke to a similar pattern in the eastern Alps centuries ago.

In the East, the Sierras find a parallel in the southern Appalachian region. The Southern Appalachians stretch from Pittsburgh, Pennsylvania, to just north of Atlanta, Georgia, a distance of almost 600 miles. Along the crest lie the Appalachian Trail, made famous in Bill Bryson's *A Walk in the Woods*, and the Blue Ridge Parkway, America's first scenic highway. The southern Appalachians are also home to Great Smoky Mountain National Park, the most visited national park in the USA with 4 million visitors per year. It is estimated that 100 million people live within a half-day's drive of the Southern Appalachian forests (Southern Appalachian Forest Coalition 2002, 10).

J.L. Wescoat, Jr. and D.M. Johnston (eds.), *Political Economies of Landscape Change.*
© Springer 2008

Perhaps no other rural region of the United States has been as dramatically transformed over the last few decades as southern Appalachia. More than 2 million people left the region between 1950 and 1970, mainly because of hard times caused by the loss of jobs from the mechanization of the coal mining industry, sharp declines in agriculture and manufacturing, and a shift from rail to highway transportation. While the region still has few metropolitan areas and remains mostly rural, many conditions have significantly improved. Job growth in southern Appalachia is increasing faster than in several regions and the nation as a whole.

Poverty rates in southern Appalachia have been cut in half since 1970, and rural unemployment rates are lower than in every region of the country except the Midwest and Plains. Since 1970, all of the states of the region except Alabama and West Virginia have population growth rates that exceed the nation as a whole. Three of the states (Georgia, Tennessee, and North Carolina) rank in the top ten states for net domestic migration. Moreover, much of the population growth in southern Appalachia has been due to the arrival of in-migrants who were attracted by the region's high quality of life, rural mystique, and expanding and diverse economy. "Many of these "in-migrants" have moved to rural areas around the region's two national parks (Great Smoky Mountains, Shenandoah), the Appalachian Trail, the Blue Ridge National Parkway, the Little River Canyon National Preserve, eight national forests, and along the banks of the regions' many lakes and rivers" (Jones et al. 2003, 223).

This comparison of two regions is offered as a way of understanding whether the transformation of these landscapes is a unique phenomenon, driven by local conditions, or if broader principles are at work that might also apply to other similar regions around the USA or, indeed, internationally. This paper relies heavily on existing published sources but also on 25 years of working in both landscapes, most recently from professional offices in Stateline, Nevada, at South Lake Tahoe, and Asheville, North Carolina.

We would offer three theses for your consideration: First, that the growth in both regions is driven largely by broader demographic trends, most notably the aging of the baby boom generation in the country, rather than disenchantment with urban America or the presence of new technologies that allow Americans to live and work at greater distances from urban centers. Nor are jobs the primary driver for this migration. The processes of (re)urbanization, suburbanization, and counter-urbanization are all at work in the USA today.

Second, that there is a logical pattern of use, from visitation to national parks, forests, scenic rivers, and ski resorts that in turn motivates second-home ownership. As with the railroad suburbs of Chicago, Naples and Palm Beach, Florida, or Beverly Hills, California, a century ago, these second home communities are not mere recreational havens, but emerging primary home communities.

Third, that the primary impacts of these changes are social in nature effecting the quality of community life rather than environmental. Planning and community building, therefore, must focus as much, if not more, on the creation of great communities, as on the regulatory aspects of environmental protection. This latter conclusion is similar to findings in similar examinations of the Roaring Fork Valley, the Yampa Valley, and the Interstate-70 corridor in Colorado (Culbertson, Jackson and Kolberg 1992; Culbertson, Kolberg and Turner 1991).

To identify and understand these forces at work, one must first consider the first three rules of real estate: Location, Location, Location. But what does that mean?

Location as proximate to what aspects of the landscape? To understand the situation, we have used the county as a unit of measure. This is because the boundaries of these units are not only stable over time, but also because important background research utilizing the county as a unit of measure has been completed by others, providing an important understanding of the situation. Planning within both regions is largely governed on a countywide basis. To understand the anticipated future of both areas, an understanding of activities at a county level is useful. Those counties that experienced the greatest population change in the last decade fall into one of these three categories: they have been attractive for the strength of the technology industries to which they are home, they are highly desirable as retirement destinations, or they are prized for the recreational amenities they contain.

The Economic Research Service, a division of the US Department of Agriculture, classifies counties based upon their primary characteristics such as metro and nonmetro. The metro counties with the highest concentration of high-technology industries realized the greatest population growth during the 1990s. These are generally those communities that received high scores on the Milken Institute Tech Pole index. Nonmetro counties on the other hand, grew at a rate of 5.9% between 1990 and 1996. In total there are 2,260 nonmetro counties excluding Alaska and Hawaii. The most explosive growth was found in the 190 counties whose economies are based on retirement and 285 whose economies depend upon recreation.

Demographer Harry Dent has suggested that technology in the field of communication, energy, and transportation will prompt major migration from suburbs to small towns and "exurbs" (communities located farther out from the suburbs). "We are going to see at least 20% of the population of North America, or approximately 70 million people, migrate to exurban areas, small towns and new-growth cities in the next three decades" (Dent 1998, 210). Other than in response to employment opportunities, the impact of technology on counter-urbanization is inconclusive.

While advances in the technology economy help to explain the growth of metropolitan areas, the rural renaissance of the 1990s cannot be explained by job growth in the technology sector. And yet, the "2000 census data shows that the country's rural population grew by roughly 10%, a sharp contrast to the 1980s, when nonmetropolitan areas barely registered a net gain, following a brief growth spurt during the 1970s" (Westphal 2001, 1).

If employment growth is greatest in metropolitan areas with high-technology economies, what has driven this rural migration? Why have some rural counties grown while others continue to lose population? Some have sought to describe an area's attractiveness in terms of climate. Jordan Rappaport (2007) in his article "Moving to Nice Weather," suggests that populations are concentrated in counties with moderate winters and moderate summers, as well as, in counties with relatively high rain and humidity but low snow (Figure 1). Rappaport gave preference to counties with temperate climates. As a result his analysis does not fully explain population change over the last 40 years. Again, there are other factors at work, such as man-made attractions, access, or the proximity to small-town life that moderate the importance of climate as a factor in location choice. Others have

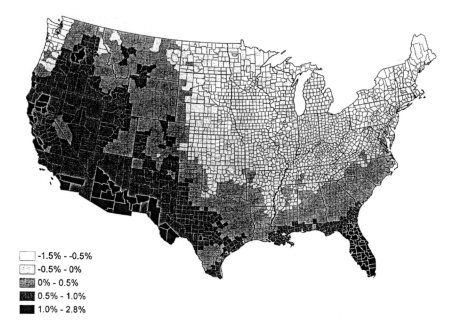

```
  ☐ -1.5% - -0.5%
  ▒ -0.5% - 0%
  ▓ 0% - 0.5%
  ▓ 0.5% - 1.0%
  ■ 1.0% - 2.8%
```

Figure 1 Expected Population Growth from Weather (1970–2000). Fitted annual population growth rate, controlled for coast, topography, initial density, concentric population, and industry. (Rappaport 2007, 300). Reproduced courtesy of Elsevier Limited and the author

found a similar positive correlation between temperate climates and population growth, yet acknowledge that such analysis may not stand up when measured against other factors (Poston and Musgrave 2005).

In attempting to capture other factors in this migration beyond climate, David McGranahan (1999), of the ERS, developed a rating scale to measure an area's attractiveness to immigrants. In preparing the scale, he cataloged the counties, and added two aesthetic measurements: the amount of water a county has, plus its topographic variation (Figure 2). For the latter measure, he defined 21 separate landforms ranging from "high plains" to "high mountains." What he found was that from 1970 to 1996, in nonmetropolitan counties low on the natural amenities index, population change was 1%. For counties high on the index, population change was 120%! McGranahan's analysis examined natural amenities that pertained to the physical environment and excluded much of what is man-made, such as historical buildings, scenic small towns, or such recreational developments as ski resorts, golf courses, or casinos. By his own admission, McGranahan's evaluation also gave greatest value to temperate climates, and thus failed to give full measure to counties with ski resorts, or the lake district of Wisconsin, Michigan, or Minnesota. In the latter case, cold winter temperatures were offset by wonderful summer weather that attracted boaters.

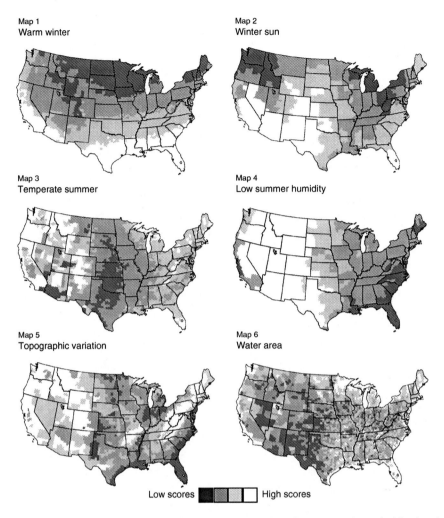

Figure 2 Amenity Measures that affect Growth (From http://www.ers.usda.gov/publications/aer781/aer781b.pdf, McGranahan 1999, 3)

Many of these counties are also federal land counties, those where 30% or more of the total land area is owned by the Federal government. These counties derive their natural amenities from the abundance of permanently protected public open space. There are 270 federal land counties in total. Reflecting the impact of retirees and tourism, the population of these counties grew at a rate of 9% versus 0.6% for nonmetropolitan counties. Similarly, people in these counties were slightly better off economically than other nonmetropolitan counties. Earnings from service jobs in these counties grew at 17% compared to 13% for other nonmetro counties.

In attempting to capture the benefits of small-town life, cultural offerings, and man-made amenities, others have sought to express an area's attraction in broader terms of quality of life. The American City Business Index ranks quality of life based upon 20 factors. A perfect score on this index would be 100%. Perhaps it is not surprising that the fasting growing counties in the Sierra Nevada, Placer (94.59%), Mono (94.78%), El Dorado (87.23%), rank with Marin (95.29%), Contra Costa (94.84%), San Mateo (93.15%), Santa Clara (91.53%), and Sonoma (91.21%) with the highest quality of life in California! Nor is it surprising that along the Blue Ridge, Buncombe (77.96%) (Asheville), Henderson (74.97%), and Transylvania (73.95%), North Carolina, rank among the top 20 counties in the state in terms of quality of life. Botetourt, Virginia (90.41%) is among the top 25 counties in that state.

But the economic benefits of natural amenities and favorable climate are not shared equally among the counties of the Sierra Nevada or southern Appalachia. Tulare (2.83%) and Yuba (1.11%) counties contain portions of the Sierra Nevada yet rank among the poorest counties in the country in terms of quality of life. Madison, North Carolina (19.49%) falls within the lowest quartile in the Blue Ridge, and Dickenson, Virginia (2.17%) is among the poorest in the country.

What might explain the variation in migration and economic vitality? Two factors may contribute to these differences within a region. The first of these is access. Placer County, the fastest-growing county in Sierra Nevada lies along Interstate 80 which connects San Francisco, Sacramento, and Reno. South shore of Lake Tahoe easily connects to Sacramento and Reno via US Highway 50. Approximately 15 million people live within a 3 hour drive of the north shore of Lake Tahoe. Many of these 15 million people earn substantial incomes in the Bay Area's high-tech industries. Conversely residents of Lake Tahoe can enjoy the commercial, medical and social services, and cultural offerings of these metropolitan areas far more easily than residents of more rural counties farther south.

A great deal of research is focused on travel costs as a determination of recreational location decisions. Although we know of no empirical data to support this theory, many real estate professionals suggest that concerns about security following 9/11 are leading many Americans to vacation closer to home and expanding the typical driving distance for second-home ownership from 180 miles to twice that distance. We would suggest that concerns about the reliability of air travel, coupled with increasing costs, are driving this decision.

In a similar way, Buncombe, Henderson, and Transylvania counties are among the first counties reached along the Blue Ridge Parkway as one heads north from Atlanta and Greenville along US Highway 64, sometimes referred to as the South Carolina autobahn because of the concentration of automotive industries along the corridor. Similarly one can reach Asheville directly via interstate from Charlotte, the nation's banking capital, and from Greensboro/Winston-Salem and the cities of the Research Triangle. Proximity to metropolitan centers therefore, is important at two levels. First, visitation from major urban areas helps to fuel the tourism economy and introduce future migrants to the region (Schmidt and Courant 2003). Second, proximity to urban areas provides a "best of both worlds" lifestyle for mountain residents.

Where the magnetism of certain portions of the Sierra Nevada or southern Appalachians to immigrants can be explained by climate, natural amenities, and quality of life, the magnitude of this migration cannot by explained by these factors alone. There are other forces at work. The greatest of these is the aging of the American population. The combination of the recreational and natural amenities of these regions with the impending retirement of millions of Americans is a powerful cocktail. America is aging in part because birth rates are at replacement levels, meaning that couples have an average of only two children. Second, baby boomers (those born from 1946–1965 when Americans averaged more than three children per family) are aging. After 1965 the birthrate subsided, so as baby boomers age, American society ages. The population at age 65 and older more than doubled from 16.6 million in 1960 to 35.0 million in 2000, while the rest of the population rose by just one half (Fuguitt, Beale and Tordella 2002) (Figures 3 and 4). From all indications, the aging of the baby boomer market is driving demand for second homes. The effect is made even more dramatic by the improved health of older people, earlier retirement ages, and higher retirement incomes made possible by a healthy stock market over the last decade and 401(K) plans. The second-home market is expected to double by 2009, putting price pressure on even the most desirable locations – those with either year-round temperate climates, or those with distinct seasons.

Anecdotally, most realtors in resort communities will tell you that the private motivation for second-home ownership is a place "where your grandchildren will come visit you." What better location, therefore, that a home on a mountain lake or beside a ski slope? Combining with the forces of retirement, the desire for

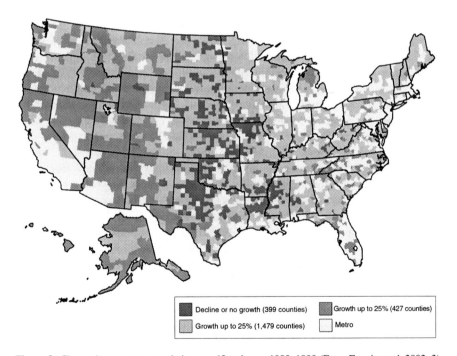

Figure 3 Change in nonmetro population age 65 and over, 1980–1990 (From Fuguitt et al. 2002, 3)

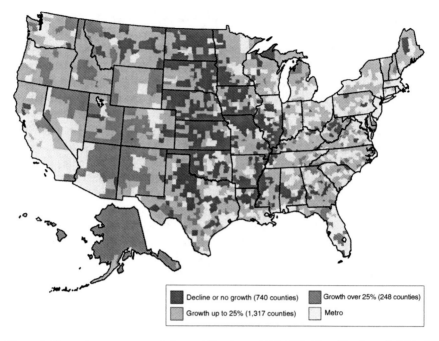

Decline or no growth (740 counties)   Growth over 25% (248 counties)

Growth up to 25% (1,317 counties)   Metro

Figure 4 Change in nonmetro population age 65 and over, 1990–2000 (From Fuguitt et al. 2002, 4)

recreation-based quality of life communities are transforming unlikely areas of the USA. A record number of second-homes sales occurred in 2003 with 445,000 transactions, approximately 5–6% of total transactions. According to a 1999 survey of the American Resort Development Association, about 9 million households alone currently own recreational property, a figure that is escalating at about 2.4% annually (Miner 1999). The National Association of Realtors estimates that there may be as many as 7 million second homes in the USA. The median price of a second-home rose 26.8% from 1999 to 2001, increasing from $127,800 to $162,000. This increase in second home sales coincides with tax-law changes in 1997 that eliminated capital gains taxes on the sale of these properties. Of people buying second homes between 2000 and 2002, 16% used equity in stocks or bonds. Prior to that period only 7% of buyers used this source of funds.

Given the recent declines in the stock market, one might suspect that the second-home market would slow as well. Ironically, the reverse is the case, as 34% of second-home buyers in the last 2 years were more likely to be planning to purchase an additional home as a result of recent stock market declines, compared to 18% of respondents 2 years earlier (Realtor Research 2002). Where investments in stocks and bonds as a source of funds has declined with the stock market, appreciation in the value of one's primary home provided a key source of equity, as "56% of second-home buyers, financed their property with a mortgage loan (52% of vacation-home owners versus 68% of investment owners)" (ibid., 1).

A survey of second-home owners is also revealing in terms of the use patterns for these residences. Approximately 51% of homeowners purchased the home for strictly recreational use. Eighteen percent plan to retire to it and 16% use it to diversify investments (ibid.). Only 15% sought income from renting their property. Eight-four percent of second-home owners never rent their properties. "Seventy-six percent want to be near an ocean, river, or lake; 38%, close to the mountains or other natural attractions, and 37%, in a specific vacation area" (ibid., 1).

While most vacation homes are located relatively close to the owner's primary residence, with a median distance of 185 miles, wide variations of distances are noted. One third are more than 500 miles and one third less than 100 miles. Other studies have suggested that homebuyers are willing to travel longer, more than 4 hours for recreation (American Lives 2003).

Retirees and second-home owners are being forced to explore new locations in traditional vacation locations such as Nantucket, Rhode Island (Realtor Research 2002). From 1990 to 2000, the total number of homes in Nantucket grew by 31%. The population of Hilton Head, South Carolina rose by 43% over the same period. This market demand is driving price appreciation. "In Cape May County, New Jersey, where seasonal housing accounts for 48% of the market, home prices increased 68% between the fourth quarter of 2000 and 2003. In Barnstable County, Massachusetts, better known as Cape Cod, 32% of all homes are seasonal and prices are up 59%. Prices in Lake Tahoe are up 51% during this period, while prices in and around Sarasota and Fort Myers increased 42–40% respectively" (Max 2004, 1).

Facing these market pressures, second-homeowners are starting to look to new locations to try to maximize their real estate dollars. At the Cliffs at Keowee Springs in Six Mile, South Carolina, at the edge of the Blue Ridge, the starting price of a custom home exceeds $1 million. Mountain Air in Burnside, North Carolina, is more attractive at $800,000, approximately $250 per square foot. In Ft. McHenry, Maryland, retirement and second homes are selling at $350 per square foot and moving higher. Homes at The Greenbrier in White Sulphur Springs, West Virginia, are selling at $350 per square foot. At Virginia Hot Springs, adjacent to the Homestead in Bath County, Virginia, prices are $450 per square foot. This is slightly below the $475 per square foot being realized at the Snowshoe Ski Resort in West Virginia. As high as these prices may seem, they are well below the $500–750 per square foot realized in major Western ski resorts, or the $1,000 per square foot being realized in selective areas of the Colorado Rockies, or coastal California or Florida. The first phase of the new redevelopment at Squaw Valley near North Lake Tahoe sold for $648 per square foot. With regional or national market demand and a limited supply of such special places, price gains in the second home/retirement market are far outstripping the real estate market in general.

What is beginning to emerge is a new pattern of second-home use. A comparison of data from the American Housing Survey and the Housing Vacancy Survey, suggest that in both the Sierra Nevada and the southern Appalachia, between 1999 and 2001 more units were classified as "usual residence elsewhere" rather than rental or recreational properties. This suggests a higher level of at least seasonal use or the conversion of second homes to more permanent use (Carliner 2002, 9). Similar findings by Ford Frick in Colorado suggest a similar pattern elsewhere (http://www.bbcresearch.com/).

J.P. Morgan suggests that that America's wealth culture is focused in this decade on wellness and wisdom. For the last decade skier days nationally have been flat. At Mammoth Mountain, California, emplanements fueled by direct 757 flights from places like Dallas and Chicago are steadily increasing yet skier days are relatively flat. Increasing home and condominium sales suggest that visitors are coming for other reasons. In small towns like Roanoke, Virginia, Asheville, North Carolina, and Truckee, California, residents are not only being attracted by the quality of the natural environment, recreational amenities, and the presence of state and federally protected lands, but also by the proximity to health care and the entertainment offerings of small-town life. Asheville has been referred to as the "Santa Fe of the East" because of the strength of its art market. The real estate industry often refers to the market's desire for "urban amenities in a wilderness environment."

Growth in the Sierra Nevada and southern Appalachia are likely to continue. Much of the employment decline related to the loss of extractive industries such as timber harvesting and mining has already occurred. In the Sierra, the Sierra Nevada Ecosystem Project a national mandate to plan comprehensively across the national parks and forests has provided the framework for long-term enhancement of the environment after decades of extractive use. In a similar way, the southern Appalachian Forest Initiative is working to restore the great Eastern forest. Agriculture in the region is in being reduced, returning cleared fields to forests. Population counts of bear, turkey, and other species in the East are now growing rapidly.

The species under perhaps the greatest stress is man. The transformation of entire economies from extractive industries to recreational and retirement-based industries is disruptive to local communities. The influx of major new populations into former quiet towns is disruptive to as well. It is the social transformation brought by this new population, more than environmental or economic impacts that is creating the greatest change.

What then can we conclude from this analysis? First, the impact of major urbanization in cities such as San Francisco or Atlanta extends far beyond the immediate boundaries of the community. These growing metropolitan are linked economically and socially to distant rural regions such as the Sierra Nevada or southern Appalachia. As cities such as Chicago grow through (re)urbanization, and Geneva, Illinois through suburbanization, so are communities such as Lake Geneva, Wisconsin, transformed by counter-urbanization. Dallas, Houston, Austin, and San Antonio are linked to the Hill Country and the Edwards plateau. The region around Bend, Oregon, is being transformed by residents of northern California, Portland, and Seattle, who desires to escape the rain of the Pacific Northwest and find sunshine. The wood and lakes of northern Michigan and Minnesota are being transformed by residents from Minneapolis and Detroit. The Panhandle of Florida, sometimes referred to as the Redneck Riviera, is joined to Atlanta and Huntsville. The Ozarks of Arkansas and Missouri are also being transformed as playgrounds and retirement communities for Dallas, Oklahoma City, St. Louis, and Memphis.

Second, residents are being attracted by the natural environment, recreational amenities, the presence of state and federally protected lands, and also by the proximity to health care and the entertainment amenitie of small-town life. Local and national economic policies might best be directed at enhancing the quality of life of residents and protecting the environment, rather than seeking to attract industries to remote locations or subsidizing extractive industries.

Third, many counties are being left behind, particularly those that either lack the employment base or the natural amenities to attract retirees, tourists, and second-home owners. America is becoming a landscape of larger urbanizations, green landscapes full of retirees and recreationalists, and poor counties often inhabited by minority populations. As Charlotte, North Carolina grows, what becomes of the residents of Anson county to the south of the city that lacks either the natural amenities or employment base to attract new residents? This is a similar phenomenon to the one addressed by Frank and Deborah Popper in their call for a Buffalo Commons on the Great Plains (Popper and Popper 1987).

Fourth, in the retirement and recreational counties of the Sierras and the Southern Appalachians, the natural landscape is increasingly being restored from the region's former days of natural resource extraction. The change that is being felt more acutely is a social change, as in-migration modifies both the community composition and the social contract between citizens.

Fifth, there is a sense that this rural migration may also be working in parallel with the renaissance of the inner city as well. Retirees and empty nesters, no longer dependent upon large homes in the suburbs for their families or tied to the quality of local school districts may be downsizing their homes and moving into smaller condominiums in the city. In 2001, nationwide condo sales hit 738,000, up 3.8% from 2000, as aging Americans put their big homes on the market and downsized their living space. "They're using some of that equity [from the sale of their first home] to buy a second home," says Walter Molony, an analyst with the National Association of Realtors (Carroll 2002, 45). Here they can enjoy the entertainment and cultural amenities of city life and easily "close up" the house when the head to the mountains or travel. One great example of such a project is Riverfront Park in Denver, a 60-acre redevelopment of the city's rail yards. Mark Smith, president of East/West Partners, the developer estimates that 20% of the company's sales to date have been to primary residents from Colorado mountain towns like Aspen and Vail. In a similar way, the emergence of urban timeshare products in San Francisco, New York, and other cities may also be a reflection of this counter-urbanization.

Sixth, as rural communities make the transformation from extractive, natural resource-based economies to tourism or quality-of-life economies, a key element of their success will be their ability to react quickly to change. After decades of economic decline, will these communities be too eager to welcome the big-box retail stores and fast-food outlets that have so greatly homogenized the American landscape or will they have the patience and wisdom to craft a vision for their future. Time will tell whether the lives of those who live in these regions will involve decades of conflict or merely be a "walk in the woods."?

References

American Lives, Inc. (2003) *The Second Home/Vacation Property National Study, study conducted for Centex Destination Properties (CDP).* American Lives, Carmel Valley, CA.

Carliner M (2002) Second Homes: A growing market. *Housing Economics*, July 2002: . 7–12

Carroll J (2002) My (other) house. *American Demographics* 24(6): 42–48

Culbertson K, Kolberg J, and Turner D (1991) Toward a Definition of Sustainable Development in the Yampa Valley of Colorado. *Mountain Research and Development.* Centre for Tourism Policy and Research, Simon Fraser University, Burnaby, British Columbia, pp 359–369

Culbertson K, Jackson S, and Kolberg J (1992) Loving the mountains to death: toward a definition of sustainable development in the Roaring Fork valley of Colorado. In Gill A and Hartmann R (eds) *Mountain Resort Development Conference Proceedings.* Centre for Tourism Policy and Research, Simon Fraser University, Burnaby, British Columbia, pp 41–52

Dent HS Jr. (1998) *The Roaring 2000's, Building the Wealth and Life Style You Desire in the Greatest Boom in History.* Simon & Schuster, New York

Fuguitt Glenn V, Beale Calvin L, and Tordella Stephen J (2002) Recent trends in older population change and migration for nonmetro areas, 1970–2000 *Rural America* 17(3): 11–19

Jones, Robert Emmet, Fly, Mark J, Talley, James, and Cordell, Ken (2003) Green migration into rural america: the new frontier of environmentalism. *Society and Natural Resources* 16: 221–238

McGranahan David A (1999) Natural Amenities Drive Rural Population Change. Economic Research Service, U.S. Department of Agriculture, Agricultural Economic Report No. 781, pp 1–24

Max Sarah (2004) Bought your second home? *CNN Money*, April 22: 2

Miner Steven S (1999) *American Recreational Property Survey.* American Resort Development Association, Chicago

Popper Deborah E and Popper Frank (1987) *The Great Plains: From Dust to Dust, Planning*, December 1987: 12–18

Poston Jr., Dudley L, and Musgrave Marcella E (2005) The Effect of Climate on Migration: United States, 1985–90 and 1990–98, Working paper, Department of Sociology. Texas A and M University, College Station, TX http://sociweb.tamu.edu/Faculty/POSTON/Postonweb/research/climate/climate.html. Consulted 12/28/05

Rappaport Jordan (2007) Moving to Nice Weather. *Regional Science and Urban Economics* 37(3): 375–98

Realtor Research (2002) *The 2002 National Association of Realtors Profile of Second-Home Owners.* National Association of Realtors, Washington, DC http://www.realtor.org/PublicAffairsWeb.nsf/Pages/2ndHomeSurvey02?OpenDocument. Consulted 7 June 2007

Schmidt Lucie and Courant Paul N (2003) Sometimes Close is Good Enough: The Value of Nearby Environmental Amenities http://www.williams.edu/Economics/wp/schmidt_courant.pdf. Consulted 12/28/05

Southern Appalachian Forest Coalition (2002) *Return the Great Forest, A Conservation Vision for the Southern Appalachian Region.* SAFC, Asheville, NC

Steinicke Ernst and Hofmann D (2004) California's High Mountain Regions as New Areas for Settlement, the "migration tournaround" in California and the population growth of the Sierra Nevada. *Petermanns Geographische Mitteilungen* 148: 12–15

The Wilderness Society (2004) *The Sierra Nevada, Range of Light Report* http://65.110.78.8/Library/Documents/upload/Sierra-Nevada-Factsheet.pdf. Consulted 12/27/05

Westphal David (2001) Shifting Tide: Some Cities Grow Despite Flow of Residents to Rural Areas.s *Sacramento Bee*, April 2, 2001

Part II
Political and Economic Driving Forces
of Landscape Change

Top : Franklin Delano Roosevelt Memorial, Washington DC. Bottom : All-American Canal, US-Mexico border (Photos: jlw)

Chapter 4
Constructing the Politics of Landscape Change

Susan E. Clarke

Introduction

In order to understand the political forces shaping landscape change, three constructs – or lenses – are used here to articulate key political trends and conditions. The first construct is Harold Lasswell's *garrison state* notion. Lasswell coined this phrase in 1937, 12 years before Orwell's chilling account of *1984*, to warn that extensive security concerns and the constant threat of war could lead to the creation of a garrison state where "specialists on violence" and their civilian allies become the most powerful group in society. Lasswell predicted a "crisis in democracy," with suppression of civil liberties in the name of national security. Now, in a post-9–11 era, these narratives are resurgent, accompanied by powerful forces to control access to public space and "design out terrorism."

The construct of *splintering urbanism* links spatial and political trends. Graham and Marvin (2001) characterize the "unbundling" of urban infrastructures such as transportation and communications into public and private segments as "splintering urbanism." This lens moves us beyond a focus on how privatization measures affect landscape changes. Rather, it directs attention to the ways in which contemporary processes unbundling local public authority also selectively reconnect some people and some places to political power in advantageous ways.

The third construct – *democratic ecologies* – is more speculative and incomplete. It pushes the familiar notion of just ecologies to encompass democratic practice as well. The familiar contrast of socially just and ecologically efficient resource patterns still tends to focus on different distributional patterns rather than the processes by which such choices are made. A perspective on democratic ecologies, however, would view environmental inequities and ecological dilemmas as matters of citizenship rather than distributional politics.

Constructing the Politics of Landscape Change

The notion of a landscape is inherently political. Olwig (2002) reminds us that one of the first uses of the term occurs in a theatrical piece by Ben Jonson and designed by Inigo Jones ("The Masque of Blackness" 1605). Jonson and Jones used the theatrical landscape to create a new political mindscape – the "image of the British nation-state as a body politic in a body geographic" during the Stuart dynasty. These historical origins highlight the political motivations behind landscapes. They also underscore the importance of our ideas of landscape, particularly the tension between notions of landscapes as reflecting community and culture and the views of landscapes as the geographic arena for exercises of national power. Such tensions seem sharply delineated today as we consider the types of political forces influencing landscape change.[1]

Three Constructs Linking Driving Forces and Steering Factors

Many of the familiar political forces shaping landscape change are still in play – patronage politics, regulatory regimes, policy initiatives – but they appear to be taking on new forms and new directions, with distinctive images of potential future landscapes. The difficulties and uncertainties in anticipating landscape change stem, at least in part, from the need to understand changing trends and conditions that may not appear to be related. We can get a better sense of these complex situations by using constructs that help make sense out of seemingly disparate and confusing situations. The three constructs considered here include: the garrison state, splintering urbanism, and democratic ecologies. Each of these constructs acts as a different set of *lenses*: looking at the same contemporary moment through alternative lenses, we see varying factors as significant and can reach alternative conclusions about the future. It is not a question of which construct is "right" or more accurate; rather it is a matter of how these constructs draw our attention to features and processes that we might not otherwise recognize as significant.

More or less explicit assumptions about the political driving forces and steering factors shaping landscape change are embedded in each construct. Savitch and Kantor (2002, 47) clarify these political forces using the analogy of the automobile: the drive train furnishes power to propel the car, while the steering mechanisms set it in a particular direction. Both are important factors in anticipating landscape change. The driving forces provide the economic and political power and resources to cause certain things to happen while steering factors indicate there are choices about the direction, orientation, and content of these changes. Most driving forces are exogenous and beyond local control but steering factors are more likely to be amenable to local actions. Without revisiting debates on structure and agency,

---

[1] My understanding of the landscape changes set forth here is that they include "purposeful and inadvertent modifications of landcover in urbanized areas (first-order measurements), land use, settlement, and transportation system change (i.e., the "proximate human causes and effects" of landcover change = second-order measurements), "as well as "the values associated with landcover, land use, and ecosystem changes (i.e., "underlying human causes and effects" = third-order measurements) (Wescoat 2004, conference overview).

the recognition of steering resources suggests the possibilities for change – that we can influence future landscapes and possibly even challenge some of the driving forces that appear to be structuring landscape change. Understanding the interplay of these driving forces and steering resources will provide the greatest insights on the political factors shaping landscape change, including the prospects for altering the trajectories sketched out in each of the three constructs.

The Garrison State and Landscape Change

Lasswell coined the "garrison state" phrase in 1937, 12 years before Orwell's chilling account of 1984, to warn that extensive security concerns and the constant threat of war could lead to the creation of a garrison state where "specialists in violence" and their civilian allies become the most powerful group in society. Lasswell predicted a "crisis in democracy," with suppression of civil liberties in the name of national security.

His original depiction of the garrison state is chilling (Fitch 1985; see also Lasswell 1941, 1962). The emergence of this new form of nondemocratic rule is in response to a sense of "total" war and the fear that the entire population is at risk; as a result, the line between combatants and noncombatants becomes blurred. National security is seen as contingent on domestic awareness and commitment; this supports the use of symbolic manipulation and coercion as means of internal control. Resources are diverted toward military and security expenditures; to legitimate these shifts and forestall objections based on other priorities, the garrison state depends on war scares more than on actual fighting.

The increased expectation of violence and the growing prominence of experts in violence are key trends anticipated by Lasswell. The expectation of violence legitimates demands for conformity, morality, and "patriotism" and the use of coercion to ensure compliance. The more centralized and complex is modern technology, the more vulnerable to terrorism and sabotage, again encouraging the blurred line between internal and external enemies.

Fitch (1985) points out that Lasswell's later work, in which he anticipates a garrison state emerging within the USA or Europe, recognizes that the external forms of democratic institutions would continue to exist but that power shifts to those traditionally seen as part of a military–industrial complex. Or in Gross' words, a "techno-urban fascism," stemming from "a cancerous growth *within* and *around* the White House, the Pentagon, and the broader political establishment" (1973). More elegantly but equally direct, in 1970 Senator William Fulbright warned, "Violence has become the nation's leading industry" (cited in Light 2002, 612). Eisenhower's farewell address echoed these concerns, introducing the phrase "the military-industrial complex" into everyday conversations.

But given the difficulty of detecting trends toward the garrison state when outward forms of democracy remain stable, Lasswell's cautionary words remain a matter of debate. Fitch's (1985) analysis of presidential State of the Union addresses from

1946 to 1982 finds increasing expectations of violence – a central element of the garrison state construct – and a strong focus on the Soviet Union as the enemy of the USA since 1976. With the collapse of the Soviet Union in the late 1980s, it is likely that these expectations declined somewhat. Indeed, some historians now argue that the USA did not turn into a "garrison state," as many feared at the start of the Cold War. Cultural and institutional factors, particularly anti-statism ideologies, and a weak state apparatus dampened drives toward a powerful central state (Friedberg 2000). This suggests that the garrison state is not a question of more or less state authority but the form in which it is expressed (Sherry 2003): the particular form the garrison state would take in the US would be shaped by its distinctive political structures and processes.[2]

Now, in a post-9–11 era, these garrison state narratives are resurgent, accompanied by powerful forces to control access to public space and "design out terrorism" in landscapes of security, surveillance, and political control. Lasswell's construct directs our attention to how political driving forces and steering factors highlighted by the garrison state construct are contributing to landscape change (Figure 1).

Figure 1 A more elegant example of security design at the US General Services Administration building in Chicago (Jacobs/Ryan Design) [jlw]

---

[2] Sherry (2003) characterizes this as a "hidden-hand" garrison state oriented toward air power, high technology, and quasi-private initiative rather than a highly centralized, statist version.

Driving Forces for Landscape Change

This mutually constitutive relationship between a garrison state mentality and political forces is one of the key political conditions now shaping future landscape changes. Two driving forces highlighted by the garrison state debate merit further attention: federalism and values. A focus on intergovernmental structures and public policies for homeland security draws our attention to the ways in which the federalist structure linking national, state, and local governments in the USA creates disincentives to cooperate, even around such profound threats, and mis-specifications of the threats themselves. To the extent that security issues are framed in political rhetoric and discourse as competing values of access, mobility, and security, these ideational elements must also be considered.

Federalism and public policies for homeland security. There is no question that there are serious on-going threats to public well-being and national security. These are real and important concerns. The expectations of violence and sense of risk, the priority given to security and military expenditures, and the dominance of military and public security interests parallel Lasswell's characterization of the garrison state mentality. Given the extraordinary circumstances giving rise to these concerns with homeland security since 9/11, it perhaps is not surprising that the immediate response resembles the image projected by the garrison state construct. The inter-governmental structure in the USA, however, is a major factor in determining whether this mentality persists, what form it takes over time, and what its impacts will be on landscape change.

All terrorism is local....but homeland security politics are federal. Although the trends appear to suggest the emergence of a garrison state in the 21st century, the driving force of intergovernmental structures could reshape these trends in the USA. Our decentralized federal structure portends the weak state apparatus noted by Friedberg (2000) in an earlier historical period. As Savitch and Kantor (2002, 76) point out, US federalism features loose and weak integration of different governmental authorities, little horizontal integration or coordination across differ-ent jurisdictional and regional scales, notoriously low levels of intergovernmental funding, and few integrative mechanisms, such as strong party systems, to over-come these structural features (Clarke and Chenoweth 2006). More integrated intergovernmental systems might pursue more coherent strategies that would cush-ion and support local security. But more coherent strategies are also likely to be more centralized, thereby increasing the odds of a garrison state. In the weaker US system, localities face a deficit in hometown security provisions but the specter of a garrison state also seems to take on a less coercive form.

Yet the national security crisis is an urban crisis. It is useful to remember that the urban crises of the 1960s were presented as national security crises, inviting numerous contracts between defense and aerospace firms and city officials (Light 2002). Now the homeland security crisis is a distinctly urban crisis, in the sense that critical infrastructures, highly dense populations, and concentrations of emergency personnel are massed in urban areas. There are tremendous increases in budget expenditures toward military and security priorities, with significant shares directed to state and local governments. The Urban Areas Security Initiative (UASI) program, for example, began in 2002 by directing funds to seven urban areas (New York City, Washington DC, Chicago, Houston, Los Angeles, San Francisco, and Seattle) seen as at high risk of terrorist attack; it now distributes funds to 50 cities based on risk assessments by the Department of Homeland Security but has recently adopted a regional – rather than city – orientation.[3] These funds require establishment of Urban Area Working Groups, conduct of an Urban Area Assessment, and development of their own Urban Area Homeland Security Strategy. Other federal programs direct Homeland Security funds to port security, railroad security, and mass transit security although many critical infrastructure facilities are privately owned, particularly in the West (Plant 2004). These facilities see little return on the enormous investment required to harden all their infrastructure networks. The national government has yet to develop a funding program to assist in this process, whether through incentives for private investment or through direct financial aid.

But the integrative potential of this funding is distorted by the slow distribution of these funds to state and local governments and the reliance on conventional political distribution formulae for funding allocations rather than assessments of risk. Despite the appeals of urban mayors for direct allocations of funding, with the exception of the categorical UASI program, homeland security funds are allocated to the state to "pass-through" to subnational units. States were required to pass-through no less than 80% of the allocated funds but, in most cases, did so in a lax and haltingly manner. Moreover, many directed funds to counties rather than to cities. There is some increased regional cooperation on homeland security in the past few years (NLC 2002) but few sustainable or durable cross-jurisdictional coalitions.

Cities are concerned with hometown security, of course, but deal with many competing priorities (NLC 2002; Clarke and Chenoweth 2006; Eisinger 2004), including conventional public safety, economic concerns, and budget problems (especially the lack of reimbursement for security expenses in response to federal mandates). Even within the security agenda, state, and local priorities favor responsiveness and protection of assets, while officials such as Governor Mitt Romney of Massachusetts urge them to take on intelligence and surveillance functions (Task Force 2004). As a result, the "management of expectations" has become a major policy issue within the federal system. In a recent survey of local government officials on dealing with disasters and threats of terrorism, Gerber et al. (2005, 2) pinpoint this expectations issue: "While the national government has strong incentives for promoting hazard mitigation and preparedness, state and local governments face certain disincentives to proactive management and often lack the administrative capacity or commitment for effective policies. As a result, state and local government

---

[3] The USAI formula (redesigned in 2004 and again in 2007) considers population and population density; critical infrastructure; threat information; formal mutual aid cooperation, and law enforcement investigations and enforcement activity (Somers 2004).

frequently do not develop a level of capacity for, and commitment to, effective disaster policy that matches their responsibilities [sic]." Their findings indicate that threat perception does not affect preparedness efforts as much as internal administrative capacity, underlining the importance of basic resource availability and the deficiencies created by the national budget process (Clarke and Chenoweth 2006). Overall, the decentralized federalism in the USA appears to continue to be capable of refracting and diffusing these any initiatives for a more centralized and coherent security response.

Competing policy frames and values: access, mobility, security. Using the lens of the garrison state also underscores the significance of values and framing. Values are not easily changed and they emerge from habits and historical experience that produce particular attitudes, beliefs, and norms. But people hold multiple, competing values with priorities often shifting depending on the situation or circumstance. For many architects and planners, the homeland security issue is framed as competing values of access, mobility, and security. Current policies emphasize control of access to public spaces and physical facilities as a solution to security concerns. While many points out this only shifts the weak points rather than eliminates them, it is a dominant response with a "chilling effect" on design of public spaces.

Given the constraints on information, it can be difficult to understand the competing frames in play and their priorities. But there is a growing sense that we have learned some of the wrong lessons from 9/11 in our responses to threats to the physical fabric and landscape of our cities (Linenthal 2005). This partly reflects a tendency to view intelligence as "perpetrator-centered and event-focused" (Carter 2002) leading to efforts to find individuals and prevent their plots from unfolding by limiting all access to weak points. In contrast, intelligence could be directed to surveillance and monitoring of the multiple means by which catastrophic terrorism could be delivered. This may still involve selective access but is less likely to mean the shifting of weak points by erecting physical barriers around a growing number of sites; the result would be less impact on the landscape (Carter 2001, 2002). Rather than physical barriers and imperfect security systems, for example, a system of sensors and monitors able to detect dangerous substances might be more effective and less obtrusive than the fortifications currently favored (ibid.).

More generally, there is a sense that policies need to be grounded in an understanding of vulnerability as well as risk (Clarke and Chenoweth 2006; Mitchell 2003; Pelling 2003; Vale and Campanella 2005). A focus on vulnerabilities – inevitable in an open society and competitive economy and concentrated in urban areas – directs attention to critical infrastructure design issues, particularly fixed infrastructure in cities. It now appears that many of the features adopted to improve infrastructure efficiency – agglomeration, interdependency – now increase the vulnerability of these systems (Branscomb 2004). There are many technical solutions proposed to these vulnerabilities but a common theme is a new view of infrastructure that is relevant to landscape design: not expanding systems and customers but increasing flexibility, resilience, redundancy, responsiveness, and adaptability of existing "systems of systems" (Branscomb 2004; Prieto 2003). It is also clear that safer food supplies, better public health services, more secure communication systems, more reliable electric power, safer chemical and energy industries could result from efforts to improve homeland security if they are cached in terms of these dual (Branscomb 2004) civil and security benefits.

Steering Resources and Future Landscapes

The garrison state lens leads us to expect that the expenditures necessary to create a fortified and secure landscape increasingly will displace other budget priorities at every level of government. And whether approximating a garrison state or some hybrid version of one, territorial approaches to ensuring security will contribute to the sense of "splintered urbanism" as experts carve up the city into areas of more or less risk (Coaffee 2004). The emotional context of the garrison state is one of anxiety, fear and threat; this skews power to the "violence specialists," most of who will be external to any given community. As a result, the administrative management of the garrison state – one requiring contingent coordination (Kettl 2003) and cooperation on an unprecedented scale and complexity at every level of government – could crowd out traditional democratic practice. At a minimum, it will raise difficult questions of transparency and accountability.

As noted above, however, the driving forces of our decentralized federalist structure indicate that this chilling scenario of a garrison state is likely to be unevenly experienced and imperfectly realized in the USA In part, this is because our institutional arrangements and cultural practices make any highly centralized and coherent practices difficult to carry out without substantial and significant variations – the disincentives for cooperation and coordination in our "weak state apparatus" are not to be underestimated.

But the limits to a fully articulated garrison state are not just structural. Even given the force and unique character of these driving forces, several steering factors are available to direct or guide everyday practices in ways that thwart or mitigate trends toward a garrison state landscape of limited access and mobility. Three steering factors in which landscape designers and practitioners are likely to be influential include: civic and grassroots activities that contest the garrison state mentality, the institutions and practices emerging from local governing arrangements demanded by these new security issues, and the role of design education in developing security-based design.

Contesting the garrison state security frame. The garrison state construct leads us to anticipate a grim future landscape, dominated by surveillance, deterrence and detection mechanisms limiting access, and mobility, particularly to public spaces and buildings. The values articulated by these structures privilege security at the expense of other cultural and political values. It is important that professionals, academics, practitioners, and citizens become aware of the security dilemmas facing public officials but current homeland security policies are contested by many groups because they allow security values to trump access and mobility values in ways that erode the democratic nature of public spaces. These challenges do not deny security values but focus on how the framing of security threats can delegitimate other values. Since the ways in which situations are framed can lead people to put a priority on some values rather than others, seeing framing as a steering resource directs our attention to political activities centered on defining how to understand a situation and what value priorities should guide our policy choices.

There is some evidence of grassroots activity resisting and challenging elements of the homeland security policy but these are dampened by constraints imposed by the Patriot Act. The role of civic groups and professional associations is more visible. Note that where the Fein Report in the 1960s anticipated landscape architects as mediators of environmental disputes, it is likely that one of their roles in the 21st century will include championing access and mobility values in the face of rashly produced, security-based design policies. At its annual national meeting in 2004, for example, the National League of Cities went on record in calling for repeal of parts of the Patriot Act granting law enforcement agencies broad powers, requiring public universities to collect information on selected students, and violating other civil liberties and rights (Hudson 2004).

Creating new local governance arrangements on security issues. These security issues raise essential questions about the politics of landscape – who owns the land or decides how it "should look?"(Walker and Fortmann 2003). Landscape architects involved in major redevelopment projects with rescaling of urban spaces are well aware that these projects involve the cultural landscape as well (Prytherch 2003). As such they are often contested; we now must ask whether the rescaling of the city for security purposes will give rise to similar cultural and social conflicts – and if not, why not?

The institutions, arrangements, and practices bringing together citizens and public officials to deal with these conflicts and choices about security are critical steering features. Yet local governments will be only one of many players in these governance arrangements. They are likely to feature new local governance arrangements constructed to deal with security issues that reach beyond formal government institutions. Already emerging in cities across the country, the local governance arrangements demanded by security agendas involve multiple stakeholders, reach across jurisdictions and bring together both public and private actors (Eisinger 2004; Savitch 2003; Pierre 2000). Each controls strategic resources necessary to "solve" the problem of local security (Clarke and Chenoweth 2006).

In these governance arrangements, there is no one hierarchical authority in charge so there is an unprecedented need for cooperation among stakeholders who seek mutual benefits but have little experience dealing with each other. While these actors are not necessarily – and even unlikely – partners in coalitional regimes, their cooperation is essential to achieving mutual goals. These new coalitions include fire/police/emergency personnel but also public health officials, universities, and other diverse actors including private facilities and personnel, e.g., corporate medical departments, private engineering and construction firms, private infrastructure. This brings resources and skills previously not considered to the table but the involvement of landscape architects, planners, and others involved in design of local plans appears more problematic. Given the narrow definition of security threats, design issues are likely to be perceived as engineering tasks in the absence of a design presence at the table.

Rethinking security-based design curricula. The impact of this garrison state mentality on design curricula is an important consideration (Hopper and Droge 2005). At one level, it is ironic that the resurgence of physical design occurs just when security issues threaten to dominate design values. For planners and architects, it is important to remember that the "security threats and vulnerabilities" and even the security plans and standards are contested issues. But it is likely that security-based design will not immediately transform design education. Note that design for sustainability has yet to make a major impact on design curricula: only 14% of the administrators surveyed in 2003 by Metropolis said their institutions were developing programs for sustainable design (McDonough 2004) despite the decades-long emphasis on sustainable design. There may be more money available to support security-based design than has been available for sustainability projects but this is yet to be demonstrated.

Splintering Urbanism and Landscape Change

One of the hallmark conditions of contemporary life is the sense of blurring – accelerating technological development, shifting authority, rapidly transforming urban spaces. Very much in the tradition of Lewis Mumford, Graham and Marvin (2001) introduced the construct of "splintering urbanism" to characterize the "unbundling" of urban infrastructures into public and private segments. This second construct moves us beyond a focus on how privatization measures affect landscape changes, although they play a part in these processes. Rather, it directs our attention to the ways in which contemporary processes fragmenting local public authority also selectively reconnect some people and some places to political power in advantageous ways.

This is very much a "big picture" perspective on urban change. Other scholars, such as Ed Soja (2000), also focus on the "intensification of social and spatial control" with new developments in the privatization, policing, surveillance, governance, and design of the built environment. Soja depicts this postmetropolitan landscape as encompassing protected and fortified spaces, islands of enclosure and anticipated protection against the real and imagined dangers of daily life (2000). But the splintering metaphor is useful at analyzing the everyday consequences of these changes.

We all understand infrastructure as the means by which basic goods, services, information, and people move throughout urban areas. These very processes shape and define the urban setting and the ways in which people and neighborhoods are linked together. To Graham and Marvin, these networks are intrinsic elements in socioeconomic, cultural, political, and ecological change in the city. As these authors point out, these unbundling processes create "premium spaces" for some, where the infrastructure networks are customized to serve a favored few. As they reconnect these groups, they "bypass" less powerful users and spaces. As a result, these premium, customized networks splinter urban areas into enclaves and archipelagos of privilege and power. Think of gated communities, privatized Business Improvement Districts, self-enclosed shopping malls, "tourist bubbles," (Judd 1999) and edge city spaces as illustrations of these premium networked spaces. These gaps between the connected and unconnected places and people contribute to and sustain the physical and social fragmentation and polarization of the city (Figure 2).

They contrast these contemporary secessionary trends with the historical albeit modernist infrastructural ideals of universal, integrated, standardized, mass service provision through invisible and neutral technologies. A nationally integrated infrastructure surely allowed the state "to impose its own rationality on to the territorial scales, and social processes, within it," as they put it. But Graham and Marvin also underscore how universal provision of some public goods histori-cally created a sense of connection and community. At both the neighborhood and city level, proximity meant similar services, and similar citizenship. While careful not to romanticize a past solidarity and coherence in American communi-ties – women and ethnic and racial minorities rarely shared these privileges – Graham and Marvin emphasize the ways in which common infrastructure supports the urban fabric. As these infrastructures become splintered and public goods are privatized or selectively distributed, the disconnect between proximity and coher-ence increases. New networks emerge, selectively connecting favored people and

Figure 2 Millennium Park, Chicago, with spaces named for their principal patrons, has enhanced the already premium residential and commercial real estate along the lakefront. (jlw)

places rather than territorially cohesive places (ibid. 16); by implication, less-favored people and places are hived off to lesser levels and quality of services.

By treating privatization issues in terms of social and spatial segregation rather than as matters of bureaucratic efficiency, Graham and Marvin highlight the normative citizenship dimensions of the growing trend of privatizing previously public goods and services. Now we see the shift toward individual choice, the dominance of private and often transnational corporations, market-based pricing, the recommodification of public goods into separate circuits, and the incursions on public spaces.

MacLeod and Ward (2002) characterize these emergent landscapes as resembling "a patchwork quilt" of fortified spaces and neighborhoods that are at once physically proximate but institutionally estranged. The adjectives characterizing the contemporary situation are telling – "unbundled," urban archipelagos", "privatopias,' "floating", "partitions," "enclaves." As metaphors, they reflect the emotions that run through our experience of place (Klinkenborg 2004). They also signal the ideological and political context in which infrastructure is established, particularly underscoring the ways in which infrastructure reflects power and legitimacy.

Driving Forces for Landscape Change

Some of these splintering processes are encouraged by private market forces supported by state actions – such as in the creation of business zones, business improvement districts, enterprise zones, business parks, and other areas linked more closely to extra-local markets than to local communities. Market conditions, particularly the profit margins available through segmenting markets, are critical driving forces in splintering urbanism but they are insufficient, in themselves, to construct the landscape envisioned here. The different institutional forms and political arrangements necessary for these market forces to unfold are necessary factors. These include the migration of authority across governmental levels as well as less formal aspects, such as the emergence of new forms of power brokers and patronage around security agendas. It is the interplay and cumulative effects of these market forces and shifting authority structures that push splintering processes with important consequences for landscapes.

Private power, segmented markets, and authority migration. The sheer volume of unbundling processes, and the absence of significant shifts in the other direction – from unbundled to more bundled, from private to public – indicate that there are profit margins available in segmented markets for premium spaces and formerly public goods. But labeling these processes as "privatization" or "deregulation" is too simple: it overlooks the multiple pathways to unbundling, the many diverse institutional forms around unbundling, and the roles of political choice in these new arrangements. Graham and Marvin are careful to emphasize that the infrastructure networks themselves are not the agents of urban change, merely the expression of shifting power relations (385).

Within the last two to three decades, the changing political climate emphasized "reforms" that would devolve power away from the national bureaucratic structures, shift toward market pricing mechanisms, allow alternative, competitive delivery systems, and create more of a market environment for provision and distribution of basic services. Public regulations continue to set standards for provision and distribution but public organizations are not necessarily the builders or providers of public goods. In contrast to the expectations voiced in the Fein Report (1972), landscape architects are less likely to be on the firing line of public service delivery systems since many service delivery systems and infrastructures are less likely to be public.

An emerging research approach characterizes these shifts and driving forces as the migration of authority (Gerber and Kollman 2004). Rather than analyze devolution and centralization as separate processes, the focus is on a more unified framework for analysis of the movement of power within a political system overall and the political choices underlying these shifts. So the authority migration allowing and supporting splintering processes is neither "natural" nor "mechanistic." Rather it is a contingent and strategic political choice by elites who are responding to technological and social changes in ways that enhance their positions and increase their control over the distribution of new resources. Each migratory "direction" creates different types of incentives and constraints on policy makers at every level. As power and authority is unbundled and rebundled by splintering processes, we need a better understanding of what those new incentive structures are.

New forms of power brokers and patronage. The disjuncture of economic power and local political authority sketched by Graham and Marvin do not mean the diminishment of local political power. Nor do they necessarily mean the substitution of private power for local governance. At a minimum, the forces driving landscape change contribute to more diffuse power networks: the days of power brokers like Robert Moses are fading away, displaced by less visible and less coherent partnerships and quasi-public authorities. And to the extent that a garrison state mentality becomes more entrenched, we may see a new type of power broker reshaping landscapes: a security based elite, embedded in a complex intergovernmental homeland security network with even less accountability and access than the old style Moses-type brokers.

Graham and Marvin depict architects in a rather passive role, managing the programs, and processes attendant to splintering rather than actively engaged in resisting these processes or mitigating their consequences. This is not necessarily the case. The role of architects, planners, and landscape architects in a landscape of premium networked spaces should be the starting point of an extended discussion, beginning with the question of who "the public" might be in this splintered landscape. The notion of how to serve the "public interest" amid a city of emerging gated enclaves, privatopias, and secessionary trends is unsettling (MacLeod 2003).

Steering Resources and Future Landscapes

The scenario for future landscape change from this perspective is seemingly less austere and less foreboding. Indeed, the premium spaces created in these reconnecting networks are marketed to be attractive and entertaining settings for those able to access them. But as the wealthy and privileged reconnect in premium spaces, the urban landscape becomes marked by social polarization and spatial segregation. MacLeod and Ward's (2002) description of these competing future scenarios as "patchwork quilt urbanism" reflects a "best of times, worst of times" dimension. We are all familiar with warnings of a "revanchist" urban landscape (Smith 1996) or "fortified" cities (Davis 1999; Coaffee 2004) but Graham and Marvin's perspective is especially powerful because it captures a series of coterminous trends – privatization, the migration of authority, rescaling or re-territorialization processes – and casts them as unbundling processes occurring in a spatial, political, and cultural setting.

This view of urban dystopia clearly forces us to ask about the implications of unbundling and splintering for democratic practice, particularly within cities. It also directs our attention to the steering resources that might shape these unbundling processes and their social and spatial consequences into more democratic and equitable outcomes. A steering factor of particular relevance to landscape architects and planners is the potential for mobilization for collective action around the juxtaposition of premium and non-premium spaces within common institutional settings.

Mobilizing around the boundaries of the privileged and the peripheral. Graham and Marvin offer a prescriptive manifesto, a call to explore more democratic ways of constructing network spaces. Their empirical analyses sketch out the ways in which the unbundling of the historical "infrastructural ideal" links up premium spaces and segregates the poor and less privileged. Yet this very juxtaposition of privileged, premium spaces, and more peripheral spaces contains the seeds of discontent and change. It is not at all clear how the boundaries between the privileged and the peripheral are regulated and maintained, for example. The interaction of these spaces, particularly within the same metropolitan institutional context, and the interdependence of these spaces and processes, opens up opportunities for potential political mobilization and collective action at the local level.

In contrast to some US versions of urban dystopias (e.g., Davis), Graham and Marvin see splintering and reconnecting not as a wholesale historic shift but as a series of processes, characterized by inertia and discontinuities. Indeed, they note the continued publicness of spaces, the diverse mixes of unbundling processes, and the ineffectiveness of many efforts to control public spaces (2001, 388; see also, Coutard 2002). Given post-9–11 conditions, there may be additional constraints on public places but their urging to consider the processes of governance and politics that support and resist splintering merits our attention.

As noted above, one of the immediate responses to the increased demands for homeland security was to erect physical barriers controlling access to important public places, increase surveillance, and create new security systems for perceived weak points in transportation and communication infrastructures. Graham and Marvin argue that these splintering processes are making the "normative ecologies" of who "belongs" in urban public spaces more tightly defined and self-reinforcing. Many seemingly public spaces also are now under the direct or indirect control of corporate, real estate or retailer groups which carefully work with private and public police and security forces to manage and design out any groups or behavior seen as threatening to the tightly "normalized" use (MacLeod 2003). Mobilizing around public space and design proposals maximizing access may be one path to creating diverse constituencies for less-segregated networks.

These conditions, however, will not result in collective action unless they are framed in ways that articulate the values diminished by greater social and spatial segregation – echoed currently in political rhetoric such as "the other New York," "the two Americas" – and lead to viable solutions. At a minimum, these unbundling processes constitute a threat to the public realm and public spaces through privatism. As Graham and Marvin ask, under what conditions can coalitions resist tendencies to construction of secessionary networks and spaces and support traditions of more equitable networks? (2001, 419) Can cities manage the production and regulation of premium networked spaces through planning and regulatory mechanisms that mitigate their more negative consequences? (2001, 397) These points suggest that prospective interventions are likely to be context-specific, shaped by the local political and regulatory environment; the outcomes of these larger unbundling processes, therefore, are likely to be variable over time and space.

The Potential for Democratic Ecologies and Landscape Change

The third construct – *democratic ecologies* – is more speculative and incomplete. It pushes the familiar notion of just ecologies to encompass democratic practice as well. Often, for example, ecological dilemmas appear to pit socially just distributions of amenities, such as trees, that would benefit all local residents against ecologically efficient distributions with benefits spreading to larger scales. This contrast of socially just and ecologically efficient scenarios still tends to focus on different distributional patterns rather than the processes by which such choices are made.

The lens of democratic ecologies, however, frames environmental inequities and ecological dilemmas as matters of citizenship rather than distributional politics. It anticipates future landscapes in which cities are ecologically rational and also supportive, for example, of human social relations that are egalitarian, non-domineering, and cooperative in character (Watts 2000). Thinking in terms of democratic ecologies captures the networked complexities of contemporary cities as well as the problematic roles of local government institutions.

The expectation is that different forms of urban governance produce distinctive ecologies – reflecting, for example, how cities mediate relations between human and nonhuman nature, uneven development between cities and nonurban environments, and the different ideological contexts for urban planning – and how these issues are matters of deliberation and debate. To the extent that we consider nature and landscape – and politics – as constructed entities, these ecological dilemmas need to be matters for democratic deliberation and engagement. To do so requires putting a stronger understanding of "the political" into notions of political and landscape ecology.

Not that ecological arguments always overlook political dimensions. To Swyngedouw and Heynen (2003), "the political programme, then, of urban political ecology is to enhance the democratic content of socioenvironmental construction by identifying the strategies through which a more equitable distribution of social power and a more inclusive mode of environmental production can be achieved." But these declarations often lack the specificity and analytical edge necessary for a truly political ecology.

Driving Forces and Steering Resources for Future Landscape Change

As Delores Hayden notes (2004), architecture and design cannot, in themselves, contend with the economic and political driving forces shaping contemporary landscapes. But we can understand these roles and possibilities for steering resources more clearly by looking at empirical cases of efforts to achieve more just and democratic ecologies. These are useful antidotes to scholarly rhetoric and offer some diagnostics for future action.

Sellers' (2000) comparison of Freiburg, Germany and Madison, WI, for example, highlights the importance of "translocal orders" – institutions, organizations, and policymaking at higher levels of government – in determining whether progressive coalitions will be able to provide collective environmental goods or more private, divisible and selectively provided environmental goods. In both cities, ecological objectives became the rallying point for mobilization and coalition-building. In both cities, these values actually allowed coalitions to link developmental and redistributive goals with ecological agendas – exemplifying the steering forces highlighted by the democratic ecologies construct. But in Madison, place-based disparities transformed these goals into "Upscale" strategies that improve environmental amenities and expand development but give selective and private benefits – "premium" gains – to the more privileged.

This was not a matter of weak leadership, corruption, electoral ambitions, or other flaws: to Sellers, it illustrates how larger "translocal" structures can encourage or discourage recognition of collective interests. In Madison, in contrast to Freiburg, officials lacked the legal mandates, financial resources, technical competence, and organizational capabilities necessary to gain leverage over groups seeking more privatized distributions. The different contexts in which local officials in Madison and Freiburg operate are not just a question of national policies but of the multilevel governmental infrastructure making some strategies more feasible than others. In Germany, the structured formal representation of economic sectors in national policymaking lessens their role in local politics and contributes to more stable local policy choices. In addition, the proportional representation system and stronger party mechanisms meant that Greens and socially progressive groups gained influence more easily in Freiburg. Once in elected office, they were able to institutionalize their priorities and thus contribute to the local capacity for sustained action on economic, environmental, and democratic practices.

But, as noted above, the weak translocal infrastructure and the absence of horizontally integrative mechanisms meant that Madison officials needed to approach issues of a just and democratic ecology through very particularistic channels – neighborhood groups, business, and others. On the one hand, this appeared to grant democratic control to the lowest levels but it also sustained the wide place-based disparities in amenities. Ironically, the progressive coalition in Madison came to depend increasingly on selectively provided amenities to privileged neighborhoods despite the ideological preferences of members (140). As a result, Sellers contends that environmentalist groups in the USA have generated less environmental and social justice and worse environmental conditions overall than in countries with translocal orders able to foster more public provision of environmental goods (118).

This instructive comparison seems to indicate driving forces will determine the prospects for democratic ecologies. The lesson from Freiburg and Madison, however is that the strategy need not be to alter these driving forces but to supplement them with alternative institutional channels. In Freiburg, public–private organizations and nonprofits were especially effective in bringing together environmental, economic, and equity concerns. These are familiar options in the USA but tend to lack an emphasis on values of justice and democratic practice. One of the limitations may well be the tendency to associate notions of justice with rights and group identities rather than capacities. Fainstein's (2005) argument that a just city is defined in terms of the capacities available to citizens to achieve their desired potentials rather than by group rights exemplifies the types of questions highlighted by the democratic ecology construct. It also raises the prospect that trade-offs among desired values and capacities – equity, environment, democratic practice – may be necessary to create a landscape conducive to nurturing citizens' capacities.

Conclusion

Using these constructs or lenses to make meaning out of the complex reality we are facing at this point in time is instructive. These three lenses identify some of the key political driving forces that structure the decisions possible – particularly the intergovernmental structure and the trend toward market segmentation – but also highlight steering resources that will shape what types of choices are made and with what consequences. It is the interplay of these driving forces and steering resources that provide insights on landscape change. To prevent a fortress landscape or to mitigate or equalize the consequences of splintering processes requires identifying and drawing on the steering resources available. Over time, it more likely requires building up those steering resources, especially if we seek not only just ecologies but also democratic ecologies.

References

Branscomb LM (2004) Protecting civil society from terrorism: The search for a sustainable strategy. *Technology and Society* 26: 271–285

Carter AB (2002) The architecture of government in the face of terrorism. *International Security* 26: 5–23

Clarke SE and Chenoweth E (2006) The politics of vulnerability: constructing local performance regimes for homeland security. *Review of Public Policy Research* 23: 95–114

Coaffee J (2004) Rings of steel, rings of concrete and rings of confidence: designing out terrorism in central London pre and post September 11th. *International Journal of Urban and Regional Research* 28: 201–211

Coutard O (2002) Premium networked spaces: a comment. *International Journal of Urban and Regional Research* 26: 166–174

Davis M (1999) *Ecology of fear*. Random House, New York

Eisinger P (2004) The American city in the age of terror: a preliminary assessment of the effects of 9/11. *Urban Affairs Review* 40: 115–130

Fainstein SS (2005) Cities and diversity: should we want it? Can we plan for it? *Urban Affairs Review* 41: 3–19

Fein A (1972) *Study of the Profession of Landscape Architecture*. ASLA Foundation, Alexandria, VA

Fitch JS (1985) The garrison state in America: a content analysis of trends in the expectation of violence. *Journal of Peace Research* 22: 31–45

Friedberg AI (2000) *In the Shadow of the Garrison State: America's Antitstatism and Its Cold War Strategy*. Princeton University Press, Princeton, NJ

Gerber BJ, Cohen DB, Cannon B, Patterson D, and Stewart K (2005) On the front line: American cities and the challenge of homeland security preparedness. *Urban Affairs Review* 41: 1–29

Gerber ER and Kollman K (2004) Introduction: authority migration: defining an emerging research agenda. *PS* 37: 397–401

Graham S and Marvin S (2001) *Splintering Urbanism: Networked infrastructures, Technological Mobilities, and the Urban Condition*. Routledge, New York

Gross B (1973) Friendly fascism: a model for America. In Franklin Tugwell (ed) *The Search for Alternatives: Public Policy and the Study of the Future*. Winthrop, Cambridge MA, pp 287–301

Hayden D (2004) *Building Suburbia: Green Fields and Urban Growth, 1820–2000*. Vintage, New York

Hopper L and Droge MJ (2005) *Security and Site Design: A Landscape Architectural Approach to Analysis, Assessment and Design Implementation*. Wiley, New York

Hudson A (2004) Cities in Revolt over Patriot Act. *The Washington Times*, January 5

Judd D (1999) Constructing the tourist bubble. In Dennis R Judd and Susan S Fainstein (eds) *The Tourist City*. Yale University Press, New Haven, CT, pp 35–53

Kettl D (2003) Contingent Coordination: practical and theoretical puzzles for homeland security. *American Review of Public Administration* 33: 253–277

Klinkenborg V (2004) Without walls. *New York Times Magazine* May 18: 15–16

Lasswell H (1941) The garrison state. *American Journal of Sociology* 46: 45–468

Lasswell H (1962) The garrison state hypothesis today. In Samuel Huntington (ed) *Changing Patterns of Military Politics*. Free Press, New York, pp 51–70

Light JS (2002) Urban security from warfare to welfare. *International Journal of Urban and Regional Research* 26: 607–613

Linenthal ET (2005) The predicament of aftermath: Oklahoma city and September 11. In Lawrence J Vale and Thomas J Campanella (eds) *The Resilient City: How Modern Cities Recover From Disaster*. Oxford University Press, New York, pp 55–74

MacLeod G (2003) *Privatizing The City? The Tentative Push Towards Edge Urban Developments And Gated Communities In The United Kingdom*. Report for the Office of the Deputy Prime Minister, University of Durham, ICRRDS

MacLeod G and Ward K (2002) Spaces of Utopia and Dystopia: landscaping the contemporary city. *Geografiska Annaler: Series B, Human Geography* 84: 153–170

McDonough W (2004) Twenty first century design, *The Chronicle of Higher Education* July 23, 50: B6

Mitchell JK (2003) Urban vulnerability to terrorism as hazard. In Cutter S, Richardson D, and Wilbanks TJ (eds) *The Geographical Dimensions of Terrorism*. Routledge, New York, pp 17–25

National League of Cities (2002) Cities See Biological, Cyber-Terrorism as Top Threats, One Year After 9–11. Press Release, NLC, September 4

Olwig K (2002) *Landscape, Nature, and the Body Politics: From Britain's Renaissance to America's New World*. University of Wisconsin Press, Madison, WI

Pierre J (2000) *Debating Governance: Authority, Steering, and Democracy*. Oxford University Press, Oxford

Pelling M (2003) *The Vulnerability of Cities: Natural Disasters and Social Resilience*. Earthscan, London

Plant JR (2004) Terrorism and the railroads: redefining security in the wake of 9/11. *Review of Policy Research* 21: 293–305

Prieto R (2003) Business community views. *Technology in Society* 25: 517–522

Prytherch DL (2003) Urban planning and a Europe transformed: the landscape politics of scale in Valencia. *Cities* 20: 421–428

Sellers J (2000) Translocal orders and urban environmentalism: lessons from a German and a United States city. In: Terry N Clark and Keith Hoggart (eds) *Citizen Responsive Government*. JAI, Westport, CT, pp 117–147

Savitch HV (2003) Does 9–11 portend a new paradigm for cities? *Urban Affairs Review* 39: 103–127

Savitch HV and Kantor P (2002) *Cities in the International Marketplace*. Princeton University Press, Princeton, NJ

Sherry M (2003) A hidden-hand garrison state? *Diplomatic History* 27: 163–166

Smith N (1996) *The New Urban Frontier: Gentrification and the Revanchist City*. Routledge, London

Soja E (2000) *Postmetropolis*. Blackwell, London

Swyngedouw E and Heynen NC (2003) Urban political ecology, justice and the politics of scale. *Antipode* 35: 898–918

Task Force on State and Local Homeland Security Funding (2004) *DHS Homeland Security Advisory Council*. US Government Printing Office, Washington DC

Vale LJ and Campanella TJ (2005) *The Resilient City: How Modern Cities Recover From Disaster*. Oxford University Press, New York

Walker P and Fortmann L (2003) Whose landscape? A political ecology of the "exurban" Sierra. *Cultural Geographies* 10: 469–491

Watts M (2000) Political ecology. In Barnes T and Sheppard E (eds) *A Companion to Economic Geography*. Blackwell, Oxford

Chapter 5
Institutional Dynamics, Spatial Organization, and Landscape Change

Tom P. Evans, Abigail M. York, and Elinor Ostrom

Introduction

Landscape change is a highly complex process both in terms of the drivers affecting changes to natural and built environments and the outcomes or impacts of those changes. Reflecting this complexity, researchers have explored the process of landscape change from a variety of disciplinary perspectives. The goal of this chapter is to demonstrate the role of social institutions in the process of landscape change within the complexity of social-ecological systems. Here we define institutions as the formal and informal rules that govern human behavior in a particular situation (Dietz et al. 2003; Tucker and Ostrom 2005). Some fields consider institutions mostly in terms of regulations and constraints, such as with land-use zoning. In this context institutions are viewed as tools to limit the impact of undesirable landscape changes. An example is zoning ordinances designed to avoid development in environmentally sensitive areas. However, institutions are also tools that can be used to facilitate or encourage desirable landscape changes. State and federal tax incentives for forest management are examples of institutions designed to produce a particular landscape change outcome. We present both of these types of objectives in exploring the role institutions play in landscape change in rural and urban areas.

The term "landscape change" has various meanings within the academic literature. In terms of dialog within the global change community, landscape change often refers to landcover transition or land degradation (also often referred to as "landcover change" or "land use/landcover change"). Examples include deforestation in the Brazilian Amazon or selective harvesting of valuable timber from private forests in the Eastern USA. Another interpretation of the term "landscape" is more associated with individual perceptions of built and non-built environments. As discussed in this paper, changes from mesic to xeric landscaping practices (xeric landscaping, or xeriscaping, refers to the practice of using vegetation adapted to dry environments) can result in dramatically different visual landscape appearance as well as landscape function (hydrology). But a transition to xeric landscaping would not be considered an example of landcover change because it entails a relatively small-scale change. In this chapter we provide several examples of institutional impacts on landcover change processes. We also include selected examples of landscape change that would not be considered changes in

J.L. Wescoat, Jr. and D.M. Johnston (eds.), *Political Economies of Landscape Change.*   111
© Springer 2008

landcover. While the clarification of these definitions may seem pedantic, this exercise is important because the study of landscape change is clearly the domain of numerous disciplines and fields of research.

There is a vast array of institutional types that affect landscape change processes. Institutions vary in terms of scale, actors, overlap, coordination, and resilience among many other factors. Adding to the complexity of the relationship between institutions and landscape change is the fact that many environments – especially urban environments – are affected by multiple institutions, presenting a case of institutional interplay that is difficult to dissect much less predict. All too often, policymakers, and many academics, have been confused by the complexity of the institutional ecology and have not recognized that complex landscapes and public economies need complex institutions that are well tailored to solving diverse problems at multiple scales. Researchers are accustomed to defining a study area and then identifying institutions operating in this area. However, because institutions may exist at many different organizational levels, it can be a challenge to identify the complete domain of institutional effects. But it can help to assess the scales at which institutions may exist in order to assess how and why institutions have evolved in particular ways and the consequences of new or modified institutions.

The development of local and city rules governing water use in the southwestern USA provides an example of the cross-scale interactions that exist between institutions and the processes driving the creation of those institutions. Water use in urban and rural areas of the southwest has been highly contentious (and sometimes litigious) for many years. Battles have been waged between cities, county, and state governments, as well as between the residential homeowners and the agricultural industry. A primary driver in this context is the growth of metropolitan areas such as Phoenix and Las Vegas. Much of the population growth in these metropolitan areas has come from migrants from other regions of the USA as well as first- and second-generation Hispanic immigrants. This population growth has impacts on both regional and local levels. The general problem of water scarcity is in part considered a regional problem in that metropolitan areas in the southwest compete for water with rural land uses as well as other distant metropolitan areas. Figure 1 presents a conceptual diagram of some of the relationships between drivers, institutions, and landscape change in this system. Institutions to reduce water use have developed through city ordinances as well as neighborhood covenants at a very local level. Cities like Aurora, CO, place restrictions on what outdoor water uses are acceptable by residential type and require permits for certain landscaping choices such as increasing the amount of turf/lawns on properties. In 2006 the city adopted ordinances that require permits for residential irrigation systems, place restrictions on water use depending on current water availability, and changed landscaping requirements to xeriscaping-focused designs with limits on the amount of turf grass allowed in residential areas (City of Aurora 2006). At an even finer level some individual neighborhoods have developed highly detailed covenants prohibiting non-xeric landscaping such as turf lawns altogether (among other restrictions). Other neighborhoods have no such restrictions and expectedly the landscapes between communities with and without these types of covenants differ dramatically. Thus there are city-level water restrictions affecting

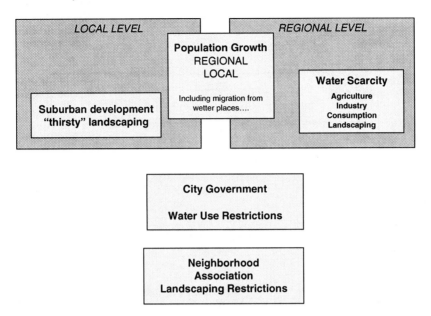

Figure 1 Urban growth, water use restrictions and cross-level interactions (note: this figure is not intended to portray a comprehensive set of relationships in this complex situation)

entire metropolitan areas and a heterogeneous pattern of neighborhood institutions affecting landscapes within metropolitan areas. The complexity in the evolution of institutions is apparent when one considers how cultural preferences affect the perception and reaction to local institutions. One study of landowners in Phoenix found that Arizona natives were more likely to prefer non-xeric/"wet" landscaping compared to residents who had migrated to Arizona from other regions of the USA (Martin et al. 2003). The same study hypothesized that xeric landscaping policies were often enacted at the neighborhood level but the overall popularity of this design was predominantly a product of a top-down process directed by public and private interest groups. Thus heterogeneity at a very local level can lead to particular challenges in the development and design of institutions to address negative impacts of landscape change, as discussed in the next section. These simple examples are basic demonstrations of the diversity and complexity of institutional arrangements that can affect landscape change. The following section presents a general framework to consider the spatial and temporal dimensions of institutional diversity discussed in this chapter and more generally elsewhere (Ostrom 2005).

Figure 2 portrays a series of domains that can be used to describe different types of institutions. While it is a simplification to try to position a particular institution at precisely one place on any of these axes, the characteristics presented here do provide some foundation for exploring the diversity of institutions affecting landscape change. These characteristics serve as themes that will be drawn upon in examples presented later in this chapter.

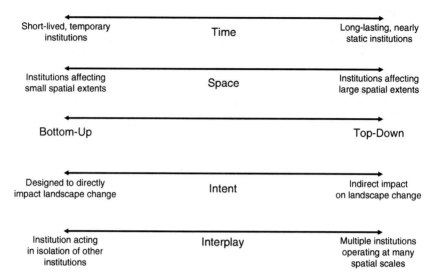

Figure 2 Institutions are diverse and vary across a many domains

Table 1 Spatial scale of selected institutions

Neighborhood or local level	Landowners agreeing to maintain vegetation in city constructed, traffic calming barrier
	Neighborhood associations restricting landscaping and architectural choice
Subregional level (e.g., city)	City ordinances on landscaping (e.g., xeric), municipal zoning, growth policy plans
	City park programs, urban forestry
Regional level	County-level zoning, new road/highway construction, road widening
National level	US Forest Service forest thinning policy, creation and location of national highway system
	Crop subsidies
Global level	Kyoto protocol, carbon credits, climate change policies, tariffs

One characteristic that can be used to describe an institution is the spatial extent or jurisdiction affected by that institution. In terms of spatial extent, institutions can develop from community action at a very local level as well as be imposed from top-down actions at national or global levels (Table 1). Likewise, institutions may affect very small jurisdictions (neighborhoods) or very large jurisdictions (nations). Time is another scale that can be used to describe institutions. There are some long-lasting institutions that have existed for decades or even centuries. There are also institutions that rapidly evolve or that are removed, perhaps because they are not effective or because a groundswell of public sentiment results in their retraction.

The interaction, or "interplay", between institutional levels poses particular challenges to predicting the impact of new institutional formation. For example, many cities have growth policy plans and sometimes the counties in which these cities reside themselves have growth policy plans. There is a certain degree of friction or discord when government entities at different levels try to guide the management of the same resource. The levels listed in Table 1 such as "city" and "county" may seem somewhat discrete, but there is even additional complexity when hybrid entities are developed as with the case of a combined city/county government organization in Indiana discussed later in this chapter (which exists simultaneously with preexisting city and county government structures).

The axis labeled *intent* in Figure 2 is an attempt to acknowledge that while some institutions have a clearly identifiable and direct impact on landscape change, other institutions have an indirect effect but also important to consider in studying the role of institutions in complex systems. An example of an institution designed to directly affect landscape change is a zoning restriction. With these types of institutions it is a simpler process to see the connection between rules and outcomes, although given the complexity of social-ecological systems and the dynamic interactions within these systems often makes it difficult to predict exactly how a particular institution will affect subsequent landscape change processes. Other institutions have just as important effects but the connection between the institution and landscape change is less direct. For example, efforts to control emissions affect local and regional climate, which in turn affects vegetation albeit over long time periods. This theme is further developed in discussing the role of policing, neighborhood characteristics, and intra-urban migration later in this chapter.

One key to the puzzle of understanding how institutions affect landscape change is the temporal dynamics of the interaction between rules and landscape change outcomes. Long-term, slow, and small landscape changes are more difficult to detect than rapid and extensive landscape changes but are not less vital to how ecosystems adapt and change. Thus, one challenge is to understand factors that affect both rapid landscape change processes (e.g., clear-cutting) as well as those changes gradually occurring over several years or decades (clearing firewood from the edges of a forest). One component of this challenge is understanding the role of institutions in these different types of landscape changes.

Another key characteristic of institutions is whether rules are developed by and for stakeholders rather than by public officials that are intended to change the behavior of stakeholders. The ability of stakeholders to create and mold existing institutions can be a factor in the perceived legitimacy of the institutions. For certain location-specific problems, stakeholders may be able to provide information about the landscape that is unknown outside the community. Institutions may also be imposed by private, local, state, and federal governments, as well as created by private entities. One type of private government, property owners' associations, often impose institutional changes on property owners. But like traditional government, property owners have a voice in these changes through hearings and elections. Typically there are several overlapping jurisdictions with overlapping institutions that impact the landscape. These overlapping institutions are created by all levels of government, as well as private citizen groups. This complexity and diversity of institutions reflects the complex social-ecological issues impacting areas of landscape to different degrees. In our chapter, we explore this diversity through examples from land-use planning, collaborative management, policing, and education in order to illustrate the interrelationships between institutional dynamics, spatial organization, and landscape change.

A type of institution that we explore in Indiana and North Carolina is the plan commission and communities' growth management strategies. Many municipalities have planning commissions designed to guide development including requests for new projects requiring a modification or variance to the existing land-use zoning for a parcel or group of parcels. These commissions are typically composed of nominated individuals who evaluate development proposals and make recommendations to an elected city/town council that approves development projects. These municipalities have planning policies outlining strategies for long-term development. Legally, zoning must be accompanied by these comprehensive plans to prevent planning decisions from being arbitrary (Ellickson and Been 2000). However, these comprehensive plans, as well as supporting documents like growth policies, are not formal institutions but rather intended to provide guidelines for implementation of municipal rules and codes.

Institutions impact land-use changes through restrictions, such as zoning or the Endangered Species Act, as well as via inducements, like urban forestry programs or tax increment financing. Frequently, inducements are voluntary, while restrictions are imposed on landowners, although there are many examples of voluntary restrictions such as conservation easements. Furthermore, some institutions include both restrictions and inducements, like Indiana's property tax abatement program, the Classified Forest Program, which restricts development and livestock stocking within the designated area while providing some tax relief.

Institutions do not impact the landscape in a vacuum; rather, institutions (in a democratic polity like the USA) are typically a part of a polycentric system with overlapping jurisdictions (McGinnis 1999; Oakerson 1999). These overlapping institutions may have differing impacts on the landscape, which designers and analysts need to consider. For instance, a landscape may have zoning, conservation easements, property tax relief programs, forestry programs, and historic preservation. A property tax relief program may encourage development, while zoning, conservation easements, and historic preservation attempt to either restrict or direct construction. Without careful consideration of other institutions impacting the land, an institution may have unintended consequences. Recently, many organizations have started to use institutional interplay self-consciously to promote ecosystem management by coordinating local, state, and federal regulations with private initiatives (Yaffee 1996).

Institutions that Affect Landscape Change Processes

The following sections describe a series of cases and situations where institutions have had an impact on the trajectory, rate, or types of landscape changes. Among the most pressing challenges facing public officials today is how to manage urban growth, including the negative impacts of some kinds of urban growth, and to protect greenspace (Bengston et al. 2004; for interpretations of urban growth see also chapters 1 and 4 in this volume by Mitchell and Clarke). Here we focus on a somewhat broader set of landscape changes, some associated with rural areas, some with urban areas. The policy tools used in urban versus rural contexts differ somewhat, but exploring the diversity of institutional types present in both of these domains can provide some insight into the range of options available for the preservation of scarce resources. The purpose here is not to present a comprehensive list of institutional types but rather to demonstrate the diversity of how institutions affect landscape change and how institutions are developed. Examples included in this chapter draw particularly from research we have conducted in south-central Indiana, with additional cases drawn from areas with alternative institutional contexts.

Community Forestry in South-Central Indiana as a Method of Land Management

While the vast majority of forested land in Indiana is owned by private individuals or households, several community-based groups in south-central Indiana own and manage some forested areas as well. Within these communities, there is great variation in the size of the communities, the legal ownership, and the goals of forest management. The communities range from three households to a neighborhood of several hundred households. Each of these communities struggles to govern their property using a variety of institutions including a traditional property owners' association council, an elected governing board based on service in a spiritual forest, and meetings to encourage the development of consensus among households about preferred land-use practices that all landowners will undertake individually.

Many of these communities have existed since the 1960s. Their histories illustrate the struggles to maintain a community and manage a forest, while their longevity provides an example of the possibilities with alternative management strategies. Communal management through legal ownership is one means to coordinate management activities. In the next section we focus on public and private initiatives to coordinate land use across public and private lands.

Land Conservancies and Institutional Interplay

Public land acquisition by state and federal governments is one mechanism that has been used to manage urban growth and protect greenspace (Bengston et al. 2004; Ruliffson et al. 2002). Land trusts are a more bottom-up means to coordinate management of private land holdings through institutional arrangements. The land held by land trusts is either owned outright or the land trusts hold conservation easements. The impact of land trusts on the landscape is not entirely understood, as they have only been around for about a half century, but their presence in communities often leads to other types of conservation activities.

In Brown County, Indiana, The Nature Conservancy has established a priority management area and is helping the Indiana Department of Natural Resources obtain Forest Legacy conservation easements with private land managers. The ability of land trusts to serve as a leader in the community by aiding in collaboration efforts between other NGO, private land managers, and public land managers is fairly widespread (Yaffee 1996). In Indiana this role is particularly important as The Nature Conservancy is in a unique position to serve as a conduit between the government and private individuals because of its well-known and trusted reputation for environmental protection in the public eye. In this area there is a fairly prevalent mistrust of government officials, which may partially be due to public land take-overs in the early 1900s. Thus, The Nature Conservancy has been especially important in gaining the trust between private, NGO, and government actors.

Private landowners interested in preserving their forestland often contact national land trusts, such as the Nature Conservancy, or local land trusts, like the Sycamore Land Trust (a land trust organization active in southern Indiana), in order to place easements on their property or to sell or donate their property to the land trust. Officials from the land trusts often are knowledgeable about public cost-share, tax, and easement programs that private landowners could benefit from. Thus, contact with land trusts can lead to participation in public programs, such as Indiana's Classified Forest Program.

Increasingly, public officials and land trust officials are working together to focus on important ecosystems within the state. Environmental NGOs and public officials sometimes find themselves in opposition over land management techniques on public and private lands, but recent efforts in cooperation in Indiana and throughout the USA indicate that public and private officials can be powerful allies (Yaffee 1996). Through cooperation public and private organizations with limited resources can pool efforts to produce results that would not be possible if these groups were not working in coordination.

Zoning and Land Use in Indiana

Zoning and planning mechanisms have been used to both accelerate and decelerate the pace of urban growth, especially when used in combination with economic development incentives, like tax increment financing, or disincentives, such as development impact fees. The impact of zoning on land-use decision-making is not widely understood, although some theoretical work indicates that zoning may inhibit development of land for urban uses (Fischel 1985). Others argue that zoning does not impede growth, but rather may cause sprawl through large lot requirements that are common in traditional ordinances (Carruthers 2001; Dowall 1988). Local governments often face tough choices in determining the tradeoffs between ideal land-use policy, and socioeconomic and political contingencies.

Minimum lot size restrictions, as found within agricultural reserve zones, can lead to residential development on larger parcels than would be found without this requirement (Esparza and Carruthers 2000). Therefore, the impact of zoning may not be unidirectional with respect to land-use change; some rules may push urbanization outward, while other rules will restrict urbanization. Furthermore, inconsistent zoning across jurisdictions can cause leap-frog development where investors develop land in pro-growth counties and cities while "leaping" over more restrictive areas (Carruthers 2003).

Many jurisdictions attempt to reduce environmental impacts on the ecosystem, particularly watersheds, through zoning. In Monroe County, Indiana, there are restrictions against tree cutting within a 1,000 ft buffer around a major reservoir in the area. These ordinances are enforced with fines and threats of legal action, but sometimes these fines are ineffective (Tucker and Ostrom 2005). In particular Tucker and Ostrom, found one landowner that seemed relatively immune to the fines and legal proceedings, and continued to cut trees over a 4-year time period. Thus, even when zoning ordinances are focused on environmental protection, their effectiveness is limited by enforcement, as well as the relative cost of fines versus the benefits for violation.

Zoning in some states, like Indiana, is bottom-up with limited state government involvement. In other states, like Vermont and Oregon, state commissions and regulations guide local or regional zoning ordinances. Zoning impacts the landscape within its jurisdiction, as well as the neighboring jurisdictions through spillover effects. Zoning is one of the most universal institutions impacting land management and landscape change. Zoning is also increasingly used in combination with other institutions to promote particular types of development, reduce environmental impacts, and maintain community aesthetics and character. Frequently within jurisdictions a small group of landowners desire more restrictive controls on land management. Under these conditions, zoning, by itself, can be ineffective. In the following section, we explore a recent attempt to promote collaborative land management in Indiana.

Designing Institutions for Collaborative Private Land Management

A variety of fee programs have been used by communities and governments to provide some financial benefit when new development occurs. These fees can then be used to provide public services and facilities that are needed to support the infrastructure needs of the new development (Nelson and Duncan 1995). There are also programs at state and federal levels that provide positive incentives to encourage the preservation of wetlands and forest areas by existing landholders. In order to qualify for some programs a landowner must have a certain minimum threshold of wetland or forest area. Most of these programs were designed with individual landowners in mind. But in areas where there is a high degree of land ownership fragmentation these existing programs may not provide an effective tool because many landowners do not individually have the minimum amount of wetland or forest on their property. Several Indiana communities recently contacted the Indiana Department of Natural Resources (IDNR) requesting assistance in collaborative land management with the goal of preserving forested area on their property. The IDNR currently is evaluating the array of mechanisms available to private landowners and communities that wish to restrict uses on private property in order to conserve forestland. There are several mechanisms that have been identified that may enable this collaboration including: conservancy districts, property owners' associations, conservation easements with land trusts and government agencies, and contracts.

Conservancy districts in Indiana primarily focus on water resources, although the enabling statute is quite broad (Indiana Conservancy District Act). These districts are special-use governments that are created through a court petition by the freeholders or by a municipality. The districts are able to collect fees from freeholders and impose restrictions on use within the district. In this way conservancy districts may enable landowners to maintain a forested area through a new government entity.

Property owners' associations (POAs), including homeowner and condominium owner associations, are typically created by a developer prior to property sale to individual owners. Thus frequently POAs are imposed by a private developer on new homeowners, although information is disclosed regarding mandatory compliance with POA rules. Many POAs focus on issues of architecture, signage, or noise issues. However, POAs also have a potential for guiding land management for environmental conservation.

Conservation easements are negotiated between private landowners and land trusts or government agencies. Conservation easements are important means to restrict development of land, although many landowners do not want to preserve their land in perpetuity. Furthermore, local land trusts are often unable to afford to buy easements from willing sellers. Land trusts also turn down easement requests because they are unable to effectively monitor easements due to limited resources. Thus, the potential use of conservation easements across a landscape is limited, but the tool is important at small scales or for important landscape features.

In order to enable collaborative management, a combination of these public and private institutions may be the best means to achieve the goal of forestland preservation. Each of these institutions has strengths and weaknesses, which can be improved through use of overlapping restrictions and inducements. As can be seen, there is a portfolio of institutions that could be used in combination to meet the needs of private landowners hoping to conserve forestland in Indiana. The ability of landowners to coordinate management informally is limited over time, as property changes hands or management goals change, but some of these formal legal mechanisms may ensure forestland conservation for long time periods or even in perpetuity. The experiences in Indiana are both similar to and different from the attempts of communities to regulate growth in North Carolina. South-central Indiana has had relatively slow population growth in comparison to the Triangle area of North Carolina, which has experienced both rapid population and urban growth in the last 15 years. As will be discussed below, urban growth presents particular institutional challenges in regard to landscape change that contrast the context in south-central Indiana.

Growth Policies and Land-Use Change in North Carolina

The Triangle area of North Carolina (defined by the three cities Chapel Hill, Durham, and Raleigh) presents a particularly complicated development history and one affected by numerous economic, social, and institutional factors. Each of the cities composing the Triangle area extent has experienced dramatically different growth trajectories. Raleigh is the state capitol, and state government offices and associated state organizations such as NGOs have characterized this part of the Triangle for many years. North Carolina State University also is a major component to the Raleigh landscape. Durham, home of Duke University, has a history of manufacturing and tobacco-based industry, which has declined from their prime in the early to mid-1900s. Chapel Hill is a prototypical college town, relatively small and dominated by the University of North Carolina. In 1959 leaders from business, academia and industry created the Research Triangle Park (RTP) as a public/private entity to foster economic growth and development in the area. The park initially grew slowly in the 1960s until IBM and the National Institute of Environmental and Health Sciences moved major operations to the area. The Park encompasses 7,000 acres of what was previously largely undeveloped pine forest. Businesses in RTP now employ over 38,500 people and their combined salaries exceed $1.2 billion.

In the 1990s the synergy between RTP and the surrounding cities resulted in dramatic employment and thereby population growth (Figure 3). However, the development of urban areas occurred very differently in the three counties and three cities most affected by this growth. The Chapel Hill town council has been reticent to approve zoning modification requests in an attempt to retain the unique quality of life in this university town. Here the mechanism to slow growth is to control the

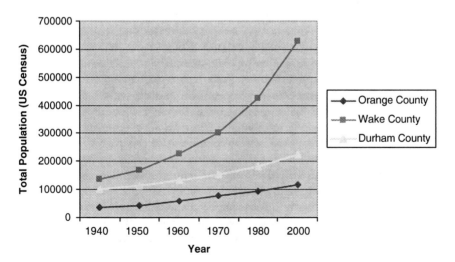

Figure 3 Population growth in Orange, Wake, and Durham counties, 1940–2000 (US Census Bureau 2000)

process of rezoning. In other communities, rate of growth controls have been used to more directly address the problems associated with rapid urban growth (Kelly 1993; Nelson 1992). Areas outside the municipal boundary of Chapel Hill and locations in Durham and Wake counties did not have the same degree of "slow growth" or "no growth" policies. These policies in Chapel Hill resulted in spillover effects in surrounding areas that absorbed the bulk of the residential and retail development associated with the economic growth in the area. At the same time, housing prices in Chapel Hill now are among the highest in the state due to the high demand but low supply of housing in the city limits.

Studying Institutional Interplay in Local Public Economies

As discussed earlier in this chapter, institutions not specifically designed to affect landscape change can indeed impact the manner in which cities grow, neighborhoods change, and landscapes evolve. The following section discusses research on the provision of community services, policing and different types of municipal government organization. The discussion here frames a debate about the level at which the provision of government services is most effective as well as residents' perception of the provision of those services. The service discussed here, policing, is not traditionally considered among those affecting landscape change. However, we use this example to demonstrate not just the diversity of institutional solutions to urban problems, but the breadth of government institutions that ultimately impact landscape change. Among the criteria used by residents considering where to buy a home are certain quality of life indicators. Crime and policing play an important role in how desirable a particular community is perceived. A tremendous number of major metropolitan areas in the USA have experienced dramatic changes in urban neighborhoods. Although there are clearly exceptions, there is a trend in many cities of general decline and out-migration from city center areas to subdivisions and new developments in suburban areas outside the city boundary. While the growth of suburban areas is related to many factors, safety and crime levels are cited among the reasons individuals prefer suburban areas to urban areas. Here we discuss in some detail the case of policing and government organization in Chicago and Indianapolis as a means to explore different types of government organization and the impact on the provision of services in those areas. Much of the literature on public policy is dedicated to describing policy options rather than evaluating the effectiveness of those policies (Hollis and Fulton 2002). Here we summarize empirical research testing the provision of public services, but we agree that more empirical analysis of policy instruments directly related to landscape management is needed to move beyond qualitative assessments of program effectiveness.

The August 2, 2004, headlines in the *Indianapolis Star* announced that "Vast Plan Would Revamp City, County Government." Indianapolis Mayor Bart Peterson proposed "sweeping changes to Indianapolis government... in a plan that would expand his powers, create a new police force, merge fire departments, and abolish most township offices" (*Indianapolis Star*, August 8, 2004, 1). The next day, headlines in the same paper screamed that a "Big Battle is Brewing Over Uni-Gov Overhaul." In all of the Mayor's announcements, he stressed that consolidation would streamline services, improve efficiency, and save the citizens of the county over $35 million.

The mayor's proposals echoed those proposed for metropolitan consolidation that were articulated frequently during the last century. The sheer complexity of the delivery arrangements existing in American metropolitan areas has long perplexed many observers. Many articles, books, monographs, and reports have recommended the elimination of smaller jurisdictions and the creation of a few, large, general-purpose governments to produce all local services in any given metropolitan area. Amos Hawley and Basil G. Zimmer summarized the dominant academic view of the 1970s:

> A diagnosis of the metropolitan malady is comparatively easy and its logic is too compelling to admit disagreement. Given the diagnosis the treatment seems just as apparent: consolidate the many political units under a single, over-arching municipal government. With one stroke the many conflicting jurisdictions could be eliminated and a fragmented tax base could be combined into an adequate source of revenue for an entire community. Nothing, it would seem, could be more obvious or more rational (Hawley and Zimmer 1970: 3).

This view has been reiterated continuously. In the May 1997 issue of *The New Leader*, for example, Michael Lind echoes the same theme in an article on "A Horde of Lilliputian Governments." Lind vigorously complains about the multiplication of little electorates like coral polyps, which pile together in reefs that lack any ordering principle other than propinquity (1997, 7). Observers have frequently focused on the incomprehensibility and irrationality of metropolitan systems and have not asked why these systems have evolved the way they have. Scientific progress is difficult when the phenomena of interest are perceived to be incomprehensible.

Unfortunately, the view that consolidation of units in metropolitan areas increases efficiency and equity is based on a simple view that institutional interplay does not exist and that when many units exist in a metropolitan areas, they cannot achieve coordinated outcomes at multiple scales. This issue is important for understanding urban landscapes as one of the forces leading to ever greater suburbanization is the desire of many families to move to safe communities where their children can go to good schools. Instead of improving urban services, evidence derived from a long-term study of policing in Indianapolis and Chicago – and multiple other sites – provided contrary evidence.

During the late 1960s and early 1970s, in response to concerns about police effectiveness in the face of increasing crime rates, proposals to slash the number of police departments serving urban and rural areas were placed on the national agenda. Underlying these proposals was the assumption that bigger would be better, that is more professional, more responsive, and most important, more effective. Some proposals recommended moving from the over 40,000 police departments that then existed to under 500 police departments across the country. *No systematic empirical evidence supported these reform proposals.* Colleagues associated with the Workshop in Political Theory and Policy Analysis began what became a 15-year intensive research program on urban policing with a relatively simple most-similar systems study in the Indianapolis metropolitan area and eventually conducted a comparative study in 80 metropolitan areas throughout the USA (for an overview, see McGinnis 1999).

Alternative predictions about police performance in metropolitan areas. From an analysis of the nature of producing and consuming police services, we derived an alternative set of predictions (to those of the consolidationists) from our theoretical work on polycentric, local public economies (McGinnis 1999). First, we distinguished between *direct* police services, such as patrol and immediate response service, and *indirect* police services, such as crime laboratories and jails (that are basically provided to direct service producers rather than directly to citizens). Due to the labor intensive nature of direct police services, the essential role of citizen as coproducer of safety, and the problem of measuring output, we assumed that small- to medium-sized, direct-service producers would be more effective and efficient than large, direct-service producers under similar service conditions. Thus, for *direct* police services, we predicted that small governmental units that arrange for the supply of direct services by small- to medium-scale producers would perform better than larger jurisdictions.

Given that indirect police services tend to be capital intensive and are easier to measure than direct services, large production agencies should be more effective and efficient than smaller agencies in producing indirect services. If local police departments face pressures to become more efficient, they should search out larger police departments or other producers to supply most indirect services. To the extent that institutional arrangements facilitate contracting or other intergovernmental arrangements, we predicted we would find that: (1) substantially fewer indirect-service producers exist in metropolitan areas than direct-service producers, (2) most indirect producers are large, and (3) small direct-service producers obtain most indirect services from large producers.

A third set of theoretical predictions was that the performance of direct-service producers of police services would be enhanced in metropolitan areas containing a large number of producers at multiple scales of organization. In these areas, the larger producers can efficiently and effectively produce crime laboratory services, training, and communications while smaller agencies produce immediate response services. It is the potential for complementarity that leads to this prediction. Substantial empirical support exists for all three predictions that can only be briefly reviewed here.

Small- and medium-sized police agencies are more effective in producing direct services. In conducting studies of this question in the Indianapolis, Chicago, St. Louis, Rochester, and Tampa–St. Petersburg metropolitan areas, the severe problem of measuring police performance was met by collecting performance data from interviews with a random sample of households served by small and large departments. Information was obtained about victimization, willingness to call the police, speed of police response, amount of police follow-up, satisfaction levels with police contacts, and general evaluations of the quality of policing in a neighborhood.

By studying matched neighborhoods with similar service conditions, we controlled for many of the other factors that can be expected to affect performance.

The general findings from this series of studies is that small- and medium-sized police departments perform more effectively than large-sized police departments serving similar neighborhoods and frequently at lower costs (Ostrom and Parks 1973; Ostrom et al. 1973; Ostrom and Whitaker 1974). Victimization rates tend to be lower, police response tends to be faster, citizens tend to be more willing to call on police, citizens tend to more positively evaluate specific contacts with the police, and citizens tend to rate police higher across a series of other evaluative questions. Further, citizens living in small communities tend to be more informed about how to change local policies, tend to know more policemen serving their neighborhoods, and call the police more frequently to obtain general information than citizens living in large cities. Citizens served by small departments tend to receive *better* services at *lower* costs than their neighbors living in the center city. Instead of being a problem for the metropolitan area, small departments frequently contribute to the improvement of police services in the area. And, more recent research demonstrates that the relationships found in Indianapolis in the 1970s were still valid almost 30 years later (Parks 1995).

Our study conducted in two independent black communities in the Chicago metropolitan area (Phoenix and East Chicago Heights) and matched black neighborhoods inside the City of Chicago generated particularly noteworthy findings. While in many of our other studies, we found that victimization rates tended to be lower in the independent departments, we found a similar and relatively high level of victimization in Chicago and in the independent communities. We also examined the cost of policing in these neighborhoods and found that the Chicago police department was allocating 14 times more resources to policing the Chicago neighborhoods than were the poor black communities. It is quite noteworthy that with 14 times more resources, that Chicago Police Department could not outperform the independent communities in regard to providing safer communities.

Small police agencies arrange for indirect services from large police agencies. In our major study of police organization in 80 Standard Metropolitan Statistical Areas (SMSAs) (see E. Ostrom et al. 1978), a total of 1,159 direct-service producers were found to serve residents in these 80 metropolitan areas. Most of these agencies produced general area patrol, traffic patrol, accident investigation, and burglary investigation services. About 70% of these agencies produced homicide investigations while citizens served by the other 30% of the direct-service producers received homicide investigation services from a large producer in the area usually an overlapping sheriff office or a metropolitan-wide homicide unit.

In regard to indirect services, we found 70% of the direct-service producers also produced their own radio communications, but only a small proportion of any of the direct-service producers produced the other indirect services. In all 80 SMSAs, indirect services were made available to *all* direct-service producers. In most SMSAs, direct-service producers had a choice between at least two large-scale, indirect producers. Where agencies can work out interjurisdictional contracts, set up regional facilities, and exchange services with one another, small agencies are able to obtain highly professional, indirect services at low costs without the need to become fully integrated departments.

Police performance is enhanced in metropolitan areas with larger numbers of police agencies. In order to examine the effect of interorganizational arrangements on police performance, we relied on measures of performance such as: the allocation of police personnel to on-the-street assignments and the relative efficiency of agencies in producing response capacity and solving crimes. For each of the 80 SMSAs, we calculated the number of producers of each type of service (multiplicity) and the proportion of the population being served by the largest producer of each type of service (dominance). Metropolitan areas with low scores in regard to multiplicity and high scores in regard to dominance come closest to approximating the "consolidated" model. Metropolitan areas with high scores in regard to multiplicity and low scores in regard to dominance come closest to approximating the "fragmented" metropolitan area criticized by these same proponents.

Parks (1985) found a distinct difference in the availability of sworn officers to conduct patrol in the metropolitan areas depending upon the structure of interorganizational arrangements. While there are more officers per capita in the most consolidated areas, a lower percentage of these officers are actually assigned to patrol divisions in these SMSAs. The ratio of full-time sworn officers employed in the area to actual officers on the street at 10:00 p.m. is highest in the most consolidated areas. One third more officers are required in the most consolidated SMSAs to place the same number of officers on patrol as compared to the least consolidated SMSAs. Citizens living in the most fragmented metropolitan areas receive more police presence on the streets for their tax expenditures than do citizens living in the most consolidated areas (Parks 1985).

Parks and Ostrom (1981) estimated production possibility frontiers in metropolitan areas that varied in regard to multiplicity. These production possibility frontiers show the maximum combinations of clearances by arrest and cars on patrol (both standardized by the number of sworn officers to control for agency size) that were obtained by departments in metropolitan areas with differing amounts of multiplicity. The frontiers show a significant upward shift in output possibilities as the number of patrol producers in a metropolitan area increases. The most efficient producers supply more output for given inputs in high multiplicity SMSAs than do the most efficient producers in lower multiplicity areas. Thus, the presence of many other producers for comparison enhances the efficiency of direct-service producers.

There Is No One Best System for All Local Public Economies

In addition to the research on police, scholars have conducted rigorous empirical research that has challenged the presumptions that larger public school districts achieve higher performance (Hanuschek 1986; Kiesling 1967; Niskanen and Levy 1974; Teske et al. 1993) and fragmentation of governments leads to higher costs (Dilorenzo 1983; Schneider 1986; Wagner and Weber 1975), and have provided further insights to the way local governments are constituted (Oakerson and Parks 1989; Stephens and Wikstrom 2000). As a result of extensive empirical and theoretical research, the presumed self-evident truth that constructing one government for each metropolitan area is the best way to achieve efficiency and equity has slowly been replaced with a recognition that judging a structure directly on the single criterion of uniformity contributes little to the advancement of research or reform (Oakerson 1999, 117). Instead of a single best design that would have to cope with the wide variety of problems faced in different localities, a polycentric theory generates core principles that can be used in the design of effective local institutions when used by informed and interested citizens and public officials (ibid., 122–124).

The experience in policing and education has recently been echoed in the land-use planning arena. The fragmentation of planning authority is seen as one of the main contributors to urban sprawl (Carruthers 2003). There are no comprehensive studies that demonstrate that consolidation of authority will lead to more effective policy, as limiting sprawl and preserving landscape features. Thus, a polycentric system with local planning, regional coordination, and some state and federal goals may be the most effective means to deal with policy that impacts every parcel within a jurisdiction.

Discussion and Conclusion

We have surveyed a wide range of institutions that impact the landscape. These institutions may be designed to directly impact the landscape, such as zoning, or, like policing and education, indirectly impact the landscape. These institutions are created and implemented on a variety of spatial scales and political levels. Frequently the most effective means to a particular goal, such as forestland conservation, may be through the coordination of a variety of public and private mechanisms at varying scales. As demonstrated in the discussion of collaborative management, several institutions could be used separately or in combination for the goal of forest preservation. There is no one single solution or approach to designing institutions that affect landscape change processes. Communities may use the same type of institution for different goals, such as the variation we see in the North Carolina growth management policies.

One particularly important aspect of rules affecting landscape management is the issue of enforcement. Rules without enforcement are often ineffective and many government entities with the resources to create rules do not necessarily have the resources to enforce those rules. Particularly striking examples of the importance of enforcement include resource use in government-owned forest preservations created in areas formerly utilized by native populations. One example is the case of the Monarch Butterfly Special Biosphere Reserve created by the Mexican government in 1986. The creation of this reserve included the development of rules restricting the use of this resource by residents who had previously relied on this area for their livelihoods (Merino 1999). Government organizations had difficulty enforcing these access rules because of the complications caused by the perception of rights and preexisting uses among the residents in the area (Tucker 2004). Likewise, each landowner in many areas of the Brazilian Amazon along the TransAmazon Highway is prohibited from clearing more then 50% of his or her parcel. Nevertheless, many parcels have been almost completely deforested. The insufficient amount of resources the government commits to monitoring combined with the difficulty in traveling in the region result in many landholders not being penalized for these large-scale clearings.

Our preliminary survey of institutions impacting landscape change illustrates the diversity of institutions that directly or indirectly impact our cities, towns, and country-side. Instead of attempting to seek to develop universal institutions with standardized growth policies, forest conservation plans, education, and policing, we should recognize that this institutional diversity complements the diversity of our world. The complexity found in social and environmental factors in the real world suggests that it will take a diverse set of institutions to effectively manage natural resources. Landscape change processes are driven by different factors in different locations. The magnitude of impact of particular drivers of landscape change is mediated by the complexity of the interrelationships that exist in social-ecological systems. It is reasonable to suggest that a diversity of institutional tools is needed to address the wide range of landscape management challenges found around the world.

Acknowledgments This research was supported by a grant from the US National Science Foundation Biocomplexity in the Environment initiative (NSF SES008351) and by center funding provided by the National Science Foundation to the Center for the Study of Institutions, Population, and Environmental Change at Indiana University (SBR9521918).

References

Indiana Conservancy District Act (1957) In *IC 14–33, Indiana Legislature*

Bengston, D.N., Fletcher, J.O., and Nelson, K.C. (2004) Public policies for managing urban growth and protecting open space: policy instruments and lessons learned in the United States. *Landscape and Urban Planning* 69: 271–286

Carruthers, J.L. (2001) *Growth at the Fringe: The Influence of Political Fragmentation in United States Metropolitan Areas.* The North American Meetings of the Regional Science Association International, Charleston, SC

Carruthers, J.L. (2003) Growth at the fringe: the influence of political fragmentation in United States metropolitan areas. *Papers in Regional Science* 82: 475–499

City of Aurora (2006) 2007 *Water Management Plan.* Aurora Water Department, Aurora, CO. Accessed January 30, 2007 from http://www.auroragov.org/stellent/groups/public/documents/article-publication/014178.pdf.

Dietz, T., Stern, P., and Ostrom, E. (2003) The struggle to govern the commons. *Science* 302: 1907–1912

Dilorenzo, T. (1983) Economic competition and political competition: an empirical note. *Public Choice* 40: 203–209

Dowall, D.E. (1988) Land policy in the United States. In Hallett G (ed) *Land and Housing Policies in Europe and the USA: A Comparative Analysis.* Routledge, London

Ellickson, R.C. and Been, V.L. (2000) *Land Use Controls: Cases and Materials.* Aspen Law & Business, New York

Fischel WA (1985) *The Economics of Zoning Laws: A Property Rights Approach to American Land Use Controls.* Johns Hopkins University Press, Baltimore, MD

Hanuschek EA (1986) The economics of schooling: production and efficiency in public schools. *Journal of Economic Literature* 24: 1141–1177

Hollis LE and Fulton W (2002) Open space protection: conservation meets growth management. Discussion Paper. Center on Urban and Metropolitan Policy, The Brookings Institution, Washington, DC

Kelly ED (1993) *Managing Community Growth: Policies, Techniques, and Impacts.* Praeger, Westport, CT

Kiesling H (1967) Measuring a local government service: a study of school districts in New York state. *Review of Economics and Statistics* 49: 356–367

Martin C, Peterson K, and Stabler L (2003) Residential landscaping in Phoenix, Arizona, U.S.: practices and preferences relative to covenants, codes and restrictions. *Journal of Arboriculture* 29: 9–17

McGinnis, M.D. (ed) (1999) *Polycentricity and Local Public Economies. Institutional Analysis.* The University of Michigan Press, Ann Arbor, MI

Merino L (1999) Reserva Especial de la Biósfera Mariposa Monarca: problemática general de la region. In Hoth J, Merino L, Oberhauser K, Pisanty I, Price S, and Wilkinson T (eds) *1997 North American Conference on the Monarch Butterfly.* Commission for Environmental Cooperation, Montreal, Quebec, Canada

Nelson AC (1992) Preserving prime farmland in the face of urbanization: lessons from Oregon. *Journal of the American Planning Association* 58: 467–488

Nelson AC and Duncan JB (1995) *Growth Management Principles and Practices.* Planners Press, Chicago, IL

Niskanen W and Levy M (1974) *Cities and Schools: A Case for Community Government in California.* University of California, Graduate School of Public Policy, Berkeley, CA

Oakerson R and Parks R (1989) Local government constitutions: a different view of metropolitan governance. *American Review of Public Administration* 19: 279–294

Oakerson RJ (1999) *Governing Local Public Economies: Creating the Civic Metropolis.* Institute for Contemporary Studies, Oakland, CA

Ostrom E and Parks R (1973) Suburban police departments: too many and too small? In Masotti LH and Hadden JK (eds) *The Urbanization of the Suburbs,* vol. 7. Sage, Beverly Hills, CA

Ostrom E, Parks R, and Whitaker G (1973) Do we really Want to consolidate urban police forces? A reappraisal of some old assertions. *Public Administration Review* 33: 423–433

Ostrom E and Whitaker GP (1974) Community control and governmental responsiveness: the case of police in black communities. In Rogers D and Hawley W (eds) *Improving the Quality of Urban Management.* Sage, Beverly Hills, CA

Ostrom E (2005) *Understanding Institutional Diversity.* Princeton University Press, Princeton, NJ

Parks R (1985) Metropolitan structure and systemic performance: the case of police service delivery. In Hanf K and Toonen TAJ (eds) *Policy Implementation in Federal and Unitary Systems,* pp 161–191. Martinus Nijhoff Publishers, Dordrecht, The Netherlands

Parks R (1995) Do we really want to consolidate urban areas? In *Polycentric Circles,* vol. 1, pp 7–8

Parks R and Ostrom E (1981) Complex models of urban service systems. In Clark TN (ed) *Urban Policy Analysis: Directions for Future Research,* vol. 21, pp 171–199. Sage, Beverly Hills, CA

Ruliffson JA, Gobster PH, Haight RF, and Homans FR (2002) Niches in the urban forest: organizations and their role in acquiring metropolitan open space. *Journal of Forestry* 100: 16–23

Schneider M (1986) Fragmentation and growth of government. *Public Choice* 48: 255–263

Stephens GR and Wikstrom N (2000) *Metropolitan Government and Governance. Theoretical Perspectives, Empirical Analysis, and the Future.* Oxford University Press, New York

Teske P, Schneider M, Mintron M, and Best S (1993) Establishing the micro foundations of a macro theory: information, movers, and the competitive local market for public goods. *American Political Science Review* 87: 702–713

Tucker C (2004) Community institutions and forest management in Mexico's monarch butterfly reserve. *Society and Natural Resources* 17: 569–587

Tucker C and Ostrom E (2005) Multidisciplinary research relating institutions and forest transformations. In Moran EF and Ostrom E (eds) *Seeing the Forest and the Trees: Human-Environment Interactions in Forest Ecosystems,* pp 81–103. MIT Press, Cambridge, MA

Wagner R and Weber W (1975) Competition, monopoly, and the organization of government in metropolitan areas. *Journal of Law and Economics* 18: 661–684

Yaffee SL (1996) *Ecosystem Management in the United States: An Assessment of Current Experience.* Island Press, Washington, DC

Chapter 6
Green Landscapes: Exogenous Economic Benefits of Environmental Improvement

Douglas Johnston and John Braden

A past study of the landscape architecture profession and resulting marketing strategy emphasized the value added by design services (Bookout 1994). It supported the notion that design was not necessarily a luxury, a loss-leader, or other marginal(ized) component of the built environment, but had real value. Nonetheless, the marketing still smacked of triviality – the notion that landscape architectural contributions were something akin to an "after-market" product of land development rather than a fundamental element of the building process. We argue here that the benefits of environmental improvement through mitigation and prevention form a more core component of land-use decision-making.

The environment provides numerous goods and services to communities. Of course it provides life-sustaining elements for food, air, water. It provides raw materials for production of other goods and services. It also provides regulation of ecological processes, habitat, recreation, identity, pleasure, and many other tangible and less-tangible benefits. Variations in the quality of environmental goods and services quite logically lead to variations in their potential valuation.

The production of particular qualities and quantities of environmental goods and services falls well within the scope of the design and planning professions. As such, they act as agents of landscape change in both direct (the construction of particular places, in particular ways) and less direct ways (through the generation of economic – among other – benefits). A proper accounting for the benefits of particular landscape goods and services can lead to different decisions about the provision of those goods and services, affecting the future state of the landscape.

There are numerous challenges to examining the benefits associated with environmental change. A major challenge is that many of the potential benefits must be imputed from other measures, as they are not directly accounted for in the marketplace. The indirect accounting is due to several factors, but of particular interest here is the classic problem of public goods.

The landscape, in addition to being a source of resources, is also used as a sink for waste products. When a pollutant is added to the environment, the benefits (the avoidance of treating or eliminating the pollutant) accrue to the entity that produced the pollutant. However, the costs, in terms of environmental degradation, are borne by entities not receiving the benefits (such as downstream or downwind residents).

J.L. Wescoat, Jr. and D.M. Johnston (eds.), *Political Economies of Landscape Change.*   131
© Springer 2008

Because of the distribution of costs (among other things), it is difficult to obtain compensation or collective action to minimize the burdens of those costs. In decision-making by the entity producing the pollutants, the benefits of the products of which the pollutant is a by-product are counted, while the costs to other entities are not, therefore providing incentive to continue production of the pollutant.

As another example, we use the provision of a public park. Development of a park has costs in terms of land, and capital and operating expenses. However, there is no direct charge for use of the park, so it is difficult to construct an argument on economic valuation terms for determining the number or qualities of parks. We generally turn to a variety of indirect measures to determine the value or provide them based on attitudes or conventions.

The principle employed here is that people make consumer choices based on comparison of characteristics of alternative goods and services. The willingness to pay more to live near a park (all other factors being equal) is a measure of the value of that proximity. The willingness to pay to live in a neighborhood relatively free of pollution, or crime, is an indicator of the value of that change in condition.

Methodology

The environmental services provided by the landscape are the subject of increasing study. The demand for these services is not usually expressed directly (as in the purchase of consumer goods and services like refrigerators or cars) but is embedded in other valuation decisions, such as the choice of residential property.

Investment in residential property reflects numerous considerations such as house size, lot size, construction type, neighborhood, school district, proximity to work, proximity to community services, etc. Differences in the willingness to pay for particular properties can be attributed to differences in the characteristics of the property (number of bedrooms, nearness to water, etc). Thus the value of these characteristics is considered, and accounted for, in property value. Of course property values are but one expression of value for environmental goods and services, but since housing remains, for most people, a major investment relative to their income, we can safely assume that variations in property value reflect relatively important values of goods and services desired by a community.

If variations in the level or type of characteristics are reflected in differences in value, then we can, without major gymnastics, suggest that changes in those characteristics should be reflected in changes in values. A given property then may be undervalued relative to its potential if the level of one or more of its attributes is suppressed. For example, numerous studies have shown that a residential property is valued more highly if it is near a park, or conservation area, or a water body. Thus, if a neighborhood is without a park, property values are suppressed below potential levels, and the difference in property values (all other factors being held constant) is a lower bound on the value of the park (the park may impart values in addition to its effect on neighboring properties).

One of the important constructs here is that value is a function of both on-site characteristics, (the size and type of residence) and off-site characteristics (the quality of the school, the quality of proximal resources such as parks, or water quality). Changes in on-site conditions are generally under the direct control of the property owner. Off-site conditions are generally not (except through location choices).

Our working hypothesis is that degraded environmental conditions suppress market value and that changes in environmental qualities will have real economic benefits that could be captured to pay for those changes. To illustrate these principles, we use two case studies recently completed. In one we apply fairly traditional measures of benefits accounting by both cost and value-based methods, while in the other, hedonic methods are compared with a discrete-choice tradeoff method to assess changes in value associated with changes in environmental conditions.

Case Study 1: Downstream Economic Benefits from Conservation Design

Managing storm water is a major challenge in most urban areas (Arnold and Gibbons 1996; Schueler 1995). Buildings, roads, and compacted soils reduce absorptive capacity. In suburban areas, 20–50% of the land is impervious to precipitation. In inner cities and commercial zones, imperviousness can exceed 80%. According to Schueler (1994, 2003), the hydrologic functions of streams change with as little as five to 10% imperviousness, and they change profoundly when imperviousness approaches 25%.

Increased runoff exacerbates flooding and increases conveyance requirements. Less water is left in the soil to recharge aquifers, replenish wells, and maintain base stream flows. Faster run-off increases erosion, scours stream banks, and entrains more sediment, landscape chemicals, petroleum residues, pet wastes, and other anthropogenic detritus. A consequence is surface water quality that is less able to support beneficial uses.

For several decades, detention basins have been the customary prescription for managing storm water. They have received criticism however, because while they reduce peak flows, they generally increase damaging bank-full flows, and do not contribute to remediation of water quality or groundwater infiltration among others (Schuler 1995). More recently, "low impact" or "conservation design" principles have been promoted that use measures such as porous paving, narrower streets, "green" roofs, vegetated swales, and constructed wetlands to maintain a nearly natural water budget and improve water quality (Figure 1) (e.g., Arendt 1996; Hager 2003; Wilson et al. 1998). Residential conservation development sites typically incorporate more cluster development than conventional development to provide the same gross density of population to land area.

Streiner and Loomis (1995, 268) group the economic effects of stream corridor enhancement into two categories: (1) reductions in property damages, including residential and public structures, vegetation and parks; and (2) restoration of the natural values of the stream itself, including more stable stream banks (which may

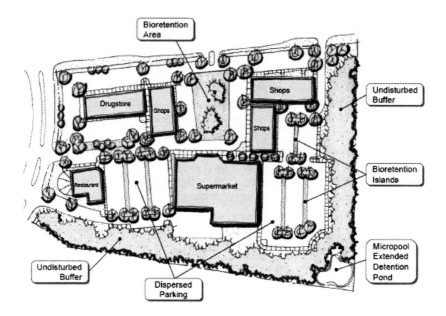

COMMERCIAL DEVELOPMENT -- BETTER SITE DESIGN

Figure 1 Conservation Design Illustration (From *Georgia Stormwater Management Manual*, Volume 2: *Technical Handbook*, 2001, pp.1.4-37.)

interfere with natural processes), enhanced aquatic habitat through restoration of pool-riffle sequences, and more attractive ecosystems. In Braden and Johnston (2003) we developed a typology of impacts and used benefits transfer techniques to develop estimates of the economic significance. Our estimates generally are conditional on property values and local factors. We concluded that the reduction of flood damages and public infrastructure costs of storm water conveyance are usually the most significant sources of change in property value, with most other benefits being case specific, or small.

The hypothesis of the case study is that, in addition to any on-site benefits that might exist for conservation design practices in the way of reduced road construction, drainage infrastructure, etc., there may exist off-site (specifically downstream!) benefits due to reduced storm water discharge. If these benefits exist and are sufficiently large, they may provide additional incentive to promote the application of conservation design.

Assessment of storm water management benefits would ideally be based on direct observation. However, because conservation design strategies have yet to be employed on a large scale, that is, at watershed scales, it is not possible to draw on monitoring research for assessing downstream effectiveness. Simulation studies are therefore required to provide comparison between two possible future scenarios:

development of the watershed with and without the incorporation of conservation design or other measures for on-site storm water retention.

Our hydrologic modeling strategy involves the following steps: (1) Perform a flood frequency analysis of the simulated stream flows to estimate the probability of different magnitudes of flood events; (2) Compute discharge (flow rates) for reaches in the watershed for the specified flood events; (3) Calculate the water surface elevation of the streams; (4) Estimate the area of different land uses contained within the flooded extent; (5) Use benefits transfer and flood damage estimates to calculate the economic benefits attributable to the differences in flooded areas; and (6) Use engineering costing methods and standard design protocols to estimate savings associated with infrastructure.

Blackberry Creek drains a 189 km^2 (73 mi^2) watershed in south-central Kane County and north-central Kendall County, Illinois. Blackberry Creek is 52 km (32 mi) long and originates north of the village of Elburn in central Kane County. It drains to the Fox River near Yorkville in Kendall County. Tributaries to Blackberry Creek include Lake Run, East Run, and several unnamed tributaries (Figure 2).

Blackberry Creek was selected for this study because it represents an urbanizing watershed. It has been the subject of numerous studies of watershed management and conservation design strategies (Kane County 1996; Blackberry Creek Watershed Committee 1999; CDF 2003). A comprehensive development plan has been prepared for the Kane County portion of the watershed (Kane County 1996). Because of data limitations in Kendall County, only the watershed in Kane County was included in this analysis.

As would normally be expected, the modeled discharges show an increase in peak discharges throughout the distribution for the conventional development scenario. The conservation scenario, however, results in discharges below not only the conventional, but also the existing levels of development (Figure 3). This result reflects precisely the potential impacts of increased storage provided by conservation design practices including permeable paving, green roofs, bioswales, use of native vegetation that increase groundwater infiltration, and evapotranspiration over conventional development types.

An implication of this is that new development can offset impacts from existing development. The magnitude of the effects are of course dependent on the scale of implementation, therefore, any analysis must include local and actual development conditions.

Floodplain extent and depth were estimated using available high accuracy digital elevation models. Because the focus is on downstream impacts, only a 17.4 km (10.8 mi) portion of Blackberry Creek downstream of its major tributaries is examined in the flood analysis (Figure 2). The impacts of upstream development patterns are progressively diluted downstream as flows from other sources enter the main channel. We then tabulated the land-use types and areas falling within the flood-risk areas.

Within the study area, conventional development would result in 20 more hectares (50 ac) of residential property within the 100-year event floodplain in the downstream reach of the creek than would conservation development (Figure 4). Data from the 2000 Census Summary File 3 for Median Owner Occupied Housing (H085001) are available

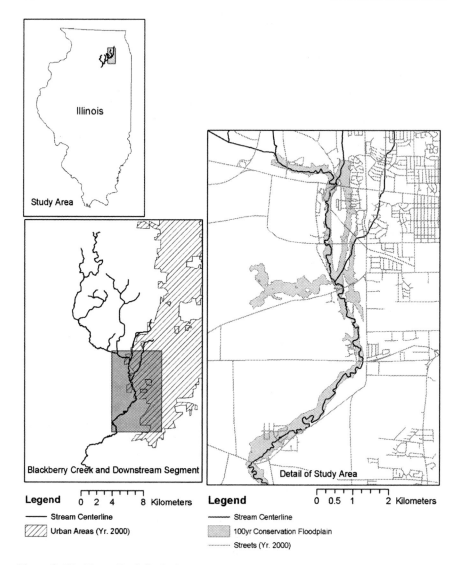

Figure 2 Blackberry Creek Study Area

at the block group level. For our study site, the area-weighted median housing value was $175,600 per unit for homes in the census block groups within the flood-risk areas.

Using benefits transfer methods as outlined by Braden and Johnston (2003), conservation design practices generate a total benefit based on property value of $391,600–2,488,500 over the downstream study area based on the location of the

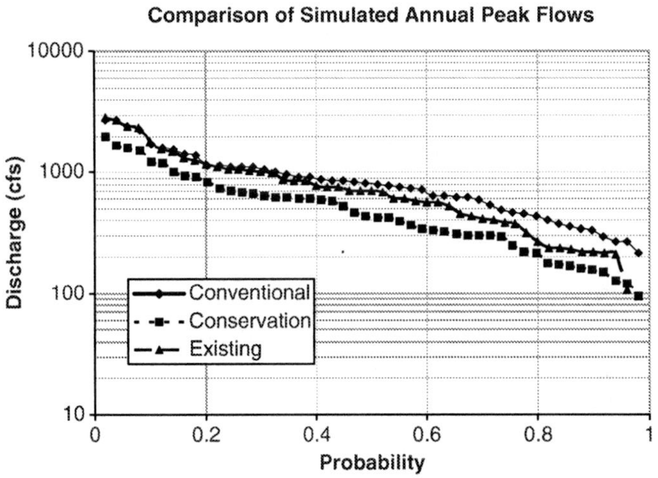

Comparison of Simulated Annual Peak Flows

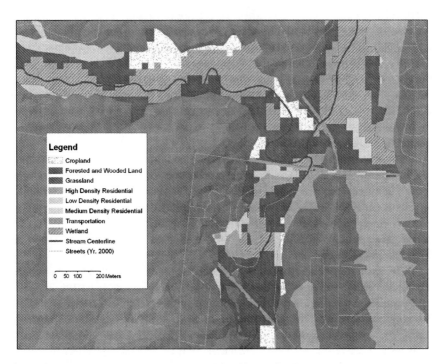

Figure 3   Probability plot of annual peak flows for blackberry creek downstream of the aurora tributary

Figure 4   Conventional scenario land uses within 100-year flood zone

properties within the 100-year floodplain generated by the two scenarios. These values range between 0.4 and 2.5% of affected property value.

Using the stage-damage approach, the upstream conservation measures produce an expected present value of downstream flood benefit for the 0.01 annual probability event ranges from $1,040,000 to $1,526,000 in structural damages and $605,600 to $838,000 in content damages. The combined value is $16,800–24,200 per hectare ($6,700–9,700 per acre) for one- and two-storey housing respectively, or $274–394 per developed hectare ($110–158 per developed acre).

The benefits attributable to infrastructure stem from avoided costs of infrastructure due to the reduced peak discharges in the conservation scenario (resulting, generally, in smaller culverts). The baseline for comparison was the conservation flow simulation with existing culvert infrastructure. Because the conservation scenario generally results in discharges below those of the existing conditions, it is likely that existing infrastructure is oversized for that scenario. Thus, the results should be viewed as a conservative estimate of benefits, rather than an absolute difference between conservation and conventional development where new infrastructure would be provided for both scenarios. Our approach represents a developing watershed that has at least basic infrastructure already in place.

The difference between the costs of the conventional solution and the conservation solution range from $430 for a small corrugated metal culvert in a small tributary to $302,000 for a long concrete box culvert on a tributary of Blackberry Creek (Table 1). The average difference between scenarios was $38,100 per culvert. In the Blackberry Creek Watershed, there are presently 87 culverts. Using the average cost, the total benefit due to smaller required drainage culverts in the basin is $3,315,000. With 4,050 ha (10,000 ac) of new development in the scenarios for the whole watershed, the downstream benefit is equivalent to $820 per developed hectare ($340 per developed acre).

In summary, the sum of the downstream flood mitigation and infrastructure benefits amounts to $920–1,440 per developed hectare ($380–590 per developed acre) following conservation design principles. These estimates are a conservative, lower-bound assessment of the property value differential gained by the employment of off-site conservation design practices to reduce flood losses. They do not include other related benefits such as improved stream water quality, increased groundwater infiltration, etc.

In this example we have examined benefits that can be construed as having purely utilitarian value of reduced damages due to flooding. Although evidence suggests it exists, we did not attempt to characterize aesthetic or other less-tangible benefits. The question arises as to whether benefits of environmental change may accrue to those who do not receive local, tangible benefits (reduced risk of damage, improved water quality on their property, etc.). To examine these issues we turn to another case study that uses a set of evaluation techniques to extract economic values from a broader set of attributes.

Table 1 Summary capital costs for culverts

Culvert	Shape	Material	Headwall Type	Length	Difference (Benefit)
1	Ellip	Metal	4	64	$1,006.51
2	Box	Concrete	1	16	$1,079.00
3	Box	Concrete	1	55	$12,027.60
4	Box	Concrete	2	230	$302,070.45
5	CMP	Metal	3	20	$429.00
6	CMP	Metal	3	68	$16,787.16
7	CPC	Concrete	4	22.5	$4,138.08
8	Ellip	Metal	4	36	$3,248.18
9	Box	Concrete	1	70	$28,541.40
10	CPC	Concrete	4	310	$52,284.18
11	CMP	Metal	3	40	$5,627.60
12	CPC	Concrete	4	68	$29,980.83
			Average Benefit		$38,101.67
			Average Benefit (w/o #4)		$17,568.29

Notes:

Headwall type

1 – Wingwall flared 30–75 degrees

2 – Tapered inlet throat

3 – Pipe projecting from Fill

4 – Square headwall

Cost Sources:

Box Culvert Material Costs from Rio Valley Pipe Co. (Labor and Equipment assumed as 40% of material costs).

Corrugated Metal Pipe (CMP), Concrete Pipe Culvert (CPC), and Headwall costs from *2003 Illinois Heavy Construction Costs*.

Case Study 2: Economic Benefits of Environmental Remediation

For more than 50 years, pollution has been recognized as a serious problem in the Great Lakes, and in many other lakes and rivers.[1] The contaminants include pollutants entrained in sediment, consisting of polychlorinated biphenyls (PCBs) and other persistent toxic substances, that is, removing the sources of the pollutant do not remove the pollutants already discharged. Some have the potential to bioaccumulate in the food chain, presenting significant health risks to aquatic organisms and their human consumers.

The primary obstacle to remediation is its cost (although there are surely political and other barriers). The estimate of US expenditures on cleanup is between

---

[1] The following discussion is based on a pending publication by John Braden et al. (2004) entitled "Contaminant Cleanup in the Waukegan Harbor Area of Concern: Homeowner Attitudes and Economic Benefits".

$160 million and $580 million for Great Lakes Areas of Concern (IJC 2003). However, only two polluted Canadian sites of this nature have had remedial efforts completed, even though they are of high national and international priority. Estimates of total cost to complete remediation of these sites are $7.4 billion (IJC 2003). To justify the remediation using economic criteria, the magnitudes of the benefits would have to exceed the costs of remediation.

The benefits of remediation are more difficult to characterize, however. Benefits include improvements in the health of the ecosystem (including reduction of human health risk). It can also be postulated that people prefer to live in less-degraded environments, and even that stigma effects of proximity (even distant) to degraded sites can affect preference. To the extent that these preferences can be captured in actual economic decisions, the economic benefits of environmental improvements can be assessed.

The premise of this study is that the presence of contaminated sediments, like other types of noxious waste, depresses the market value of properties associated with the site. Cleanup of the site should restore the market values to levels observed with properties of similar quality and context but unaffected by the contamination (e.g., Dale et al. 1999). To test this, researchers studied awareness and attitudes of residents to test the postulation of preference for less-degraded environments, and if there is evidence of preference, to use variation in property value as a measure of the effect of polluted environments.

The analysis focuses on the attitudes of homeowners and the benefits that might accrue to them through changes in the value of their residential properties. For most households, their home is the single most important and carefully considered consumption good. Decisions about housing indicate a great deal about residents' values, not only about the size and price of homes, but also about community attributes such as school quality, safety, and parks. From their housing choices, it is possible to infer the economic value that homeowners attach to those attributes.

The first and most conventional way to analyze the value of the harbor environment is to assume that people respond to a local disamenity by preferring to reside far away from it, all other things equal. The implication is that property values within the range of influence are discounted because of the associated risk or stigma. While the harbor environmental conditions may not be a dominant consideration for homebuyers, we hypothesize that it is a significant influence on the choice of a home.

Proximity to a contaminated site is a crude indicator of environmental impact. Other factors, such as school quality, access to parks, and public safety might also correlate with the location of the disamenity. To the extent that these other factors resist statistical control through the hedonic modeling process, the results will reflect changes in state of the harbor area not limited to contaminant cleanup.

The resulting model is described in more detail in Braden et al. (2004). In summary, it predicts house price as a combination of on-site characteristics such as lot size, building floor area, age, number of bathrooms, presence of a fireplace, and off-site characteristics such as distance to the harbor, and location in Waukegan versus other parts of Lake County.

As shown in Table 2, the first-stage hedonic regression produces coefficient estimates that have the expected signs and, for the most part, statistical significance. The coefficient on the variable representing distance from the harbor (HARBMILE) provides the implicit price of a small change in harbor distance. Computing the differential of price relative to the differential of distance, for Waukegan households, the mean marginal willingness to pay for a 1-mile increase in distance from the harbor is approximately $12,200 (median $10,800). The comparable WTP estimate for households outside of Waukegan is a mean of $7,080 (median $4,180).

Multiplying the distance differential times distance from the harbor provides a lower-bound estimate of the WTP per household for eliminating the proximity discount. For Waukegan, using both mean WTP and mean distance from the harbor, the WTP/household is approximately $29,500 (using medians: $25,400). The 2000 Census reported 15,697 owner-occupied residences in Waukegan, so the estimated change in mean gross value is $463 million (median: $399 million). The housing stock of Waukegan was valued at $2.5 billion in 2000 (Paulsen 2003). Thus, the estimated mean change represents approximately 19% (median: 16%) of the value of the housing stock. For the 152,604 households outside of Waukegan, the WTP/household estimate based on mean price and distance is $89,900 (using medians: $54,300), producing an estimated mean gross value change of $13.7 billion (using medians: $8.3 billion). The assessed value of the Lake County housing stock

Table 2 Hedonic regression results

Explanatory variables[a,b]	Coefficient estimates (robust standard errors)[c]	t-ratio	95% confidence interval
Ln(*LOT*)	0.0709 (0.277)**	2.55	0.0163–0.125
Ln(*HSIZE*)	0.338 (0.979)***	3.45	0.146–0.530
Ln(*HAGE*)	−0.0387 (0.0379)	−1.02	−0.113–0.0358
GRADE	0.158 (0.0494)***	3.19	0.0606–0.255
BSMT	0.261 (0.0490)***	5.33	0.165–0.357
BATHS	0.0304 (0.0263)	1.15	−0.0212–0.082
AC	0.0565 (0.0249)**	2.27	0.00765–0.105
FIRE	0.120 (0.0375)***	3.20	0.0462–0.193
ATGAR	0.0659 (0.0428)	1.54	−0.0182–0.150
Ln(*HARBMILE*)	0.198 (0.0337)***	5.87	0.132–0.264
WHARB	−0.138 (0.0940)	−1.47	−0.322–0.0467
Ln(*CLASS*)	−0.769 (0.217)***	−3.54	−1.19–0.342
Y00	0.0840 (0.0411)**	2.04	0.00323–0.164
Y01	0.0569 (0.0215)***	2.64	0.0146–0.0992
Constant	11.1 (1.09)***	10.2	8.96–13.2

$R^2 = 0.598$; n = 594
[a]The hedonic price function is double-log; dummy, categorical, and count variables are unlogged. n < 599 due to missing data.
[b]"ln" prefix for variable names stands for natural logarithm.
[c]*** – Significant at 0.01 level; ** – significant at 0.05 level; * – significant at 0.10 level.

outside of Waukegan was $54 billion in 2000, so the estimated increases amount
to15% for median values and 25% for mean values.

The second approach to benefit estimation draws on the conjoint choice experiment
in the survey. Respondents were asked to reflect upon their most recent home purchase
and to select between the home actually chosen and a hypothetical home described in
the survey. The homes were the same except for variation in six categories: lot size,
house size, class size of neighborhood schools, the amount of recreational or natural
areas in the region, degree of cleanup of the harbor, and house price.

The resulting statistical estimates are quite strong, with most variables statistically
significant and all signs in the expected direction. Households are shown to be more
likely to select homes with larger lots, more living area, public schools with smaller
classes, more public/recreation areas, a cleaner harbor area, and lower prices. The
negative and statistically significant coefficient for the variable recording the choice
of selecting the hypothetical home versus the status quo indicates that, other things
equal, the respondents reveal inertia – an unwillingness to leave their current home
for another. The harbor environmental conditions have sensible effects, with added
pollution discouraging the choice of a different home and full cleanup positively
affecting willingness to switch more strongly than partial cleanup.

For Waukegan homeowners, these calculations produce an aggregate mean WTP
of $436 million (median $462 million) for full harbor cleanup, realized as an
increase in residential property values. In the rest of Lake County, the aggregate
mean WTP for residential property in the event of full harbor cleanup totals more
than $12 billion (median $7.4 billion). These estimates for full cleanup and the
proportional changes in value of the regional housing stock values they represent
are remarkably similar to the lower-bound WTP estimates produced by the
first-stage hedonic analysis.

Partial cleanup was worth considerably less: mean aggregate WTP of $158 mil-
lion (median $158 million) and $6 billion (median $3.4 billion), respectively.
Added pollution produced perceived mean damages to residential property values
of $344 million (median $318 million) for Waukegan residents and more than $14
billion (median $9.4 billion) to homeowners elsewhere in the county. This suggests
that environmental degradation affects not only those who are exposed to the environmental problems in the conventional sense of the word, but, due to the stigma
effect of known pollution problems, even the nonexposed are materially affected
through depression of the value of residential real estate.

Conclusions

The evidence, illustrated through, but not limited to the two case studies presented
in this paper, supports numerous conclusions. First, different environmental conditions result in different, real economic values, both on and off-site, in addition to
numerous other tangible and less-tangible benefits. Differences in property values
associated with different levels of environmental quality suggest that those differ-

ences are first perceived by residents (however indirectly), that the perceptions are realized in different levels of willingness to pay, and those levels represent a potentially large portion of overall property values (2.5% baseline for flood reduction only, 18% for environmental cleanup).

Degraded environmental conditions have a real cost – in lost property value. The corollary is that improvements in environmental conditions result in real economic gains. To the extent that these gains outweigh the costs associated with the implementation of these improvements, they are beneficial to society to implement. Because many of these benefits are embedded in private property values, property owners should be willing to invest in environmental improvements (through taxes or other mechanisms) in order to realize these benefits.

In a period when local and regional governments struggle to keep up with the demands for services for expanding communities, the temptation to meet fiscal shortfalls by reducing public investments through cuts in environmental quality provision (in forms such as reduction in open-space provision, avoidance of cleanup of degraded sites, etc.) may actually result in counterproductive outcomes.

Improvements in environmental quality, through remediation, improved design knowledge, and better planning are not an economic liability to the community, but rather may serve to add economic benefits on par with (or maybe even exceeding) many other economic development strategies currently pursued. Knowledge gained by further research on the economic benefits accruing from such endeavors may provide sufficient incentive to effect landscape change.

Acknowledgments The Blackberry Creek study was supported in part by the US Environmental Protection Agency through Award No. X-97576401 to the Conservation Research Institute and by the Illinois Agricultural Experiment Station and Cooperative States Research, Education, and Extension Service, US Department of Agriculture under Project No. 0305. Any opinions, findings, and conclusions or recommendations expressed in this publication are those of the authors and do not necessarily reflect the views of the supporting agencies. Without implication, we thank Tom Brody, John Haugland, Tom Price, David Soong, and Jim Van Der Kloot for their advice.

The Waukegan Harbor research was supported in part by the Great Lakes National Program Office, US Environmental Projection Agency through Award No. 040245 of the Northeast-Midwest Institute, and by the CSREES/USDA under Illinois Agricultural Experiment Station Project No. 0305 ACE. The authors thank Vic Adamowicz, Penny Bouchard, Allegra Cangelosi, Richard Hilton, Lisa Kelly-Wilson, Ben Kennedy, Frank Lupi, John Loomis, Jordan Louviere, Pat Morris, Martin Paulsen, Jean Schreiber, Peter Schoenfield, and Jessica Taverna. Any opinions, findings, and conclusions or recommendations expressed in this publication are those of the authors and do not necessarily reflect the views of the supporting agencies or these individuals.

References

Arendt RG (1996) *Conservation Design for Subdivisions: A Practical Guide to Creating Open Space Networks*. Island Press, Washington, DC

Arnold CL Jr and Gibbons CJ (1996) Impervious surface coverage. *Journal of the American Planning Association*62(2): 243–258

Blackberry Creek Watershed Committee (1999) *Blackberry Creek Watershed Management Plan; Kane and Kendall Counties, Illinois*. BCWC, Naperville, IL

Bookout LW, Beyard MD, and Fader SW (1994) *Value by Design Landscape, Site Planning and Amenities*. Urban Land Institute, Washington, DC

Braden JB and Johnston DM (2003) The downstream economic benefits of storm water retention. *Journal of Water Resources Planning and Management, American Society of Civil Engineers* 130(6): 498–505

Braden JB, Patunru AA, Chattopadhyay S, and Mays N (2004) Contaminant cleanup in the waukegan harbor area of concern: homeowner attitudes and economic benefits. *Journal of Great Lakes Research* 30(4): 474–491

Conservation Design Forum (2003) *Blackberry Creek Alternative Futures Analysis*. Conservation Design Forum, Elmhurst, IL

Dale L, Murdoch JC, Thayer MA, and Waddell PA (1999) Do property values rebound from environmental stigmas? Evidence from dallas. *Land Economics* 75(2): 311–326

Hager MC (2003) Low-impact development: lot-level approaches to stormwater management are gaining ground. *Stormwater* 4(1): 12–25

International Joint Commission (IJC) (2003) *The Status of Restoration Activities in the Great Lakes Areas of Concern*. Windsor, Ontario, Canada

Kane County (1996) 2020 *Land Resource Management Plan*. June 11, Kane County, Geneva, IL

Streiner CF and Loomis JB (1995) Estimating the benefits of urban stream restoration using the hedonic price method. *Rivers* 5(4): 267–278

Schueler TR (1994) The importance of imperviousness. *Watershed Protection Techniques* 1(3): 100–111

Schueler TR (1995) *Site Planning for Urban Stream Protection*. Metropolitan Washington Council of Governments, Washington DC

Schueler TR (2003) Ideal urban forms to minimize land-use impacts on aquatic ecosystems in the Great Lakes Basin. Paper prepared for Great Lakes Science Advisory Board Workshop on Urban Land-use Impacts on Great Lakes Water Quality, Toronto, Canada

Wilson A, Seal JL, McManigal LA, Lovins LH, Cureton M, and Browning WD (1998) *Green Development: Integrating Ecology and Real Estate*. Wiley, New York

Chapter 7
Pricing the Economic Landscape: Global Financial Markets and the Communities and Institutions of Risk Management

Terry L. Babcock-Lumish and Gordon L. Clark

Introduction

For much of the 20th century, economic geography was preoccupied with the spatial structure of market transactions and the resulting flows of commodities across time and space. This remains a vital reference point in any understanding of the global economy, providing important insights into the changing significance of cities and regions in national and international settings. An alternative way of looking at the dynamic economic landscape is via the scope and scale of financial decision-making focused on the locales and organization of risk management, which is the approach we pursue in this paper. We begin with observations about the fluctuating geographical scale of economic relationships, specifically noting the increasing significance of integration and the decreasing hold of local relationships on market transactions. This is followed by a brief overview of recent research on the geography of finance and emphasizes the importance of risk management within and between institutions over time and space. The regulation of risk is the theme of the latter sections of the paper, linking issues such as trust and accountability with community networks and organizational integrity. We conclude by drawing implications for both the changing role of urban centers and the place of communities within the emerging global financial system.

Economic geography is about the global configuration of economic activity, as well as the prospects for inner-city residents of the developed and less developed worlds (Clark et al. 2000). Over the last 20 years or so, economic geography has focused upon the growth and decline of regions, the restructuring of economic systems, and the spatial clustering of innovation. Economic geography has grappled with the scaling-up of economic activity from the local to the global, notwithstanding the shortage of comprehensive theoretical treatments of this phenomenon elsewhere in the social sciences (Swyngedouw 2000). And yet, despite the significance of globalization, it is apparent that there remains a real premium for nation-states in sustaining centers of innovation and agglomerations of talent (Florida 2002; Florida and Tinagli 2004).

The globalization of economic activity has implications for the expanding scope and scale of geographical networks for local economic development, employment

J.L. Wescoat, Jr. and D.M. Johnston (eds.), *Political Economies of Landscape Change.*
© Springer 2008

opportunities, and income.[1] It can be shown, for example, that as European firms adopt advanced electronic communication equipment, they reach out to an expanding map of suppliers just as they search for an expanding set of markets. Some argue that technology is the modus operandi of globalization; we would suggest, however, that technology enables (as it has always done) the economic and geographical integration of profit-seeking agents and firms (see Galison 2000). Financial institutions, rather than electronic communications, are the single most important ingredient driving the expanding reach of capitalism. In this paper, we look more closely at the role of finance in a changing economic landscape and how financial institutions are organized with respect to their functions in space and time.

One of the greatest challenges posed by the enormous growth of financial markets and institutions over the last 25 to 35 years is the need to rethink the role of government and civil society. It is all too easy to look at the inherited economic landscape and identify public actors and institutions as their chief architects. Whether in mundane activities such as zoning and land use regulation or the most celebrated projects of urban development, there is a sense in which urban life is first and foremost created out of shared ideals. If examined in this way, we run the risk of underestimating both the local economic imperatives driving global integration and the enormous financial flows through cities such as Chicago into the rest of the world. Economic imperatives and financial flows leave their marks on the economic landscape – even if they are, at times, obscured by the processes of suburbanization and social differentiation, or the glittering new towers of downtown revival. Our challenge is to leave room, conceptually speaking, for the local in the face of apparent anxiety over the global (compare with Jameson 1997).

This paper provides a critical perspective on the role and significance of finance with respect to the changing economic landscape. Herein we draw upon our own research on the geography of finance, linking together work on trust and investment in innovation communities (see Babcock-Lumish 2003, 2004) with analyses of the

---

[1]Globalization is a contentious political issue, apparent in contemporary international affairs and electoral politics around the world. At one level, it is represented as an issue of job-rationing – a zero-sum game in which our jobs become your jobs, as if globalization has no net benefits for economic growth. At another level, globalization is an issue of empire-building – a veritable tidal-wave of cultural, social, and economic impulses emanating from the center (USA) and flowing out to the periphery (developing world) in ways that denude others' claims of independence and integrity. At yet another level, globalization is represented as an issue of modernization—the spread of liberal ideals of democracy and equality to all corners of the world (Florini, 2003). And yet for others, globalization is an issue of governance – making up the difference between the scope of corporations and the limits of the nation-state (Slaughter, 2004). Whatever the significance of these differing ways of representing globalization, we align ourselves with writers such as Stiglitz (2002) who, though critical of the institutions and practices of globalization, see many economic benefits of globalization if one views more and less developing countries as bilateral partners rather than as competing claimants on scarce resources (Clark, 2003).

geographical foundations of global finance (Clark 2005) and the institutional mechanisms used to manage risk in global currency flows (Clark and Thrift 2005). Our research has been intensive and case study based, and we have sought to integrate the insights gained with large-scale databases (Clark and Wójcik 2007). These reference points are useful in anchoring our discussion but are also representative of a research program shared by increasing numbers of academics concerned with the geography and sociology (as well as the economics) of how and why finance is organized and managed.[2]

The paper starts with general observations about the scaling-up of economic activity and the apparent decline of local sentiments underpinning both social and exchange relationships. This leads to a discussion of the literature under the heading of "the geography of finance," emphasizing the importance of risk management in the context of different forms of financial instruments or products. We then consider issues of risk management with respect to both intensive trust-based relationships and extensive bureaucratic relationships. This provides a means of linking the local with the global and is ultimately a story about the significance (or otherwise) of localities in a world of global financial flows and markets. In conclusion, we suggest some implications for the future of urban areas. Local urban centers may become nodes in complex financial networks drawing money up and into the global realm, and some centers may be so significant and so internally organized that they become critical points for local and global investment and innovation alike.

Inexorable Trends, Countervailing Imperatives

Powerful economic forces are shaping both local communities and global society. Today's sociocultural and physical landscapes are constantly evolving and being molded by economic actors, decisions, and transactions. However, if we look to the future in the hope of predicting the paths of social and economic change, we are left with a healthy dose of uncertainty. Two distinct societal trends emerge: increasing economic interdependence and decreasing human interaction. Increased economic interdependence heightens the need for a reliance on trust while, simultaneously, decreased social interaction reduces the societal conditioning so important for the development and cultivation of essential trust relationships. In our research, we see evidence of this tension, from venture capitalists making high-risk, early-stage investment decisions, to foreign exchange currency traders making bets about the direction of the global economy.

---

[2]Research programs are being developed around this theme in a variety of academic centers including the Social Studies of Finance group at the University of Edinburgh http://www.sociology.ed.ac.uk/finance/index.html.

Increasing Integration

Of the changes associated with globalization, three deserve special emphasis: technology, diversity, and complexity. First, improved communication and transportation technologies have lined the way for remarkable advances in labor and capital mobility. The era of affordable, accessible, reliable, and fast transnational communication and transportation has brought a manifold increase in both the exchange of ideas and physical movement across borders. Individuals are traveling further, demonstrating that technological innovation has made a substantial impact on human mobility (Metz 2004). Transatlantic trips between America and Britain that once required 6 days by boat are now relegated to an afternoon's travel, and are taken by no fewer than 180 million individuals per year (anticipated to increase to 500 million by 2030) (AmericanExpress 2003). With the advent of improved communications technologies, consumer behavior has followed in step. Cable, Internet, and wireless technologies are improving and diffusing steadily, with the costs of international communication decreasing toward effectively zero (ITU 2004). As technological communications have advanced, so too have financial transactions, as evidenced by the billions of dollars circumnavigating the globe within seconds at a keystroke (Clark and Thrift 2005).

With respect to diversity, demographic trends suggest an increasingly intercultural and multicultural global society than ever before. To illustrate, in 2003 approximately 175 million people – skilled and unskilled – lived somewhere other than within their countries of origin (IOM 2003). According to a recent survey of over 270 leading European firms, together they employed 65,000 expatriate executives, and in 1997, 840,600 people migrated *to* Germany while 746,000 emigrated *from* Germany (Niessen 2002). According to Saxenian (1999) in her work on immigrant populations in the entrepreneurial communities of Silicon Valley, Asian computer scientists and engineers dominate local high-technology firms. Similarly, Florida's (2002, 2004) work demonstrates the critical role of diversity in the prosperity of both American and European economic hot spots as our neighborhoods and workplaces grow increasingly diverse. With booming Asian and Hispanic populations, non-Hispanic whites no longer represent a demographic majority, and states such as Texas, Florida, and New York are poised to follow, underscoring the importance of demography in the context of changing US economic landscapes.

Third, increased trade liberalization has been marked by greater economic and societal complexity, as organizations and institutions scramble to specialize in talent and resource areas in order to sustain comparative advantage. Individuals are specializing further as ever greater societal interdependence is developed, and jobs in the workforce of the future will be shaped by new technologies. In fact, the fastest growing occupations at present include many that have only come into the lexicon in recent years: "network systems and data communications analyst," "computer software engineer," and "database administrator" (BLS 2004). Among specialty areas anticipated to see the strongest growth in the coming years are "Internet/Intranet development," "networking," "help desk/end-user support," and "applications development" (Half 2004). Other traditional jobs are being computerized, outsourced, or exported. Meanwhile, increased specialization requires increasing reliance on international markets and integration of these markets and communities in a dense and effective trading network.

Decreasing Interaction

As levels of global economic interdependence increase, human interaction is decreasing. Contributing to the decline of regular interpersonal interaction are trends in modern built environments that inhibit social cohesion. This is apparent in the design of transportation, residential, and commercial plans alike. Cities are often planned seemingly more for cars rather than humans, with big-box commerce and business parks on the outskirts of towns at large interchanges.[3] With suburban sprawl and heavy congestion, daily commutes are growing longer (CEA 2001), such that people are living more insular lives encased in steel rather than interacting with neighbors (Putnam 2000). As recently as 40 years ago, people still met in town squares and city centers with individual boutique-style shops serving communities' needs; today, economic exchange is increasingly less interactive with the expansion of e-commerce and full-service stores like Wal-Mart and Target. With the loss of the town square (or the economic need for it), exchange transactions have grown far less interactive. Likewise, suburban developments and decreased reliance on public transport enable individuals and families to live increasingly private lives. While urban redevelopment efforts promise revitalization of downtowns, it is impossible to ignore trends in planning that curtail what was previously regular community interface (Wrigley and Lowe 2002).

Both public and private decision-makers need to acknowledge that regions are not mere subunits of national economies. Previously, Clark (1989) cautioned that landscape dynamics must be understood in the context of communities' corporate, industrial, and regional investment strategies. In particular, he emphasized the impact of modern production and trading norms on markets, and the importance of economic flexibility in terms of firms' and communities' responsiveness to endogenous market shifts in terms of trends, competition, and the like. He emphasized the centrality of social relations: regional prospects may depend as much on internal interactions within communities as on external trading relationships with the rest of the world. Economically sustainable communities may be those that are flexible and innovative in the context of global economic integration. In sum:

> [A]s the global economy has become integrated, and as world economic events have penetrated even the most remote national economies, some localities have become more important than ever before as sites of enhanced flexibility and corporate competitiveness. Of course other sites, those not able to succeed in this competition for flexibility, have suffered the consequences of economic destruction (Clark 1989).

---

[3] For other interpretations of urban growth and sprawl in this volume see Mitchell (chapter 1) and Culberston et al. (chapter 3).

This argument was made about the relationship between global competitiveness and local institutional and technological innovation. More than a decade later, it is also an argument about the pricing policies of global financial institutions: flexible firms located in communities willing and able to adapt to global competition are the firms likely to attract a stock-price premium. Equally, firms that are less flexible or located in communities that resist the imperatives of global competition are likely to be discounted by global stock markets. This argument can be sustained empirically by comparing "domestic" firms in the S&P500 and the FT100 (US and UK), or by comparing national systems of corporate structure and governance (Clark and Wójcik 2007). But as we have indicated above, community cohesion is at risk in a world that can price the social fabric of what we count as community.

Pricing the Economic Landscape

For much of the 20th century, cities and regions were the domain of the public sector and private investors. Recurrent cycles of land speculation, building, and decay were sufficient to give the public sector a strong claim on the regulation of land use and its larger projects. Of course, in every city across the USA and elsewhere, histories can be written about the intimate relationships between public sector officials and private interests; indeed, not only have books been published about the nefarious and often secret deals that have transformed the urban landscape, Hollywood has maintained an abiding interest in any "bottom of the harbor" deal.[4] Private financial interests have always been implicated in the form and shape of our cities, and our arguments about the pricing of the economic landscape should not idealize the past.

We should recognize, however, that financial markets, especially those in the Anglo-American world, have become so significant compared to the available public resources over the last 25–35 years, that financial institutions are arguably the dominant players in landscape formation and reproduction. Given the geography of economic and racial inequality, many of the public resources of our inner cities have been devoted to the provision of welfare services rather than to economic development. Even in the wealthier suburbs, interjurisdictional tax competition combined with governmental fragmentation have conspired to empower private financial interests over public vision and plans for development. To take an example: if suburban shopping mall development is an issue of land development and transportation planning, it is also a financial product. More often than not, commercial

---

[4] The classic is, of course, Roman Polanski's *Chinatown* (Towne, 1974). However, there is also a vibrant academic literature, which we can hardly survey literature in this brief paper. Specific to Chicago, readers are referred to the seminal book by Gerry Suttles (1990), which captures both the intrigue and the institutional logic of such real-life stories.

centers are developed by private partnerships involving institutional investors and are bundled together in real estate investment trusts offered on public securities markets to individual and other institutional investors. Anglo-American pension funds are significant investors in such financial products.[5]

Financial institutions remain very wary of some parts of our cities, just as they are wary of investing in some kinds of land uses and services. Social housing in the inner cities is almost exclusively a public responsibility, save the significant roles played by some public sector pension funds. Even so, infrastructure provision, whether roads, rail routes, airports, water systems, or even electronic communication systems, are increasingly financial products managed by some of the world's largest financial institutions. For example, there has been considerable controversy about the role played by global institutional investors in the setting of tolls for the use of a "private" provincial highway around Toronto.[6] In effect, this road is owned and operated by financial institutions that desire a long-term risk-adjusted rate of return attractive to global investors with competing opportunities to invest in similar financial products in other cities around the world. Given that many cities and regions are starved of resources, financial institutions may be the only source of long-term investment for large-scale infrastructure projects (Clark 2000).

In effect, global financial markets are pricing our cities and regions. This has been made possible by the commodification of large units of function-related buildings and land. These units are added together or deleted where necessary to create investment products with well-defined risk-and-return profiles over defined time horizons. In the language of the industry, more often than not these are like bonds in that they promise a long-term flow of income set against an initial investment and perhaps capital preservation guarantees. Frequently, institutional investors prefer fixed-income products that can be traded with respect to both their expectations of competing financial market opportunities and their changing, albeit often unanticipated, liquidity requirements. These products rarely lock investors in; rather, lock-in must be compensated with a higher rate of return. Investors must be confident about the governance of such projects: governance systems set the relationships between investing partners, the time horizons over which relationships are to be maintained, and the incentives and penalties for performance on each and every partner. Governance systems may also set the conditions for dissolving investment partnerships in light of changing circumstances.

---

[5]To illustrate, just read the pages of the financial press. Shopping malls are important financial instruments with dedicated financial reporters, analysts, and investment managers. For example, see http://news.ft.com/cms/s/c04b4f2a-f2a3–11d8-b848–00000e2511c8.html.

[6]The Toronto story is worthy of a research program in its own right. Pitted against one another are financial institutions, the provincial government, and road users, all of which have stakes in the provision of urban transport infrastructure notwithstanding their very different economic and political interests. This is more than an issue of toll-road pricing: it has implicated the global financial community and the European Commission since one of the investment partners comes from Spain. See http://www.theglobeandmail.com/servlet/story/RTGAM.20040812.wroad0812/BNStory/National/.

Notice what is implied by this form of financial engineering. Given the importance of modern portfolio theory for institutional investors, it is inevitable that any investment in a particular urban setting is very small against the total volume of an investor's assets. Any individual investment offsets risk against other investments within that asset class, as well as by diversification within classes. To illustrate, an airport linked to an urban center by a large highway running over bridges and through tunnels using advanced electronic tolling equipment may together loom large for the functional performance of any city. Nevertheless, this bundle of integrated land uses remains relatively trivial in terms of the myriad investments held by any single global financial institution – and may be traded in a moment between financial institutions if so desired. Whereas urban infrastructure has a long life running perhaps over centuries, whatever the physical life span of their investments, financial markets may value geography on merely a quarter-to-quarter basis. Subsequently, the pricing of cities and regions in this manner may be stripped bare of commitments to local communities.

Global finance is not entirely ubiquitous or anonymous. Rather, institutional investors recognize that the economic landscape is highly differentiated in terms of risk and return; money tends to flow to known opportunities rather than less popular destinations. Just as equity markets are characterized by recurrent episodes of herd behavior and speculative bubbles, so too are investments in cities and regions (compare Shiller 2000 with Clark 2000). Moreover, there are fashions in the global investment industry that have national characteristics. For many years, UK pension funds were overwhelmingly invested in domestic and international equities, especially compared to US pension funds. The increasing role of institutional investors in urban infrastructure has been led by Australian pension funds with their service providers drawing on local partners from around the world to provide the insight and knowledge necessary to sustain such investments (Berry and Hall 2005). In this sense, finance has well-defined origins and destinations.[7] This may not mean "citizenship" in the sense of an obligation or commitment to local interests, but it may be manifested in distinctive patterns in the supply and demand for certain types of investment products.

The heart and home of finance is an important issue of political economy, particularly when economic competitiveness thrives on local commitment. This is evident in the debate over the investment policies of public sector pension funds in regional development. It also has ramifications for the roles and responsibilities of all institutional investors in the context of national systems of corporate governance and social responsibility (see Clark and Hebb 2005; Hebb and Wójcik 2005).

---

[7] The origins and destinations of finance map onto a variety of institutions and practices, being the object of considerable academic and industry comparative research (Allen and Gale 2000). Determinants of this map include the funding practices of pension funds and national systems of social security, as well as legal regimes and systems of corporate regulation and governance (La Porta R, López-de-Silanes F, Shleifer A, and Vishny R 1997; Clark 2003).

Financial Risk and Communities of Innovation

Financial institutions have also been crucial to the development of communities of innovation such as the Boston Route 128/495 corridor and Silicon Valley (in the USA) and Oxford, Cambridge, and London (in the UK). We have argued that communities are often forced to bear the risks associated with the shifting interests of financial markets, but we must recognize that in innovation risk is an essential ingredient, and innovation itself is a vital ingredient in urban futures, or even, at an extreme, national futures within a global economic environment. The trick is the management of risk. In the next section we consider the role of trust and antitrust in regulating risk in entrepreneurial communities.

Understanding how people make investment decisions in the face of *risk* and *uncertainty* has proven vital in understanding the geography and sociology of innovation. Despite casual usage, these terms are not interchangeable: here the concept of "risk" refers to situations in which decision-makers are able to assign probabilities to various potential outcomes. By contrast, under "uncertainty" decision-makers do not know the odds of potential outcomes, and in fact, are infrequently aware of the full range of outcomes that exist (Keynes 1921; Knight 1921). Rather than assuming that people use resources to best effect, our research programs assume that individuals have limited abilities to process information in the context of risk and uncertainty (Simon 1982).[8] In the case of innovation, it is extremely difficult to anticipate all possible contingencies, including technical, political, and economic considerations. Not only do the payoffs of investment extend far into the future, but also each stage of the long-range innovation process may be disrupted by unanticipated complications such as economic shocks and rival technological innovation.

As we consider both public and private equity investment, there are critical differences to consider. In publicly traded financial markets, information is ubiquitous but subject to relative pricing.[9] In contrast, within innovation communities characterized by private equity, information is less ubiquitous, and the quality of risk-related decision-making is dependent upon the translation of scarce information into knowledge. Knowledge, or the meaning and value attributed to information, is

---

[8] Our research also draws on the work of behavioral decision theorists such as Kahnemann and Tversky Kahneman D, Slovic P, and Tversky A (1982); Dawes (1988); Fischhoff, Lichtenstein, Slovic, Darby, and Keeney (1981); Loewenstein and Thaler (1989); Elster (1986); and Bazerman (1998) who integrate insights from psychology and economics to provide realistic assessments of and predictions for human judgment and decision-making.

[9] In perfect capital markets, knowledge is symmetric between buyers and sellers of capital, and expected returns are agreed upon between them. With respect to innovation activities, however, capital markets are imperfect and R & D is risky, such that firms must often rely on either their own funds or those raised through angel and venture capital private equity networks.

best considered a quasi-public good because more than one person may acquire and use it simultaneously. However the marginal cost of providing additional knowledge is rarely zero in cases involving complex scientific and technological knowledge since users must be able to understand and apply the information in order to derive benefit. Similarly, the notion that knowledge is non-excludable (or that by one person partaking of knowledge, it does not prevent others from also doing so) is questionable, as evidenced by intellectual property rights and widespread concerns for secrecy. A common argument runs that should knowledge be distributed freely, society runs the risk of dulling entrepreneurs' incentives to innovate. Because of asymmetries of information and knowledge between various decision-makers, innovation communities are subject to a host of valuation problems characterized as "principal-agent problems" (Spence and Zeckhauser 1971).

There are many different types of risk in financial markets and institutions. Figure 1 shows a layered pyramid of institutions with scope of behavior represented on the *x*-axis, and the pricing efficiency of value on the *y*-axis. At the apex of the pyramid are the Anglo-American equity markets, which have developed sophisticated third-party trading systems for evaluating and distributing risk via the pricing of offered stocks. By contrast, at the base of the pyramid are innovation institutions with often private valuation devices subject to a wide variety of judgment and behavior. Included within this category are angel and venture capital investment supporting early-stage, high-technology firms in regions such as Silicon Valley. In some cases, such as specialized markets for innovation, dense with institution-specific heterogeneous decisions, the development and sustenance of high-trust relationships are critical mechanisms used to cope with inherent risks. Given this, there may exist a simple but highly effective virtuous cycle, capable of turning communities of risk into communities of trust. These relationships have powerful recursive properties adding value within long-term innovation cycles, thereby sustaining urban growth and development.

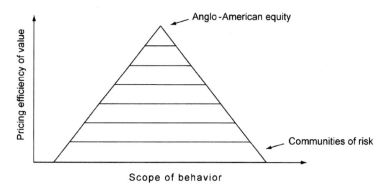

Figure 1 A pyramid of Anglo-American equity institutions [NB: The pricing efficiency of value is defined as the market's ability to return prices fully reflective of all information necessary to value a given investment.]

Critical to any consideration of how individuals and institutions cope with risk and uncertainty in investment decision-making is Spence's (1974) work on signaling. Here he discusses the role of observable actions and activities from which decision-makers draw conclusions about other individual and organizations. Recognizing that information about actions and activities may be in short supply in innovation programs, it is apparent that investors must balance the costs of searching for information against the reputations of those involved. In this sense, reputation serves as a signal. Only after commitment do investors gain fuller knowledge about the transaction already undertaken, even if not yet completed. Spence demonstrated that under certain conditions, well-informed individuals can improve their market outcomes by strategically signaling information about their prospects and reputations to those who know less.

How risky is investment in innovation? The probability of achieving success from any given technological endeavor undertaken is approximately 0.57. Given technical success, imagine then that the probability of realizing commercial success is 0.65. Given commercial success, the likely probability of financial success is 0.74. While taken individually, each is manageable; however, taken together, the probability of financial success when pursuing innovative activity is only 0.27, about 1 out of every 4 projects (Cohen 1996). Consequently, issues of path dependency, escalation of commitment, and the honoring of sunk costs, are often deeply entwined with decision-making. To manage these risks, firms, especially large ones, benefit from portfolio diversification approaches to better manage aggregate risk-return tradeoffs. In doing so, they may consider sequential approaches to projects, informed by updated information and a willingness to reconsider continuing with a project at each and every point within the development process. Firms may also pursue multiple approaches or parallel paths to achieve the same technical objective – that is, success.

Trust and Antitrust

A great deal has been written in recent times about the significance of trust in market relationships. There are now entire branches within the social sciences devoted to exploring the role of trust in sustaining bilateral transactions, underlining the importance of the institution for long-term development, if not its current status in short-term market exchange. A great deal has also been written about the decline of trust in American communities, documenting the apparent increase of anonymity in everyday experience, as well as the sense of isolation that goes with estrangement from community values and norms. In a previous section, we commented on the significance of this literature, arguing that if true, the decline of trust in modern American society carries with it implications from global economic integration all the way down to our local urban landscapes. Here, we carry through the contrast already drawn between financial products available in the market and the financial investments in communities of innovation.

Many financial products offered and traded through public securities markets are deliberately designed to ensure that buyers and sellers do not require more information than market signals of price, volume traded, and rate of return. Indeed, it could be argued that one of the great virtues of public markets is the fact that traders, whatever their location, may trade in and out of those markets free from the need to be close to the sources of knowledge, whether just gossip or detailed assessments of underlying economic and social relationships. Of course, traders can lose money if they do not pay attention to the price, volume traded, and apparent unexplained shifts in market pricing. These variables and others may, in fact, reflect information not available to all market participants but which are nevertheless channeled back through the market to signal changed expectations and therefore variations in the relative value of one product versus another. All being well, with the rapid transmission of such information into and throughout markets, market pricing should be sufficient for traders to proceed with their investment strategies.

In other words, trust is not a particularly important or, indeed, relevant variable in these kinds of trading relationships. In response, it might be argued that trust is nevertheless important in the execution of investment strategies, given that so many market agents depend on others for specialized financial services. However, even here it is hard to imagine that experienced market traders would place trust before well-calibrated contractual relationships with clearly specified incentives and punishments for performance. Indeed, it could be argued that over the last decade or so it has become apparent that contract is the single most important private governing mechanism in the market for financial services: long-term trust relationships are neither robust enough nor have the respect of market agents to withstand short-term opportunism. We would argue that this is true of most equity and bond products in Anglo-American security markets, whether those products have as their underlying focus expectations about corporate value or expectations about long-term urban value as in real estate investment trusts.

One qualification to be offered against this argument is the fact that Anglo-American markets are vulnerable to insider trading and market manipulation that may take advantage of the unwary and inexperienced trader. The scandals of corporate governance, coming at the end of the technology, media, and telecommunications (TMT) bubble are evidence enough of the opportunities for subversion of market trading processes, even if these scandals had the greatest effects on noninstitutional traders. Indeed, large institutional investors have come to realize that increased market volatility associated with inexperienced and under-resourced traders represent opportunities for increasing the short-term rate of return by traders with sufficient resources and acumen. Perhaps a more important (although maybe less relevant) qualification to our argument relates to other countries' securities markets being less efficient than Anglo-American markets.[10] In the largest continental

---

[10] To illustrate the significance of this point, it is worth reminding the reader that over the 1990s passive index-based equity investment products became very important in the Anglo-American investment management industry. By contrast, given the relative inefficiency of continental European markets and the significance of insider knowledge in driving stock market prices, such passive investment strategies were clearly a losing game. Active management was one response, even amongst the largest Anglo-American portfolio managers such as Fidelity (Clark and Wójcik 2007).

European markets, insider knowledge is an essential ingredient in any trading strategy, just as long-term relationships are important in assessing the significance of market signals. Whether these relationships are trust relationships is debatable. Nonetheless, it is clear that they must have continuity and be mutually beneficial to ensure that any long-term trading strategy is robust enough to deal with the knowledge of other better-informed investors outside the immediate circle of trading relationships.[11]

By contrast, investment in innovation depends a great deal upon trust relationships, just as it depends on instruments of governance such as contract and negotiation. As noted above, these types of investments are almost always subject to high levels of risk and uncertainty with time horizons stretching over years, rather than mere months or days. Furthermore, it is apparent from our research on the innovation investment process that investors are not always equal: whereas in public markets traders can buy and sell offered stock, investors in the innovation process rarely have the chance to trade in and out of opportunities. Rather, these types of investors may be offered the opportunity to invest in a partnership subject to rules and obligations that require them to lock-in their investments over extended periods without protection of exit clauses that could allow them to flee a dynamic (and potentially volatile) situation.[12] Moreover, there appears to be a well understood hierarchy of opportunities for investment such that those partnerships with established reputations of performance might select their partners, whereas those without such well-established reputations have less ability to discriminate between investors. In effect, private partnerships are clubs just as much as they are investments. Relationships matter a great deal in this environment.

So far, we have set the basic parameters of the investment process in innovation. We also want to argue, however, that where this investment process takes place can be extremely important, in that being a member of an investment community is one way of fostering relationships with other investors to gain access to higher-quality partnerships and investment opportunities. To put the argument crudely, assume that established and highly reputable partnerships have the power to discriminate between well-known local investors and out-of-towners who fly in carting a great deal of money but without the personal relationships that can vouch for their trustworthiness. At the peak of the TMT bubble, this was exactly the situation in many centers of innovation including Silicon Valley, Boston, Oxford, and Cambridge. Money talks. And the biggest institutional investors had considerable leverage by virtue of the money they carried. Nevertheless, their commitment was unknown,

---

[11] We should be clear, however, about the relationship between trust, contract, and related governance mechanisms. Given the ubiquity of contract in Anglo-American economies and financial services, it is often assumed that it is an accessible and responsive institution for those harmed by the less than agreed performance of others. This much is implied by La Porta, López-de-Silanes, Shleifer, and Vishny (1997), comparing the legal systems relevant to financial issues of various countries.

[12] For many, especially those caught up in long-term partnerships, to seek enforcement of contract in the courts would be effectively to terminate under duress their relationship. Therefore, trust carries a significant burden of responsibility in sustaining long-term financial relationships even if in the shadow cast by contract (Hardin 1996).

and the fact that they were, more often than not, employees rather than principals gave rise to doubts about their trustworthiness. At the margin, instruments of trust common to private partnerships were at odds with the instruments of contract common to financial markets.

In our research, we have demonstrated that trust is an essential element in the governance of partnerships for innovation. Moreover, it has been shown that the depth and resonance of trust varies considerably between communities and between potential partners according to their social, ethnic, and gender identities (Babcock-Lumish 2004). Take Boston and the surrounding Route 128 region in the USA, and in the UK, London, and its nearby innovation centers including Oxford and Cambridge. Through semi-structured interviews with approximately 120 individuals representing roles, functions, and vantage points throughout the entrepreneurial investment clusters, relationships were mapped using UCINet, Netdraw, and Pajek[13] software packages. Using single-variable matrices to determine association between subjects by location, university, organization, employer/deal, and demographics, a series of networks maps were produced, demonstrating the relative openness or closeness of each community. Through this analysis, we gain a sense of the strength of connections within the communities, and perform a variety of statistical tests on the networks, to assess the nature of the "ties that bind."

As seen in Figure 2, both the Boston (left) and London (right) clusters are tightly connected by a veritable spider web of associations, with the two intermeshed and connected by separate groups of individuals. Crossover between the clusters appears

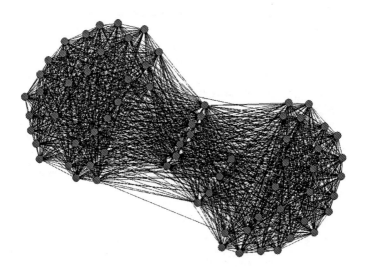

Figure 2 Boston and London innovation clusters, scaled matrix. (*Source*: Netdraw *Left*: Boston; *Right*: London.)

---

[13] Quite appropriately, Pajek means "spider" in Slovenian.

to be high, with many in each community having lived, worked, and studied in both countries and maintaining network ties in each.

Upon increasing the rigor required for two individuals to be considered associated, we are able to remove some of the noise in the data to explore the two separate clusters' internal dynamics. In Figure 3, the USA and UK communities are more clearly visible. Increasing the requirements for association further, the clusters are linked via two highly connected individuals, one in Boston, and one in London. The clusters themselves are both fairly dense; however, the UK cluster is both denser (99.0% compared to 81.6%) and more centralized (86.9 compared to 77.0), and the US cluster's connections are more dispersed (14.3 compared to 23.4) (see Table 1). To explain, in-group relations are more important to the UK cluster

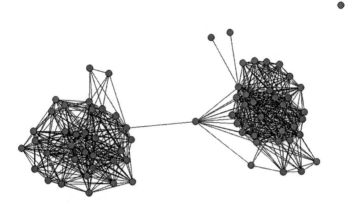

Figure 3 Boston and London innovation clusters, binary matrix with cut-off = 2. (*Source*: Netdraw *Left*: Boston; *Right*: London.)

Table 1 Density[14] of Boston and London clusters, cut-off = 2

Descriptive statistics		
	UK	US
Mean	99.0	81.6
Standard deviation	14.3	23.4
Variance	203.2	547.2
Minimum	67	0
Maximum	126	107
Network centralization[15]	86.9	77.0
Density/average value within blocks	3.0	2.6

---

[14] These measures of density represent the proportion of all potential ties that are actually present within the network.

[15] Centralization refers to the degree of inequality or variance within a given network as a percentage of that which would exist in a perfectly dispersed network of identical size. That is, a network with a higher measure of centralization would be characterized by a substantial amount of concentration and the power of individual actors varying rather substantially, such that position would be distributed disproportionately within the network.

than the US cluster, and information flows more widely and more equally in the American than the British.

By increasing the stringency of the score required for association further, the clusters become distinct from each other, as is evidenced in Figure 4. Again, the American cluster remains fairly widely dispersed, but the British one clusters relatively neatly by geography, into Cambridge, Oxford, and London cliques, from top to bottom. Finally, in Figure 5, the clusters break down; however, not by geography but by university affiliation and demographics as the dominant indicators. Remaining are a Cambridge clique characterized by white Protestant men, a combined Oxford–London clique also characterized by white Protestant men, a Harvard clique of white Jewish men, a tie between two white Protestant women with dual school ties, and interestingly, two separate MIT cliques, one of Scandinavian men and one of Jewish men.

Implications for how open or closed then these networks may be for entrepreneurial investment and high-risk or high-uncertainty transactions relate certainly to entry opportunities with respect to fundraising, market trend forecasting and analysis, deal sourcing, access to staged financing, networking, and partnering. And certainly, if one surmounts barriers to entry, there remain questions of exit opportunities. As we consider the importance of knowledge flows and learning throughout institutional investment communities, relationship economic geography – and the very nature of trustworthiness looms large.

Trust relationships are social relationships subject to all the qualities used by people to distinguish themselves one from one another and the qualities used by people to judge with whom they will find affinity rather than difference. Trust

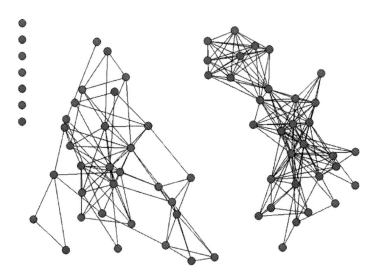

Figure 4 Boston and London innovation clusters, binary matrix with cut-off = 3 (*Source*: Netdraw *Left*: Boston; *Upper Right*: Cambridge; *Middle Right*: Oxford; *Lower Right:* London.)

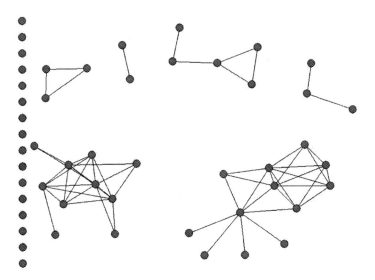

Figure 5 Boston and London innovation clusters, binary matrix with cut-off = 4. (*Source*: Netdraw *Upper Row, from Left*: 3 Scandinavian MIT men, 2 white Protestant Harvard-MIT women, 5 Jewish MIT men, 3 white Protestant Cambridge men; *Lower Row, from Right*: 10 Jewish Harvard men; 12 white Protestant Oxford–London men.)

relationships are also long-term relationships rather than short-term bilateral market transactions. In other words, they are relationships that cover an extended sequence of transactions rather than being limited and defined by only one transaction. They also include the possibility of an extended series of transactions with other people as introductions are made and networks expanded. Trust relationships are also intensive social relationships that depend upon interaction time and time again. Being part of the networks and social relationships that define that community are vital mechanisms for building the quality and quantity of interaction necessary to earn a reputation for trustworthiness -- or not.

Flying in and out of an established trading community is hardly a recipe for acquiring entry to the most exclusive clubs, much as it is an unlikely strategy for gaining access to the most reputable investment partnerships.[16] At the same time, reputation is always mediated by the realization that the entry ticket to any club is not only the ability to pay the entrance fee, but also the ability to maintain membership

---

[16] At investment management conferences over the late 1990s, it became commonplace to hear stories of the "fly-in, fly-out" opportunism of (young) global institutional investors as if (older) local venture capitalists were comparative amateurs not withstanding their noted significance as "gatekeepers" to better deals with better opportunities. As their significance increased through the TMT bubble, institutional investors used their leverage to decrease the payoff time horizon and reorient the terms of payoff to the IPO market. In effect, institutional investors sought to shift trust relationships to market relationships, exploiting the former on behalf of the latter.

162 T.L. Babcock-Lumish and G.L. Clark

in the face of changing fortunes. A number of successful interventions by institutional investors into these clubs over the 1990s were made possible, in part, by their association with individuals with demonstrable reputations in venture capital investment. After the collapse of the TMT bubble, and after the wholesale retreat of the institutional investment industry from tech-stock speculation, trust and reputation regained their significance as crucial tests of entry to investment partnerships. In a curious way, the TMT bubble reinforced the role and significance of community relationships: they became not only a means of entry to investment, but also a means of managing the crisis of confidence in technological innovation.

Trust relationships were shown to be resilient even as investment plans failed. Our research has shown that when an investment fails due to one party's inability to follow through on their commitments, it is important to differentiate between causes of failure. If the setback represented a product of exogenous *circumstance*, then partners may excuse the incident and proceed as partners. Further, when a frustrated party feels there was equality of either sacrifice or loss between partners, as per the alignment of incentives, disappointments may be pardoned. However, should the problem be a matter of *intention* or *effort*, this could represent a breakdown of the trust relationship. This is not to say that the relationship is automatically ended, but rather, a warning signal is noted. More often than not, partners are, at least in the short run, dependent upon each other. However, should betrayal be repeated or be especially egregious, behavior is eventually punished with both termination of the partnership and damage to reputation. The management of risk represents a complicated dance among shifting partners, but one that is essential for understanding the dynamism and effectiveness of innovation systems.

Implications and Conclusions

Financial markets can be found at all scales of economic activity and social life. They can be found in neighborhoods as the mechanisms for financing housing mortgages as well as for the provision of urban infrastructure such as roads, water, and sewerage systems. In fact, the use of municipal bonds to finance the provision of urban infrastructure is one of the most remarkable features of American cities when compared with much of the developed Western world. Housing mortgages are bundled together, created as investment products, and distributed amongst institutional investors seeking long-term investments promising a fair amount of certainty, if not spectacular rates of return. Likewise, municipal bonds are traded in the market: the "urban" becomes a product or commodity rather than a particular place. Our point here is simple: urban life can be seen as a traded financial product to which we owe little in terms of commitment or loyalty compared to what we desire via a risk-adjusted rate of return.

At the same time, financial markets are global. They are the switching points between national and regional systems of accumulation and innovation. They price expectations of future growth, and discount the costs of social structure and community life where they affect a warranted rate of return. At the margin, global financial markets attribute a price to local prospects even if that price is arbitrary and capricious, given acknowledged difficulties in finding a reliable reference point for valuing countries' currencies (Clark and Thrift 2005). At both local and global levels, financial markets are moments of short-term pricing stripped bare of the deeply-rooted social norms and customs in the cultures and relationships of the specific communities in which they operate. On the other hand, this is a virtue of efficient financial markets: their disembodied nature, with reliance on market prices, the volume of trading, and expectations, allow for the pooling of financial resources in ways not possible if we attribute a heart and home to each and every tranche of money. While it is sometimes fashionable to decry this characteristic of financial markets, it has given middle-class suburbs remarkable value for money.

We have also suggested that financial markets are hardly the most appropriate mechanisms for spreading financial resources evenly across a landscape. The bundling together of housing mortgages and the design of real estate investment trusts rely upon picking from the landscape *sets of opportunities* rather than an *entire opportunity set*. That is to say, these kinds of financial products are deliberately designed to reduce the risks of being exposed to troubled neighborhoods and impoverished municipalities in order to sustain both short-and long-term rates of return attractive to risk-averse investors. Just as there are highly valued communities on this score, there are many others that are virtual financial deserts. In this context, it is not surprising that state and national governments have sought to mitigate the inherent tendencies of financial flight by anchoring some banking institutions in the communities from which they derive their financial assets. If this is the mandate apparent in the Community Reinvestment Act, it is not found in the practice of mutual funds and the like.

In our view, the emerging map of financial opportunities and resources, whether local, regional, national or global in scale, will be hotly contested for its apparent asymmetries and inequalities. In effect, financial markets operate as gigantic vacuum cleaners that suck small dispersed pools of financial assets into central collection points such as financial institutions that then distribute them to service providers supplying financial instruments in markets. Characteristically, institutions profit when they are able to commingle larger and larger tranches of financial assets, thereby reaping economies of scale and the benefits of product complementarities. The financial sector is an industry, like many others, in which firms are subject to issues of scale, scope, and competitiveness. Inevitably, competition amongst financial institutions drives out small-scale investment opportunities, just as it drives out opportunities with comparatively low rates of risk-adjusted return. Not surprisingly, financial institutions are likely to blank out whole segments of urban life and even entire nation-states. In this context, new institutional forms of urban investment and new models of government regulation are two important responses, as evidenced by one of our research programs sponsored by the Rockefeller Foundation and the Ford Foundation.

We should also recognize, however, that financial institutions have come to appreciate the value of specific communities of innovation quite differently from how they treat the urban realm as a traded financial product. In this case, communities of innovation may be the leading edge of long-term economic transformation and effect profound changes in the structure of financial markets themselves. We caught a glimpse of this phenomenon through the 1990s where a few centers of innovation with distinctive modes of internal organization and compensation drove financial market expectations practically to the point of hysteria (Shiller 2000). Even if it is now deemed to have been a most remarkable instance of financial market specula-tion, on par with the Amsterdam tulip bubble centuries ago, the TMT bubble never-theless represents an important story of how the urban realm may drive the financial system, rather than the other way around. It is an instance whereby profound differ-ences in the cultures of financial markets (antitrust) and communities of innovation (trust) became reference points for pricing the future of technological change. If financial markets did not fully understand the role and significance of trust in the innovation process, analysts were willing to suspend judgment in the expectation that community-based trust relationships would remake capitalism itself.

In a curious way, the culture of trust so important to innovation communities has become a reference point for American society at large. Being preoccupied with the fragility of trust in everyday life and the realization that contract and conflict, rather than trust and trustworthiness are the glue binding together modern economies, American society has looked to centers of innovation to both recapture the past and represent the future. If a romantic vision, it was no less a vision shared by many inside and outside financial markets. How else can we explain, for example, the fact that so many individuals became active investors in the technology bubble?

References

Allen F and Gale D (2000) *Comparing Financial Systems*. MIT Press, Cambridge, MA

AmericanExpress (2003) Daily Headlines Archive – December 2003, vol. 2004

Babcock-Lumish TL (2003) Trust and antitrust in innovation investment communities: reconsidering moral sentiments. University of Oxford School of Geography and the Environment Working Paper Series WPG 04–06: 1–38

Babcock-Lumish TL (2004) The dynamics of innovation investment communities: the spatial structure of networks and relationships. University of Oxford School of Geography and the Environment Working Paper Series WPG 04–17: 1–39

Bazerman MH (1998) *Judgment in Managerial Decision Making*. Wiley, New York

BLS (2004) Occupational employment projections to 2012. *Monthly Labor Review* http://www.bls.gov/opub/mlr/2004/02/art5full.pdf (checked 9 April 2007)

CEA (2001) *The Economic Report of the President*. The Executive Office of the President, Washington, DC

Clark GL (1989) US regional transformation in the context of international economic compe-tition. In Rodwin L and Sazanami H (eds) *Deindustrialization and Regional Economic Transformation*. Unwin Hyman, London, pp 296–302

Clark GL (2000) *Pension Fund Capitalism*. Oxford University Press, Oxford

Clark GL (2003) *European Pensions and Global Finance*. Oxford University Press, Oxford

Clark GL (2004) Money flows like mercury: the geography of global finance. *Geografiska Annaler B* 87: 99–112

Clark GL, Feldman MP, and Gertler MS (2000) *The Oxford Handbook of Economic Geography*. Oxford University Press, Oxford

Clark GL and Hebb T (2005) Why do they care? The market for corporate global responsibility and the role of institutional investors. *Environment and Planning A* 37: 2015–2031

Clark GL and Thrift N (2005) The return of bureaucracy: managing dispersed knowledge in global finance. In Cetina KK and Preda A (eds) *The Sociology of Financial Markets*. Oxford University Press, Oxford, pp. 229–249

Clark GL and Wójcik D (2007) *The Geography of Finance*. Oxford University Press, Oxford

Cohen WM (1996) *The Economics of Technological Change*. Pittsburgh, PA

Dawes RM (1988) *Rational Choice in an Uncertain World*. Harcourt Brace Jovanovich, New York

Elster J (1986) *Rational Choice*. Basil Blackwell, Oxford

Fischhoff B, Lichtenstein S, Slovic P, Darby S, and Keeney R (1981) *Acceptable Risk*. Cambridge University Press, New York

Florida R (2002) *The Rise of the Creative Class: And How It's Transforming Work, Leisure, Community and Everyday Life*. Basic Books, New York

Florida R and Tinagli I (2004) *Europe in the Creative Age*. Demos, London

Florini, A. (2003) *The Coming Democracy: New Rules for Running a New World*. Island Press, Washington, DC

Galison P (2000) Einsteins's clocks: the place of time. *Critical Inquiry* 26: 355–389

Robert Half International (2004) Hot jobs report. www.rhi.com

Hardin R (1996) Trustworthiness. *Ethics* 107: 26–42

Hebb T and Wójcik D (2005) Global standards and emerging markets: the institutional investment value chain and CalPERS' investment strategy. *Environment and Planning A* 37: 1955–1974

IOM (2003) *Migration in a Globalized World*. International Organization for Migration, Geneva, IL

ITU (2004) The cost of international telephone calls, vol. 2004. International Telecommunication Union

Jameson F (1997) Culture and finance capital. *Critical Inquiry* 24: 246–265

Kahneman D, Slovic P, and Tversky A (1982) *Judgment under Uncertainty: Heuristics and Biases*. Cambridge University Press, Cambridge

Keynes JM (1921) *A Treatise on Probability*. Macmillan, London

Knight FH (1921) *Risk, Uncertainty and Profit*. Houghton Mifflin, Boston, MA

La Porta R, López-de-Silanes F, Shleifer A, and Vishny R (1997) Legal determinants of external finance. *Journal of Finance* 52(3): 1131–1150.

Loewenstein G and Thaler RH (1989) Intertemporal choice. *Journal of Economic Perspectives* 3: 197–201

Metz D (2004) Human mobility and transport policy. *Ingenia* 18: 37–42

Niessen J (2002) International mobility in a globalising world. Paper presented at ACP-EU Joint Parliamentary Assembly Workshop on Migration and Development. Capetown, March 20

Putnam RD (2000) *Bowling Alone: The Collapse and Revival of American Community*. Simon & Schuster, New York; London

Saxenian A (1999) *Silicon Valley's New Immigrant Entrepreneurs*. Public Policy Institute of California, San Francisco, CA

Shiller R (2000) *Irrational Exuberance*. Princeton University Press, Princeton, NJ

Simon HA (1982) *Models of Bounded Rationality*. MIT Press, Cambridge, MA; London

Slaughter A-M (2004) *A New World Order*. Princeton University Press, Princeton, NJ

Spence AM (1974) *Market Signaling: Informational Transfer in Hiring and Related Screening Processes*. Harvard University Press, Cambridge, MA

Spence AM and Zeckhauser RJ (1971) Insurance, information and individual action. *American Economic Review* 61: 380–387

Stiglitz JE (2002) *Globalization and Its Discontents*. W.W. Norton, New York
Suttles GD (1990) *The Man-Made City: The Land-Use Confidence Game in Chicago*. University of Chicago Press, Chicago; London
Towne R (1974) Chinatown. In: Polanski R (ed) *Paramount Pictures*, Hollywood
Wrigley N and Lowe MS (2002) *Reading Retail: A Geographical Perspective on Retailing and Consumption Spaces*. Arnold, New York

Part III
Integrative Landscape Change

Millennium Park, Chicago (Photo: jlw)

Prairie Crossing Community development in the northwest suburbs of Chicago (Photo: jlw)

Chapter 8
The Globalized Landscape: Rural Landscape Change and Policy in the United States and European Union

J.I. Nassauer and D.M. Wascher

Introduction

While some rural areas draw increasing populations to their landscape amenities and some are changed by the long reach of metropolitan sprawl, agriculture defines, and dominates rural landscapes. Amenity characteristics and ecological services of many rural landscapes occur in the context of agricultural economies. As these economies respond to international trade, international policy, notably policies of the World Trade Organization (WTO), is increasingly affecting rural landscape change. The USA and the European Union (EU), partners as well as independent players in global trade, and agriculture, employ comparable but distinct policies to strengthen both the economic competitiveness of agriculture and the sustainability of rural livelihoods and landscape management. Pushed by WTO mandates, both the EU and USA recently have given a higher profile to agricultural policy with explicit environmental goals, so-called agri-environmental policy, because it may achieve public benefits without distorting trade. This chapter compares the intent, mechanisms, and landscape effects of the different conservation and agri-environmental policies of the USA and EU, and suggests that international trade policy could drive planning for future agricultural landscapes that provide enhanced amenity and ecological values.

Agriculture and Subsidies in the USA and EU

Both American and European agricultural landscapes are increasingly affected by world trade policy, which addresses international market access and affects environmental quality as well as social equity across the globe (Jongman 1996; Hart and Babcock 2002; Hanrahan and Zinn 2005). While similar climates, economies, and technologies might be expected to create similarities in the agricultural landscapes of the USA and Europe, differences in cultural history and agri-environmental policies have led to instructive differences in recent agricultural landscape change.

J.L. Wescoat, Jr. and D.M. Johnston (eds.), *Political Economies of Landscape Change.*
© Springer 2008

Table 1 Comparison of farm structural and economic characteristics between the United States and the European Union (EU-25) (Baylis et al. 2004; Eurostat 2006)

	US	EU
GDP from agriculture	1.5%	1.8%
Employment	2%	4.5%
Number of farms	2.2 million	9.9 million
Average farm size	396 acres	48 acres

Agricultural policy affects vast areas of both the USA and Europe, with agriculture occupying more than one third of the land area of both the continental USA and Europe, and farmers are highly dependent on government policy to stabilize their incomes in both the USA and EU (Mohanty and Kaus 1999; Feng 2002). However, the EU-25 retains about 4.5% of its population in farming on about 9.9 million farms, while the USA has only 2% farmers and about 2 million farms (Baylis et al. 2004). Most strikingly, the average size of American farms is about 8 times larger than in Europe (Table 1). In area the EU-25 is less than half the size (0.98 billion acres) of the USA, where 60% of the 2.2 billion acre total land area is privately owned (EEA 2004a, Heimlich 2003). Including pasture and rangeland, farmers manage the landscape and environmental benefits of more than one third of the total US land area, and nearly half of the EU-25. Considering area alone, the potential environmental benefits or degradation attributable to agricultural landscape management are apparent.

World Trade and Agricultural Policy in the USA and EU

Since the formation of the WTO in 1994, the USA and the EU have moved closer to comparable agricultural trade policies, and WTO mandates are powerful drivers to make their policies even more comparable. Within this context, differences in recent agricultural policy of the USA and EU may allow us to anticipate possible landscape effects of possible future policies.

Past agricultural policy in both the USA and EU has been dominated by payments to landowners or farmers based on the amount of land in production or the amount of commodities produced. These policies encouraged increased production of agricultural commodities (Babcock 2002) and had the unintended negative consequences of overproduction of some commodities (Babcock 1999; Moyer and Josling 2002), concentration of subsidies among larger farmers and farm landowners (Babcock 2001; Roberts and Key 2003; Hoppe and Banker 2006), environmental degradation (Runge 1996; Babcock et al. 2001; Claassen et al. 2001; Tilman et al. 2001; Gagnon et al. 2004; Nassauer et al. 2007), and loss of agricultural markets for Third World nations (Babcock et al. 2001; Babcock 2002; Beghin 2002).

In an effort to better address and monitor the different effects of agricultural policies, the WTO presented the concept of classifying them as "amber box", "blue box," or "green box" (Claassen et al. 2001; Hart and Babcock 2002; Moyer and Josling 2002; Womach et al. 2006):

- "Amber box" policies are recognized as market price distorting, and consequently, such policies are limited to a reduced percentage of past expenditures (80% of 1986–1988 for the USA) (Hart and Babcock 2002).
- "Blue box" refers to exceptional, specified policies. They provide direct payments to farmers or farm landowners based on land area in production or commodity production during a past baseline period (85% of 1986–1988 for the USA) (Hart and Babcock 2002; USDA NRCS 2006).
- "Green box" policies are understood to have little or no market distortion effects. Their aims can include environmental benefits from agricultural landscapes that the market alone may not provide, like clean water, habitat biodiversity, or countryside aesthetic quality (Claassen et al. 2001). Green box policies also can include decoupled income support payments to farmers, natural disaster relief, producer or resource retirement programs, and domestic food aid, as well as other activities (Hart and Babcock 2002).

Policies in all boxes aim to provide income support for farmers (Hill 1999; Mohanty and Kaus 1999; Babcock et al. 2001; Feng 2002). In the 30 developed member nations of the Organization for Economic Cooperation and Development (OECD), amber and blue box output-based support and input subsidies made up 76% of support to farmers in 2002 – down from 90% in 1986–1988 – but still a very high proportion. This output-based support varies dramatically among OECD nations – from less than 5% in New Zealand and Australia – to more than 60% in Japan and Norway. As of 2002, both the USA and EU provided a high proportion of average farmer income as amber and blue box support, with wide variation among nations, states, and regions in this average.

In order to reduce policy effects on international markets for agricultural products, the OECD nations agreed to an agricultural policy reform agenda that included direct support for "green box" public benefits, like a pleasing countryside or ecological quality (OECD 2003). The OECD determined that policy that directly targeted environmental benefits would be more likely to avoid these negative consequences and be more economical in achieving adequate farmer incomes as well as broader public benefits.

As green box policies address the environmental impacts of agriculture (Claassen et al. 2001; USDA NRCS 2006), they undoubtedly will promote new trends in landscape change. What future agricultural landscapes might be the result? How might future change compare with the trajectory of rural landscape change in the recent past? Answers to these questions will depend in large part on the evolution of international trade negotiations and on the particular policies OECD nations choose in order to conform with trade mandates.

Policy Effects on Farm Income and Land Management Choices in the USA and EU

European agricultural enterprises and practices vary widely among and within Member States – from large-scale, highly intensive, and specialized commercial holdings to subsistence farming using traditional practices with varying impacts on the environment and landscape. Dramatically different from the USA, expenditures to implement the Common Agricultural Policy (CAP) account for more than 50% of the total EU budget. The CAP is clearly one of the key driving forces of landscape change in Europe. Agriculture is very important for the 10 new EU Member States and three candidate countries in 2005. The large areas of farmland of high nature value in these countries require attention and protection to ensure that they are not damaged or lost through intensification or abandonment as these countries adapt to EU policies and more open markets (EEA 2004b).

In the EU, net agricultural subsidies to the EU-15 nations in 2000–2003 averaged: 39% of total income (LEI 2004). In the USA, federal expenditure for agricultural programs have ranged from about $23.5 billion in 2000 to $12 billion in 2002 and back up to $23 billion in 2005 – averaging about $17.5 billion from 2000–2005 and net federal government transactions averaged about 20% of net farm income from 2001–2005 (USDA ERS 2004; Hoppe and Banker 2006). However, in both the EU and the USA, there are great regional differences in the degree to which government payments subsidize farm income.

While some states of the USA net a large subsidy to farm income, others receive a negative net federal agricultural subsidy – contributing more in federal tax than is received in benefits. For example, during 2001–2002, net federal government transactions averaged about 42% of net farm income in Iowa, where corn, soybeans, and hog production were the leading commodities, and about 81% of net farm income in Montana, where wheat and cattle production were the leading commodities. However, in Florida, a state that specializes in nursery crops and oranges, net federal transactions averaged as negative during those years – with Florida farmers, on the average, receiving less federal subsidy than was paid as federal tax. In North Carolina, where the commodities that accounted for the largest value were hogs and broiler chickens, net federal transactions averaged about 7% of net farm income (USDA 2002). Reflecting their different use of federal agricultural subsidies, the agricultural landscapes of Florida and North Carolina might change relatively little under different future federal agriculture policies, but Iowa and Montana could change dramatically.

In the EU in 2003, only farmers in Austria, Finland, and Sweden received subsidies to their incomes from government agricultural subsidies in a proportion similar to Montana (81%). Comparable to the average subsidy to Iowa farmers (42%), subsidies made up more than 40% of income for farmers in the Slovak Republic, Slovenia, the Czech Republic, the UK, France, Luxembourg, Germany, and Denmark (LEI 2004).

Agri-environmental Measures in EU Policy

Agri-environmental measures are central to green box strategies for supporting farming (Claassen et al. 2001; Hanrahan and Zinn 2005). However, the evolution and implementation of these policies differs considerably between the USA and EU. Since the early 1990s, the EU has shifted its production-oriented subsidies toward income support payments, and more rural development measures have been introduced, including agri-environment schemes and support for less-favored areas (Figure 1). These help to fund the protection of farmlands with high nature value and cultural landscapes. The share of the rural development budget in total CAP spending has risen slowly since 1991, from 9% between 1991 and 1993 to 13% in 2000–2002. Some 30–40% of rural development funding is used for agri-environment schemes, but levels of spending vary widely between countries. More than 70% of farming area in Finland and Austria is covered by agri-environmental schemes compared with only about 5% of the farming area in Spain and Greece. Leading among the agri-environmental measures (covered under EC regulation 2078/92) are those intended to produce environmental benefits, including landscape amenity (Table 2). Following the 1992 reforms of the CAP, expenditures for agri-environmental measures were allowed to rise in response to adoption of relevant schemes by EU member states (EEA 2004a).

In the EU, agri-environmental measures are increasingly financed by the Rural Development Fund (EARDF) which amounts currently to about 22% of the total CAP budget. Interestingly, EU Member States make use of the flexibility that is being offered by the EU and are investing more than the compulsory 25% of these

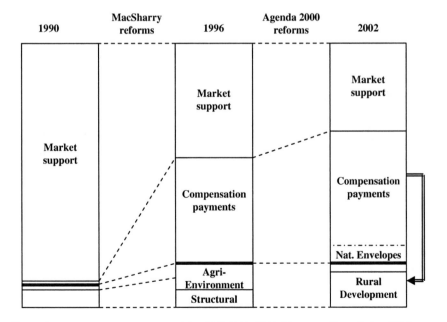

Figure 1 The changing architecture of the CAP 1990–2002 (European Commission 2004)

Table 2 List of agri-environmental measures in national programs targeting landscape conservation approved under Regulation 2078/92 (European Commission 1998)

Undertaking type	Subclassification	Environmental elements				
		Air	Biodiversity	Landscape	Soil & land	Water
Landscape conservation (whole fields)	Prevent topographical changes		B	L		
	Use sloped land		B	L	S	
	Maintain terracing		B	L	S	W
	Create new terracing		B	L	S	W
	Undertake works to cause flooding	A	B	L	S	W
	Raise water table	A	B	L	S	W
	Cause land to flood	A	B	L	S	W
	Cause seasonal flooding	A	B	L	S	W
	Prevent new drainage	A	B	L	S	W
	Reduce drainage efficiency	A	B	L	S	W
	Restrictions on works in soil or rocks		B	L	S	
	Set-aside: creation of biotopes		B	L	S	W
	Set-aside: protection of water quality			L	S	W
	Set-aside: land management			L	S	W
	Maintain abandoned farmland	A	B	L	S	
	Re-farm abandoned land		B	L	S	
(field margins)	Create unsprayed strips		B	L		W
	Maintain unsprayed strips		B	L		W
	Create uncultivated/buffer strips		B	L		W
	Maintain uncultivated/buffer strips		B	L		W
	Create beetle banks		B	L		W
	Maintain beetle banks		B	L		W
	Create stone walls/fences		B	L		
	Maintain stone walls/fences		B	L		
	Create hedgerows		B	L		

	A	B	S	L
Maintain hedgerows		B		L
Create banks		B	S	L
Maintain banks		B	S	L
Create ponds, scrapes, pits		B		L
Maintain ponds, scrapes, pits		B		L
Create biotope zones		B		L
Maintain biotope zones		B		L
Regeneration of farm woodlands		B		L
(trees) Maintain unused woodland	A			L
Maintain farm woodlands		B		L
Use grazing to maintain fire breaks				L
Maintain single trees		B		L
Pollarding and pruning		B		L
(other) Other conservation activities				L

funds for Axis 2 on "Environment and Land Management" which includes agri-environmental measures, Natura 2000 and other environmental targets. Agenda 2000 of the CAP commits few additional resources directly for rural development, and largely decouples farmer landowner payments from production. However, cross-compliance requirements will apply to direct income payments, which constitute the largest proportion of CAP payments. The final agreement on the EU's Mid-Term Review (Commission of the European Communities 2002) included new arrangements for cross-compliance requiring farmers who receive CAP direct income payments to respect a set of statutory management requirements to meet good agricultural and environmental conditions. Cross-compliance was to be phased in for all Member States by 2007. For instance, Member States were required to maintain the area that was under permanent pasture from December 31, 2001. The regulations allowed exceptions only in justified circumstances, and only if the Member State takes action to prevent any significant decrease in its total permanent pasture. This "no net loss" approach allowed Member States to continue to encourage conversion to arable land under certain agri-environment schemes for specified environmental and/or nature conservation benefits (Institute for European Environmental Policy 2003a). A minimum of 25% of the national envelope has to be spent on Environment and Land Management (Commission of the European Communities 2002).

Agri-environmental measures that may be required of EU farmers include the *protection, maintenance, and enhancement of the countryside. Maintenance* refers to situations where valuable parts of the landscape are dependent on continuous management practices, for example, grazing or hedgerow trimming. In a country-side policy context, maintenance is usually ensured through incentive instruments, although maintenance requirements are found in some regulatory measures (Institute for European Environmental Policy 2003b).

A majority of national cross-compliance policies have a principal objective of reducing negative environmental impacts – mainly by reducing fertilizers, pesticides, and livestock density (Gatto and Merlo 1999). Almost all management agreements include requirements for limiting use of pesticides, and mineral N-fertilizer, reducing livestock density, and maintaining permanent grasslands (Andersen et al. 1999). A substantial proportion also has wildlife, biodiversity, landscape, and natural environment conservation as objectives (Table 2). Most Member States appear to have used cross-compliance obligations to meet existing EU, national and/regional environmental legislation, mainly relating to fertilizer and pesticide use. Only a few countries have set standards going beyond existing legislation or covering issues of landscape and biodiversity. To set these standards, several nations are developing indicators to measure costs and benefits attributable to agri-environmental programs.

There are large differences among nations within the EU with the regard to subscribing to agri-environmental measure programs (Figure 2). Sweden, Germany, and Austria are large countries with strong involvements, and agri-environmental programs are dramatically affecting their landscapes to enhance biodiversity and cultural characteristics. Among the less-favored areas, Ireland, former East Germany, and Portugal heavily use agri-environmental schemes. Rural development is least popular among The Netherlands, Belgium, Spain, Greece, and Denmark. When comparing the details of national efforts among the EU-15

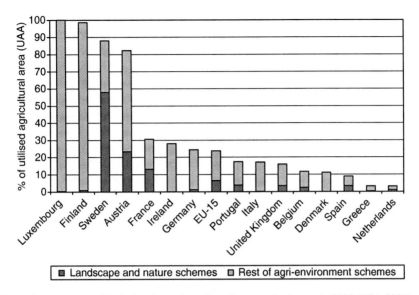

Figure 2 Percentage of agricultural area in agri-environmental schemes in 2002 (EEA 2005)

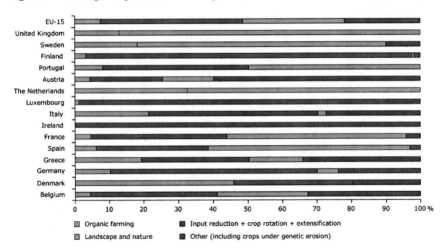

Figure 3 Proportion of four different categories of agri-environmental measures among the Member States of the EU-15, 1998 (EEA 2005)

Member States, it shows the greatest proportionate use of landscape measures in the UK, Sweden, the Netherlands, Portugal, France, and Spain (Figure 3).

In comparison with the former EU-15, use of agri-environmental measures by the 10 new Member States varies. In central and eastern European countries, problems associated with land abandonment and under-grazing because of the decline of former pastoral systems are more significant, and agri-environment schemes emphasize reintroduction of livestock and active management. At the same time, farming is scarcely viable financially in many areas of nature conservation value, and incentives are needed for reviving management that enhances nature values (Petersen 2003).

Implementation of agri-environmental schemes in most new Member States was delayed because the proposed administrative arrangements were not yet accredited to comply with EU rules. Only Bulgaria, the Czech Republic, and Latvia had achieved full EU approval for their agri-environment schemes by April 2003.

Quite apart from meeting their obligations with respect to international conventions and E U Directives, all European countries also have established national systems of protected areas, which include provisions for conserving landscapes in private ownership. While there is no common term used at the European level for landscapes that are legally protected, they share common management objectives. In countries such as Austria, Germany, Norway, Portugal, and Switzerland, *Landscape Protected Area* is a legal designation. Other countries have designations with a similar emphasis on landscape conservation, for example: Greece – *Aesthetic Forest*; Spain – *Natural Landscape* and *Natural Landscape of National Interest*; and the UK – *National Parks, Area of Outstanding Natural Beauty*, and *National Scenic Area*.

In order to simplify the diverse array of protected area designations applied throughout the world, the World Conservation Union (IUCN), through its World Commission on National Parks (formerly Commission on National Parks and Protected Areas), classified them into six types based on management objectives provided in the national legislation. Under this system, provision is made for *Protected Landscapes/Seascapes*, which are "*protected areas managed mainly for landscape/ seascape conservation and recreation*". Figure 4 illustrates that a much higher proportion of European protected areas are classified as landscape and seascape compared to North America, while a much higher proportion of North American protected areas are classified as national parks or protected habitats. By relying more heavily on protected working landscapes for agriculture, European protected areas complement the ecological functions of agri-environmental measures.

Agri-environmental Measures in US Policy

In the USA, late 20th-century history shows agri-environmental expenditures, which are termed conservation measures in the American policy nomenclature, being increasingly dwarfed by production-based commodity subsidies. However, beginning with the landmark 1985 federal agriculture law, the Food Security Act (FSA) and evolving through successive federal agricultural laws in 1990, 1996, and 2002, US agricultural policy innovations have increased the relative proportion of agri-environmental expenditures to about 15% of federal agricultural spending in 2004 (USDA NRCS 2006). These innovations demonstrate some potential landscape effects of agri-environmental measures for the future in America. Several of these innovations parallel policy concepts employed in Agenda 2000 of the CAP. These include set asides of formerly cultivated land, subsidizing the cost of implementing agri-environmental measures (or cost-sharing), cross-compliance, and decoupling farmer income payments from commodity production (Hanranhan and Zinn 2005).

Cost-sharing for working lands and land set asides as temporary land retirement have been used to achieve certain agri-environmental benefits since early US federal agricultural policy, dating from the 1936 Agricultural Conservation Program's (ACP)

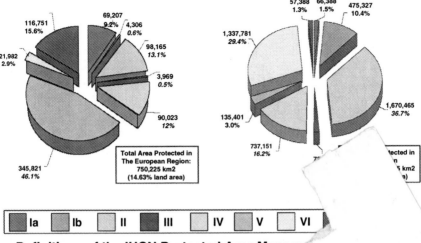

Definitions of the IUCN Protected Area Manage.

Ia	Strict Nature Reserve: protected area managed mainly for science
Ib	Wilderness Area: protected area managed mainly for wilderness protection
II	National Park: protected area managed mainly for ecosystem protection and ı
III	Natural Monument: protected area managed mainly for conservation of specifıc
IV	Habitat/Species Management Area: protected area managed mainly for conserva. management intervention
V	Protected Landscape/Seascape: protected area managed mainly for landscape/seascaȷ conservation and recreation
VI	Managed Resource Protected Area: protected area managed mainly for the sustainabl. natural ecosystems

Figure 4 Landscape protection (IUCN Category V) in comparison with other protection categorı for Europe[1] and North America[2] (UN 2003)

initial commitment to promoting soil conservation (Babcock et al. 2001; Claassen et al. 2001; Feng et al. 2003). With the 1996 farm law, cost-sharing for installation of conservation measures under the ACP was replaced by cost-sharing for conservation measures under the Environmental Quality Incentives Program (EQIP).

While land set asides have been part of US policy for more than 50 years, in 1985 the Conservation Reserve Program (CRP) was the first agri-environmental land retirement program (Zain and Lovejoy 2004), and its cost and area of impact has dwarfed all other US agri-environmental policies. Begun by the 1985 Food Security Act (FSA), the CRP has enrolled nearly one tenth of American cropland to be set aside in perennial cover, typically for a 10-year contract period. CRP land is selected to achieve certain environmental purposes including prevention of soil erosion.

---

[1] European Region contains: Albania, Andorra, Austria, Belgium, Bulgaria, Bosnia and Herzegovina, Croatia, Czech Republic, Denmark, Estonia, Faroe Islands, Federal Republic of Germany, Finland, France, Gibraltar, Greece, Hungary, Iceland, Ireland, Italy, Latvia, Liechtenstein, Lithuania, Luxembourg, Former Yugoslav Republic of Macedonia, Malta, Monaco, the Netherlands, Norway, Poland, Portugal, Romania, San Marino, Slovakia, Slovenia, Spain, Svalbard and JanMayen Islands, Sweden, Switzerland, UK, Vatican City State (Holy See), Yugoslavia.

[2] North American Region contains: Canada, Greenland, Mexico, St. Pierre and Miquelon, USA.

Figure 5 Geographic distribution of the Conservation Reserve Program (From Heimlich, USDA ERS 2003.)

The landscape effects of the CRP extend across the nation (Figure 5). About 36 million acres of US cropland are enrolled in the CRP (Hellerstein 2006) and nearly half of the $4.5 billion in federal agricultural funds for conservation in 2005 were spent on this set aside program (Zinn and Cowan 2006). The approximately $2 billion current annual cost of the CRP averages less than 10% of the cost of federal agricultural subsidies, which reached $23 billion in 2005 (Hoppe and Banker 2006). The CRP is estimated to have paid for itself in broader societal benefits, which are estimated at about $694 million per year in nonmarket benefits from soil erosion reduction and another $704 million per year in benefits from wildlife viewing and pheasant hunting (Babcock et al. 2001).

From 1985 to 1990, eligibility for the CRP was limited to fields with highly erodible soils. Eligibility was expanded in 1990 with the new agricultural law, the Food Agriculture Conservation and Trade Act (FACT). FACT 1990 introduced a multifactor score sheet of environmental benefits criteria for determining CRP eligibility. However, broad geographic distribution was a fundamental criterion, and consequently, some environmental benefits, like wildlife habitat, had greater emphasis in areas that were less vulnerable to soil erosion (Figure 6). Other environmental benefits criteria included: wildlife habitat, water quality, erosion, enduring benefits, air quality, and whether the land was inside a designated Conservation Priority Area (Feng et al. 2003). These broader criteria resulted in more good wildlife habitat and

Figure 6 The Conservation Reserve Program converted formerly cultivated highly erodible land, like this field in southern Minnesota, USA, into perennial cover for at least 10 years (J.I. Nassauer)

riparian corridor fields being enrolled in the CRP but less of the total of highly erodible land being enrolled.

The landmark 1985 FSA also introduced cross-compliance to US agricultural policy (Claassen 2006). To be eligible for enrollment in commodity subsidy programs under the 1985 law, farmers were required to develop a farm conservation plan that limited erosion on highly erodible cropland, and to implement their plan by 1995. The plans were highly tailored to individual farms, and by 1997 some 1674 different combinations of practices had been approved for different farms across America (Claassen et al. 2001). CRP enrollment was integral to achieving these goals, but practices like crop rotations, residue management, conservation tillage, contour farming, terracing, and grassed waterways were also important components (Figure 7). Under cross-compliance, farmers in the commodity programs also were prohibited from draining most wetlands or plowing previously uncultivated highly erodible land (Claassen et al. 2001; Feng et al. 2003). However, under 1990 FACT, cross-compliance requirements changed with substitution of a "no-net-loss" wetland restoration policy for outright prohibition of wetland drainage. With the 1996 agricultural law, the FAIR or "Freedom to Farm" law, cross-compliance requirements were further relaxed: eligibility for federal crop insurance was no longer linked to compliance, and local county committees could provide relief in hardship cases – exempting some of their neighbors from the cross-compliance requirement (Walker et al. 2000). Over the life of cross-compliance, monitoring for compliance has been a difficult challenge (Claassen 2006). Costs of actual performance monitoring have been perceived as impractical (Claassen et al. 2001), and for some practices, empirical studies have reported high rates of noncompliance (Swanson et al. 1999). However, by 1997, 91 million acres of US cropland, about 20%, were classified as meeting cross-compliance

Figure 7 Conservation tillage is widely employed to meet conservation compliance provisions (J.I. Nassauer)

criteria (Babcock et al. 2001), and total cropland erosion declined by 49% from 1982–1997, suggesting the success of cross-compliance and CRP together in achieving a fundamental environmental goal (Feng et al. 2003).

With the 1996 FAIR "Freedom to Farm" law, US agricultural policy began decoupling farmer payments from commodity subsidies. Under FAIR, payments to farmers were determined by the amount of land that previously had been enrolled in commodity programs, and the payments were to be gradually phased out over 5 years. While farmers were required to conform with cross-compliance requirements, they were free to manage their land for any enterprise and still receive income payments. The premise for this experiment was partly that removal of trade barriers through NAFTA and WTO's predecessor, GATT, had dramatically expanded markets for American farm products, and consequently, markets could sustain healthy farmer livelihoods. The CRP was continued but not expanded. As many of the 10-year CRP contracts of the mid 1980s expired, former CRP land, most of it highly erodible land, was returned to cultivation.

The 1996 US agricultural policy change did not result in dramatic new experimentation with new crops or enterprises. However, tens of thousands of acres of perennial cover were lost as CRP contracts expired without opportunities to reenroll. As the 1996 "Freedom to Farm" law was implemented, and farmer payments were reduced as planned, they were augmented by a series of "emergency" subsidies when commodity prices declined (Babcock 1999). The net effect was record-breaking agricultural subsidies, with lower proportionate expenditures for conservation during the "Freedom to Farm" era than in any previous period. After the passage of the 1996 farm law, the cost of federal agricultural subsidies rose from $7.3 billion in 1996 to $23.5 billion in 2000 (USDA Commission of 21st Century Production Agriculture 2001).

The most recent US farm law, the 2002 Farm Security and Rural Investment Act, changed the decoupling experiment of 1996 by introducing counter cyclical commodity price supports. However, it also introduced what has been described as the first American green box program for working agricultural lands, a nationwide Conservation Security Program (CSP) in which farmers were to be paid according to the number and type of agri-environmental measures they had already established or adopted for their entire farming operation. It also authorized funding for a reinvigorated CRP and more well-funded Farmland Protection Program (FPP).

However, funding for these measures was dwarfed by funding for commodity support programs. Concentration of overall subsidy payments among the largest farmers continued, and by 2004, 40% of all American farmers received federal agricultural subsidies, with the largest 7.5% of farms receiving 56% of all subsidy dollars (Hoppe and Banker 2006). In contrast, only 12% of US farms received payments for conservation measures, which averaged $5,446 (Environmental Working Group 2004). Currently, relatively small retirement and residential lifestyle farms receive more than 50% of their government payments in conservation payments. For retirement farms alone the percentage is 89% (USDA ERS 2004).

Implementation of the CSP and the expanded CRP were delayed and incomplete. To control costs, CSP was not implemented until 2004, and by the end of 2006, it had been implemented in only 280 (Figure 8) of 2119 agricultural watersheds nationally (Claassen and Ribaudo 2006). Appropriations for new enrollments in the CRP up to 38 million acres (6 million acres less than the 44 million allowed under the original 1985 law) were announced in August 2004, 18 months after the 2002 law was passed.

The FSRIA 2002 acknowledged countryside landscape amenities as a public good by authorizing a tenfold increase in federal support for the Farmland Protection Program (FPP). While the authorizeded $500 million over 5 years was very small compared with allocations for CSP and CRP, actual appropriations for farmland protection have ranged from 10–50% less than annual authorizations.

The FPP was begun as part of the 1996 FAIR; it provides a cost-share for state and local government investments in protecting farmland amenities. Many states have recognized the need to protect farmland as a scenic amenity to counteract sprawl, real estate development that converts agricultural land to higher rent land uses, like residential development. The USDA ERS (Hellerstein et al. 2002) found that protecting rural amenities like scenic beauty, open space, and agrarian cultural heritage are the leading goals (along with providing for locally grown foods) for state farmland protection programs, which have been adopted in some form by every US state. However, unlike most European counterparts, such farmland protection programs almost never allow for public access to farmland.

While funding for Farmland Protection has been extremely modest compared with the CRP or commodity support programs, and the capacity of existing government programs to stem the tide of exponentially higher rents offered by conversion to residential land uses is questionable, farmland protection programs do tend to recognize the breadth of rural landscape values. Their regional criteria for application may be a strong harbinger of potential innovation in landscape change as

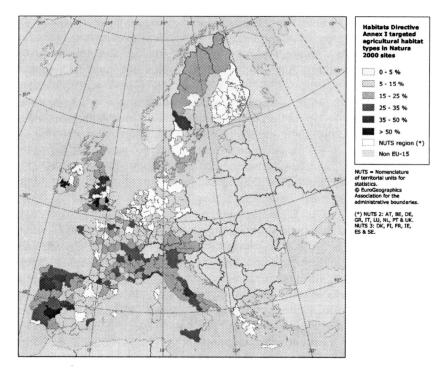

Figure 8 Habitat directive annex 1 targeted agricultural habitat types in Natura 2000 sites (EEA 2005)

affected by American agricultural policy. The trend toward increasing numbers of so-called lifestyle farms in America supports this possibility. The proportion of farms of less than 50 acres (with annual sale of at least $1,000.) has sharply increased over the last 15 years. This trend suggests that if US federal agricultural policy were to move away from commodity-based payments toward conservation payments, the geographic distribution of smaller farms, and farms owned by retirees or those who want a rural lifestyle might coincide with the distribution of landscape change to enhance environmental values.

The Green Box: Lessons for Future Agricultural Landscapes in the EU and USA

Regardless of which agri-environmental measures are included in European or American policy, the environmental effects of agricultural land use on these continents are undeniable. Nutrients moving from farmland in the Mississippi Basin have been identified as the leading cause of hypoxia in the Gulf of Mexico, which threatens fisheries there (Burkart and James 1999; Rabalais et al. 2002). Groundwater contamination from chemical fertilizer leached as nitrates threatens drinking water supplies throughout the Corn Belt. Aquatic ecosystems also are widely compromised by elevated levels of phosphorous and sediment from agricultural landscapes (Woltemade 2000; Beeton 2002). In both Europe and America, green box strategies are genuinely needed to protect soil and water quality, biodiversity, and landscape quality. Furthermore, the WTO accepts green box strategies as policies that do not distort trade. Consequently, they may be increasingly seen as a politically and societally acceptable means of providing income support for farmers.

In order to demonstrate the dimension of green box expenditures, Table 3 shows EU overall spending for notified environmental protection programs in 1995 to 1997 increasing from US$3,585 million in 1995/1996 to US$5,079 million in 1996/1997 (Wiggerthale 2004). As much as 74% of that difference is due to agri-environmental programs in EU Member States such as Austria, Finland, and Sweden, which made use of the EU cofinancing for the first time in 1996. The EU made up more than half of the total US$5,258.5 million spent on environmental protection programs in 1995 and the total US$ 7,487.9 million in 1996. With these increased European expenditures, the US share of the total WTO green box expenditure amounted to 4.4% in 1995 and 3.7% in 1996.

Table 3 Expenditure for notified environmental protection programs in 1995 and 1996 (Wiggerthale 2004, based on WTO 1999)

Expenditure for notified environmental protection programs in 1995 and 1996				
	1995		1996	
	Absolute in million US $	Relative in % of total expenditure on environmental protection program	Absolute in million US $	Relative in % of total expenditure on environmental protection program
Canada	12.5	0.2	–	–
USA	234.0	4.4	279.0	3.7
EU	3585.0	68.2	5079.0	67.7
Norway	28.5	0.5	25.0	0.3
Slovakia	0.3	0.006	0.7	0.01
Slovenia	0.2	0.004	0.1	0.001
Czech Republic	43.9	0.8	57.1	0.8
Switzerland	265.3	5.0	533.7	7.1
Argentina	–	–	0.2	0.003
Australia	89.3	1.7	157.5	2.1
New Zealand	5.5	0.1	5.4	0.1
South Africa	2.8	0.05	22.6	0.3
Korea	100.0	1.9	108.3	1.4
Japan	858.0	16.3	1225.4	16.4
India	33.2	0.6	–	–
TOTAL	5258.5	100	7487.9	100

In Europe in 2004, the Council of Europe's Committee of Ministers launched the European Landscape Convention, which aims to encourage public authorities to adopt policies and measures at local, regional, national and international levels for protecting, managing and planning landscapes throughout Europe. It covers all landscapes, both outstanding and ordinary, that affect the quality of life. The convention provides for a flexible approach to landscapes according to their specific features and calls for appropriate action, ranging from strict conservation through protection, management and improvement to actual creation. It calls for research to identify landscape types, and analyze their characteristics and the dynamics and pressures that affect them.

Different states and nations in Europe and America have widely varying dependence on agricultural subsidies. Where subsidies make up the greatest share of farmer income, agricultural landscape change are likely to be most affected by future green box policy strategies. Within these regions, agricultural landscape adaptations to choices under green box policy will vary enormously with world market competition, as well as local access to urban areas (and their markets for agricultural products and rural landscape experiences), climate, and landscape characteristics.

What might a working agricultural landscape that protects soil and water quality, biodiversity, and landscape quality look like? How would it look in different regions of each continent? How should it be managed? Drawing from recent EU and US policies described in this paper, we can anticipate some of the challenges in implementing green box policies.

Land Retirement or Set Aside Programs

In addition to agricultural programs provided as part of the Common Agricultural Policy, the EU has launched the Fauna, Flora, and Habitat Directive – better known nas Natura 2000. Under this essentially environmental policy, 12.5% of European landscapes have been designated as permanently protected habitat reserves.

Farmland located in habitats that are protected under the Natura 2000 scheme are considered as priority areas for targeting agri-environmental measures in support of nature conservation objectives. Figure 8 demonstrates that Natura 2000 sites are likely to benefit from agri-environmental measures, especially in the UK, Sweden, France, Portugal, Spain, Italy, and Austria. Combining the efforts under both schemes helps to integrate policy objectives, while ensuring efficient funding mechanisms.

Future set aside programs on both continents might draw some lessons from Natura 2000. In comparison with the 10-year set aside contracts characteristic of the American CRP program, Natura 2000 aims for set-asides much longer than 10 years and even, fee simple purchase of some lands to act as reserves. This kind of permanent commitment can enhance environmental benefits, and longer contract periods could help some farmers better anticipate their future incomes and land management options. Set aside selection criteria could further target not only characteristics of the land, like erodibility and habitat restoration, but also characteristics of landscape structure, like connectivity and patch size for habitat. The Natura 2000 program provides a strong precedent for this kind of targeting within an agricultural landscape matrix. For example, in the Netherlands, Natura 2000 EU funding is used partly to implement agri-environmental measures that prevent movement of pollutants from manure holding areas nearby (Figure 9).

Future set aside programs in US and EU landscapes might create a pattern of perennial cover that is more connected with other set aside parcels as well as other habitat parcels, and cover within set aside parcels might be established for several

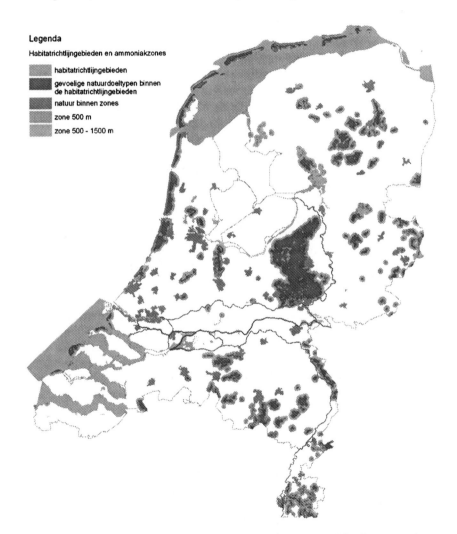

Figure 9 EU Natura 2000 funding is used to create buffers around dairy farm areas that are sources of nitrates and other pollutants moving to nearby nature reserves (Farjon et al. 2002)

decades – giving farmers more certainty in management decision-making and opening possibilities for woody crop rotations and a wider range of habitat types on set aside parcels. The agricultural landscape on both continents might be planned to create habitat "hot spots" of large patch or dense grain perennial retired land parcels where soil tends to be highly erodible or very wet, or where agricultural land could provide filters or conduits for flows or nutrients, materials, or species through nearby reserve areas.

Decoupling and Cross-compliance were tried by the USA under FAIR 1996 and are planned for the EU under CAP Agenda 2000. A key difference is that farmers' income subsidies are a large, continuing part of the EU CAP Agenda 2000, whereas farmer income subsidies were planned to diminish over 5 years under US FAIR 1996. While both policies require cross-compliance, FAIR 1996 did not emphasize enforcement of cross-compliance. Since Agenda 2000 does not allocate increased funding for agri-environmental measures, CAP achieving increased environmental benefits seems to depend almost entirely on strict enforcement of cross-compliance. If cross-compliance toward a broad platform of relatively easy to monitor environ- mental goals can be strictly enforced in the EU, it might demonstrate how agri- environmental measures can be pervasively applied to agricultural landscapes across both continents – not only to selected watersheds or regions within them. While agri-environmental measures might simply introduce a new crop rotation or residue management technique in some regions, they might suggest a landscape newly dominated by perennial cover in some other regions.

Withdrawal of commodity supports that distort world trade markets is the ultimate aim of WTO agreements. If commodity supports were withdrawn in the EU and USA, farmers would undoubtedly choose a different mix of enterprises and land covers for their land. If cross-compliance for environmental benefits were linked to substantial farmer income support (as is planned in the EU under Agenda 2000), then agricultural land cover change might likely include many practices that increase perennial herbaceous and woody cover as well as enhance the biodiversity of agri- cultural landscapes. At the same time, farmers would probably introduce a greater variety of other land covers for new agricultural enterprises as well. These might include ethanol-producing crops (whether corn, sugar, or cellulosic ethanol crops), new food crops, new rotations and cropping patterns, and new haying and pasture management regimes. Without subsidies that target particular crops or enterprises, farmers in some regions may pursue some entirely different types of enterprises, including production of wildlife or provision of outdoor recreational experiences.

Agri-environmental practices on working lands. In addition to land retirement set asides, other policies in both America and Europe suggest the types of practices that could be adopted on working agricultural land under a green box approach to agricultural support. Crop rotations, strip cropping (Figure 10), contour farming, terracing, and grassed waterways all have a long history as cost-share practices under the ACP in America. With cross-compliance under the 1985 FSA, residue management and conservation tillage (Figure 7) became the mainstay of farm con- servation plans. A more comprehensive level of agri-environmental performance is being asked of farmers in the watersheds selected for the new CSP. Management for aquifer protection, odor reduction from concentrated animal feeding operations (CAFOs), and energy savings have begun to be recognized as agri-environmental practices. Protective perennial cover around wellheads, more fencing of riparian zones, more fields of windmills or solar cell panels – all could characterize future landscape patterns under CSP in America. However, agri-environmental practices anticipated for EU Agenda 2000 are even broader in scope. In particular, these practices encourage farmers to continue to manage agricultural land that might otherwise be abandoned for its cultural and ecological values, to manage the amenity values of certain agricultural landscapes, to prevent topographical changes, to restore groundwater tables, and allow seasonal flooding in some landscapes to achieve downstream benefits.

Landscape quality practices are far more fully integrated as agri-environmental practices in the EU than in US policy. The FPP provides some support for competitive matching grants to states and local governments to protect farmland, and most state and local programs aim to protect open space, amenity, and cultural characteristics, along with local food supplies. However, systematic implementation of landscape quality protection as part of cross-compliance for farmers has not been undertaken in America. In the EU, rural landscape amenity protection is on the menu of agri-environmental practices (Table 2). Pervasive implementation of land set asides and agri-environmental practices for soil and water quality, habitat, recreation, and landscape open space, amenity, and cultural values would look different in different regions, depending upon their intrinsic landscape characteristics and cultural traditions (compare Figures 11 and 12). In response

Figure 10 Strip cropping and crop rotations could be adopted more pervasively under green box policies (USDA NRCS)

Figure 11 Agricultural landscape in the Ardennes, Belgium (Dirk Wascher)

Figure 12 Cultural landscape on Gozo Island, Malta (Dirk Wascher)

to the increasing policy relevance of landscape values, the European Environment
Agency has taken up landscape indicators as part in their agri-environmental assessment
program (EEA 2005).

Conclusion

By shifting the focus of support for agriculture in both the EU and USA to green box policies, international trade policy may reduce overproduction of some crops and trade distortions on world markets, and it may push both Europe and America to adopt more environmentally beneficial agricultural landscape patterns and practices. Choices made by the EU and USA in constructing their own green box agricultural policies could also reduce environmental pollution, increase biodiversity, and enhance and protect the amenity value of rural landscapes. Public sentiment questioning the costly agricultural subsidies employed on both continents may underscore the need for immediately apparent, broader public benefits of green box policies to be employed if farmer incomes are going to continue to be supported by public spending (Nassauer 1992). New green box policies should anticipate not only economic and ecological benefits produced, but also the appearance of the benefits produced and public appreciation for those benefits. Planning and design that is attentive to public perceptions will be necessary to the success and longevity of green box practices.

Green box strategies for taking land out of production can build on the successes of the CRP in America and Natura 2000 in the EU by targeting landscape pattern characteristics as well as parcel characteristics in set aside parcels, by employing a longer time period and programmatic consistency for set asides, by considering long-term rotations and markets for perennial vegetation within set asides, and by considering multiple uses of agricultural land for multiple markets. Green box strategies for farmer income support can learn from the very large unplanned expenditures for farmer income support under FAIR 1996 in America and from the strong link between cross-compliance for agri-environmental benefits and continued farmer income planned under CAP Agenda 2000 in the EU. These strategies can draw from the comprehensive menu of agri-environmental and conservation practices employed in both the EU and USA. In particular, farmland protection policy in American can draw upon EU experiences with landscape quality protection: the USA may want to emulate EU policy by including practices that enhance landscape amenity and cultural characteristics in the green box menu. This can assure that widely held American public values for open space, landscape amenity, and cultural characteristics are protected by public investment in agriculture. Planning for visible public benefits should be a strategy to also assure long-term public support for the less apparent food safety and environmental services benefits of sound agricultural policy.

Undoubtedly, world trade, technology, and changing markets will dramatically affect agricultural landscapes in Europe and America over future decades. WTO support for green box policies challenges both American and European policymakers to imagine the landscapes they are creating, not only the agricultural economies they are affecting, and to anticipate public reaction to the agricultural landscapes that results.

Acknowledgments This work was supported by USDA Forest Service Grant No. 02-JV-11231300-037. Integrating landscape ecological knowledge into design of agricultural landscape scenarios for improved water quality and sustainability of the Upper Mississippi River Basin. Erik Dayrell provided important assistance in data gathering.

References

Andersen E, Primdahl J, Oñate JJ, Peco B, Cummings C, Aguine J, Schramek J, and Knickel K (1999) Environmental effects of agri-environmental measures implemented under reg. 2078/92. In Schramek, J., Biehl, D., Buller, H., and Wilson, G. (eds) *Implementation and Effectiveness Effects of Agri-environmental Schemes Established under Regulation 2078/92*, Final Consolidated Report. Project Fair 1, CT95-274, vol.1, pp135–162

Babcock B (1999) Whither farm policy? *Iowa Agricultural Review* 5(4): 1–6

Babcock B (2001) The concentration of US agricultural subsidies. *Iowa Agricultural Review* 7(4): 8–9

Babcock B (2002) Local and global perspectives on the new U.S. farm policy. *Iowa Agricultural Review* 8(3): 1–3

Babcock B, Beghin J, Duffy M, Feng J, Hueth B, Kling C, Kurkalova L, Schneider U, Secchi S, Weninger Q, and Zhao J (2001) *Conservation Payments: Challenges in Design and Implementation*. Iowa State University Center for Agricultural and Rural Development, Ames, IA

Baylis K, Rausser G, and Simon L (2004) Agri-environmental programs in the United States and European Union in Anania. In Bohman ME, Carter CA, and McCalla AF (eds) *Agricultural Policy Reform and the WTO: Where Are We Heading?* Edward Elgar, Cheltenham, UK/ Northampton MA

Beeton AM (2002) Large freshwater lakes: present state, trends, and future. *Environmental Conservation* 29(1): 21–38

Beghin J (2002) Rich countries, poor countries, and the Doha Round trade negotiations. *Iowa Agricultural Review* 8(3): 10–11

Burkart MR and James DE (1999) Agricultural-nitrogen contributions to hypoxia in the Gulf of Mexico. *Journal of Environmental Quality* 28(3): 850–859

Commission of the European Communities (2002) Mid-Term Review of the Common Agricultural Policy. Communication from the Commission to the Council and the European Parliament. Commission of the European Communities, COM(2002) 394 final of 10.7.2002 Brussles

Claassen R, Hansen L, Peters M, Breneman V, Weinberg M, Cattaneo A, Feather P, Gadsby D, Hellerstein D, Hopkins J, Johnston P, Morehart M, and Smith M (2001) *Agri-Environmental Policy at the Crossroads: Guideposts on a Changing Landscape*. US Department of Agriculture, Economic Research Service 68, Washington, DC

Claassen R (2006) *Compliance Provisions for Soil and Water Conservation Chapter from the Agricultural Resources and Environmental Indicators*, 2006 edition, USDA Economic Research Service, Chapter 5.3, pp 184–193

Claassen R and Ribaudo M (2006) *Conservation Policy Overview from the Agricultural Resources and Environmental Indicators*, 2006 edition, USDA Economic Research Service, Chapter 5.1, pp 168–174

Environmental Working Group (2004) Farm Subsidy Data Base. www.ewg.org/farm/ Access date: September 10, 2004

European Commission (1998) State of application of regulation (EEC) n° 2078/92: Evaluation of agri-environment programmes, Working Document; VI/7655/98, 9.11.1998 available at http:// europa.eu.int/comm/agriculture/envir/programs

EEA (European Environment Agency) (2004a) The State of Biological Diversity in the European Union. Contribution prepared by the European Environment Agency for the event of the Stakeholder Conference Biodiversity and the EU – Sustaining Livelihoods, Malahide, Ireland, 25–25 May 2004, European Environment Agency, Copenhagen

EEA (European Environment Agency) (2004b) High nature value farmland - Characteristics, trends and policy challenges. EEA report No1/2004, European Environment Agency, Copenhagen, 26 pp

EEA (European Environment Agency) (2005) Agricultural and the Environment in the EU-15 – the IRENA Indicator Report. EEA Report No. 6 2005. European Environment Agency, Copenhagen, 138 pp

Farjon JMJ, Dirks GHP, Koomen AJM, Vervloet JAJ, and Lammers GW (2002) Neder-landschap Internationaal: Bouwstenen voor een selectie van gebieden landschapsbehoud. (Alterra Rapport 358), Alterra, Wageningen, The Netherlands

Feng H (2002) *Green Payments and Dual Policy Goals*. Iowa State University Center for Agricultural and Rural Development: 30, Ames, IA

Feng H, Kling CL, Kurkalova L, and Secchi S (2003) *Subsidies! The Other Incentive-Based Instrument: The Case of the Conservation Reserve Program*. Iowa State University Center for Agricultural and Rural Development: 29. Ames, IA

Gagnon S, Makuch J, and Sherman TJ (2004) *Environmental Effects of US Department of Agriculture Conservation Programs: A Conservation Effects Assessment Bibliography*. Water Quality Information Center, National Agricultural Library, Agricultural Research Service, US Department of Agriculture, Beltsville, MD

Gatto P and Merlo M (1999) The economic nature of stewardship: complementarity and trade-offs with food and fibre production. In Huylenbroeck GV and Whitby M (eds) *Countryside Stewardship: Farmers, Policies and Markets*. Pergamon, Amsterdam, The Netherlands

Hanrahan CE and Zinn J (2005) *Green Payments in US and European Union Agricultural Policy*. Congressional Research Service: Library of Congress, Washington, DC

Hart CE and Babcock B (2002) *US Farm Policy and the World Trade Organization: How Do They Match Up?* Iowa State University Center for Agricultural and Rural Development: 21, Ames, IA

Heimlich R (2003) *Agricultural Resources and Environmental Indicators*. USDA Economic Research Service, Washington, DC

Hellerstein D (2006) *USDA Land Retirement Programs*, USDA Economic Research Service, Chapter 5.2, pp 175–183, Washington, DC

Hellerstein D, Nickerson C, Cooper J, Feather P, Gadsby D, Mullarkey D, Tegene A, and Barnard C (2002) *Farmland Protection: The Role of Public Preferences for Rural Amenities*. USDA Economic Research Service, Washington, DC

Hill B (1999) Farm household income: perceptions and statistics. *Journal of Rural Studies* 15(3): 345–58

Hoppe RA and Banker DE (2006) *Structure and Finances of US farms: 2005 Family Farm Report*. USDA ERS, Washington, DC

Institute for European Environmental Policy (2003a) EU-Cross-Compliance Newsletter. Issue 1.This newsletter is part of a project that is funded by the Commission of the European Communities RTD programme Quality of Life and Management of Living Resources under project reference QLK5-CT-2002-02640

Institute for European Environmental Policy (2003b) EU-Cross-Compliance Newsletter. Issue 3. Commission of the European Communities RTD programme Quality of Life and Management of Living Resources. Project reference QLK5-CT-2002-02640. Institute for European Environmental Policy, Brussels

Jongman RHG (1996) *Ecological and Landscape Consequences of Land Use Change in Europe*. European Centre for Nature Conservation, Tilburg, The Netherlands

LEI (2004) Agricultural economic report 2004 of the Netherlands. In Berkhout P and van Bruchem C (eds) Agricultural Economics Research Institute (LEI), The Hague, The Netherlands

Mohanty S and Kaus P (1999) European union agricultural reforms: impacts for Iowa. *Iowa Agricultural Review* 5(4): 8–9

Moyer W and Josling T (2002) *Agricultural Policy Reform: Politics and Process in the EU and US in the 1990's*. Ashgate Publishing Company, Burlington, VTNassauer JI (1992) The appearance of ecological systems as a matter of policy. *Landscape Ecology* 6(4): 239–250

Nassauer JI, Santelmann MV, and Scavia D (2007) *From the Corn Belt to the Gulf: Societal and Environmental Implications of Alternative Agricultural Futures.* Resources for the Future Press, Washington, DC

Organization for Economic Cooperation and Development (2003) *Agricultural policies in OECD countries: a positive reform agenda.* OECD, Paris

Petersen JE (2003) Agri-environmental Programmes and the Candidate Countries. Report from a conference organised by Ecologic Institute for International and European Environmental Policy, Potsdam, Germany

Rabalais NN, Turner RE, and Wiseman WJ (2002) Gulf of Mexico hypoxia, aka "The dead zone". *Annual Review of Ecology and Systematics* 33: 235–263

Roberts MJ and Key N (2003) Who benefits from government farm payments? *Choices* 3rd qtr.: 7–14

Runge CF (1996) Agriculture and environmental policy: new business or business as usual. Working paper No. 1. The McKnight Foundation for Environmental Reform: The Next Generation Project, Yale Center for Environmental Law and Policy, New Haven, CT

Swanson DA, Scott DP, and Risley DL (1999) Wildlife benefits of the conservation reserve program in Ohio. *Journal of Soil and Water Conservation* 54(1): 390–394

Tilman D, Fargione J, Wolff B, D'antonio C, Dobson A, Howarth R, Schinder D, Schlessinger WH, Simberloff D, and Swackhamer D (2001) Forecasting agriculturally driven global environmental change. *Science* 292: 281–284

UN (2003) *List of Protected Areas. IUCN – The World Conservation Union.* UNEP World Conservation Monitoring Centre, Gland, Switzerland

USDA Commission of 21st Century Production Agriculture (2001) *Food and Agricultural Policy: Taking Stock for a New Century.* Washington, DC

USDA Census of Agriculture (2002) Washington, DC

USDA NRCS (2006) *Conservation and the Environment: USDA 2007 Farm Bill Theme Paper.* USDA, Washington, DC

Walker DJ, Wu S, and Brusven MA (2000) The efficiency and effectiveness of conservation compliance under 1996 farm commodity policy reforms. *Journal of Soil and Water Conservation* 55(4): 447–455

Wiggerthale M (2004) *EU agri-environmental policies in the context of the WTO.* Part Two. Germanwatch, Bonn

WTO (World Trade Organization) (1999) Green Box Measures. Background Paper by the Sekretariat. Document no. AIE/S9/REV.1 released on 27.5.1999, Geneva, IL

Woltemade CJ (2000) Ability of restored wetlands to reduce nitrogen and phosphorus concentrations in agricultural drainage water. *Journal of Soil and Water Conservation* 55(3): 303–309

Womach J, Becker G, Chite R, Cowan T, Gorte R, Hanrahan C, Jurenas R, Monke J, Rawson J, Schnepf R, Yacobucci B, Zinn J, and Richardson J (2006) *Previewing the Farm Bill.* Congressional Research Service: Library of Congress, Washington, DC

Zain Z and Lovejoy S (2004) History and outlook for farm bill conservation programs. *Choices_* (4): 37–42

Zinn J, and Cowan T (2006) *Agriculture Conservation Programs: A Scorecard.* Congressional Research Service: Library of Congress, Washington DC

Chapter 9
Implications for Future Landscape Inquiry, Planning, and Design

Douglas M. Johnston and James L. Wescoat, Jr.

The landscape undergoes continuous change, much of it by "design," broadly defined, that shapes the pursuit and consequences of human aims. In the last 50 years we have seen cities and farmland transformed by the expansion of suburbs into a phenomenon now called "sprawl."[1] The independent family farmer envisioned by Thomas Jefferson appears on the verge of extinction with the rise of national and transnational agricultural corporations. The displacement of locally owned business by national chains continues to attract public attention, awareness, mass patronage, and varying degrees of resistance. For all of the technologies, services, and amenities available in our communities, many still do not have access to them. However, as Nassauer and Wascher show in chapter 8, European landscape policies have begun to address these issues by connecting international political jurisdictions, land uses, ecosystems, and economic systems. They strive to fulfill Boulding's concept of an "integrative power" that seeks to harmonize the political and economic forces of landscape change on an international scale, as well as on the national, regional, and local scales illustrated by some US and European landscape conservation policies.

To attempt to understand these changes from a singular perspective is fraught with hazards. To view the landscape either as a by-product of direct action or as simply a raw material in some larger structural process would be a mistake. To view the landscape either as a passive body immutable in its essential forms, fluxes, and processes over time, or as changing in largely manageable ways, would ignore both reality and opportunity. A richer framework for understanding the landscape is required.

The Landscape Futures Initiative of the Landscape Architecture Foundation has sought to analyze future drivers of landscape change and to position the profession to respond to these drivers. The participants in this part of the initiative focusing on political and economic forces reflect a diverse range of scholars and practitioners from within landscape architecture and also from geography, political science, economics, and development studies. While risking complexity and abstraction from current patterns of design practice, this diversity challenges designers' frameworks for thinking about and acting within the landscape. By challenging our assumptions, we are led to explore new avenues of inquiry and practice.

---

[1] At the *Places of Power* conference, architectural historian Robert Bruegemann underscored the historical depth of these phenomena, extending back to antiquity.

J.L. Wescoat, Jr. and D.M. Johnston (eds.), *Political Economies of Landscape Change.* 195
© Springer 2008

In this concluding chapter we seek to bring together major points and themes identified throughout the previous chapters and discuss them in the context of implications for the practice of environmental design. It is important to note that implications for design extend well into the academic community as well as the community of practice. Both are important actors in "reading" the political economy of landscape change, positioning the profession to respond to and initiate significant social, political, environmental, and economic changes in local, national, and international arenas – and, again, to do so in ways that aspire to the "integrative power" that directs and harmonizes political and economic driving (and steering) forces of landscape change.

Reading Future Landscapes of Political and Economic Change

Landscape architecture is often defined in terms of its visual or experiential power. To be sure, the visual is a key dimension of human response to the environment, and even a dominant one in terms of sensory perception (see Harris and Ruggles [2007] on the complexities of landscape and vision). Designs, in addition to their functional aims, seek to be beautiful in the eyes of the beholder, and to elicit deep emotional responses (as in the recent passion for memorial landscapes). The experience of a landscape seeks to transform the occupant in any number of ways from physical health to knowledge or participation in a community.

But to analyze a landscape strictly on its visual appearance limits practice at best, and arguably, does much harm. Peirce Lewis's paper on axioms for reading the landscape gained particular resonance with landscape architects after its publication, as did May Watts's (1957) *Reading the Landscape of America* in different ways two decades earlier. It provided a framework for considering the landscape not as a discrete set of designed islands in an amorphous sea, but instead for realizing that the broad expanse of ordinary landscapes is structured and organized with as much care and thought as those areas traditionally defined as works of landscape architecture. Lewis further argued that the landscape, as artifact, provides clues to the values, aspirations, and pragmatics of human life.

Its resonance within the profession in the late 20th century could have stemmed from several sources. For one, it extended the definition of the designed landscape to include (although certainly not for the first time) "everything outside the building footprint" (Schwartz 2004). This is an important revelation, regardless of when it was first realized, because it admits a much broader domain for practice encompassing public as well as private, urban as well as rural, and vernacular as well as professionally designed landscapes. An enlargement of prospects provides real opportunities for professional advancement and impact.

Another dimension of "reading the landscape" that easily resonates with designers is the dominance of the visual characteristics of the landscape. Appearances *are* important, for they give the viewer information, clues, expectations, narrative, and history vital for design. As a means of studying the landscape, Lewis is right to suggest that the landscape is the repository of untold numbers of decisions made at all levels of a culture, for extended periods of time. He also suggests that this characteristic makes it very difficult to understand the stories the landscape has to tell because it is, in aggregate, a seemingly unstructured, unorganized, (but not unedited) amalgam of traces of past and present actions many of which gestured toward desired future conditions. If a profession defines itself by the visual transformations it provides in the environment, then the power of the visual becomes self-evident.

However, in his essay at the start of this book, Don Mitchell critiques Lewis's axioms with the caution – "Don't believe everything you see." Mitchell argues that the landscape is difficult to read not because the visual clues are cluttered, but because they are insufficient. Visual knowledge tells us about forms, materials, and geometry, but it does not overtly reveal motives, goals, struggles, power relations, and other material dimensions of landscape that are equally important to its understanding.

Michael Hough (1992) tells a similar tale in which he conducts an exercise with students from various departments in the university to examine a stream channel with the goal of understanding the condition of the stream's watershed. He reports that universally the landscape architecture students in the exercise developed carefully prepared illustrations of what the stream looked like. There was little apparent understanding of hydrology or the effects of urbanization and watershed development on the stream channel incision they described.

What Hough is saying about the need to consider ecological (and geomorphological) processes when interpreting the visual evidence provided by the landscape, Mitchell is suggesting regarding political–economic processes. Landscape architectural historians of the last decade have presented similar arguments, drawing upon archival and archaeological evidence of political and economic factors in Italian, French, and Mughal villa garden design (Benes and Harris 2001; Ruggles 2000; Wescoat and Wolschke-Bulmahn 1996). It is less clear whether or how these historical examples are affecting contemporary design practice in the early 21st century. In *Greater Perfections: The Practice of Garden Theory*, John Dixon Hunt (2000) points us in this direction by drawing together a wide range of regional examples that show how garden designers communicate social factors (as well as poetic expression) through texts *in* and *about* garden design.

The participants in the Landscape Futures Initiative suggested numerous ways in which current and future landscape changes may be "read". The landscape is constantly changing, and here the agents of change are not only biological or chemical, but also increasingly social. Shifting economic balances, changes in community structures, strengthening or weakening political power are all reflected in the works of landscape architecture, and indeed, landscape architecture influences these shifts through provision or withholding, and by inclusion or exclusion. Not all of these changes may be comfortable, for future landscape change can and will move in many directions.

Landscapes of Opportunity: Prosperity, Security, and Design

Whereas the essays in this book began with struggle and proceeded toward prosperity, as the majority of the world's population aspires to do, many if not most professional landscape architects work primarily with relatively prosperous people and places, which they strive to extend in varying ways and degrees to other people and places – as compared with what a 2007 exhibition at the Cooper Hewitt Museum titled *Design for the Other 90%* (http://www.peoplesdesignaward. org/design_for_the_other_90/). It is hardly surprising that landscape architects become embroiled in processes of gentrification; trade-offs between the profits, risks, and costs of growth; and efforts to mitigate harms to vulnerable people and places.

What are the implications for design? What are the "best practices" vis-a-vis "trickle down" approaches for extending the net economic and political benefits of purposeful landscape change? Several chapters in this book examined driving forces and effects of migration to rural areas, which identified numerous opportunities for designers to help shape both productive agricultural landscapes and regionally contextual communities, on the one hand, and also lifestyle communities, hobby farms, second-home developments, and other emergent rural land uses.

The attractions of these changing rural landscapes are numerous: trees, water, mountains, and low population densities to name a few. What enables people to relocate themselves to these locations in the hill country of the Carolina's or the range country of Colorado and Wyoming? Many economic forces have contributed to the movement: longer lives after retirement, improved infrastructure in rural communities, increased capital appreciation from the housing or stock market, changing communications technologies enabling separation of labor and workplace. Can these factors alone explain the movement? Possibly. But the number of forces already listed suggests that there are likely to be even more. For example, capital gains from the housing market are only valuable if reallocated to locations with lower property values. That is, the amenity migration described by Kurt Culbertson et al., is enabled by the supply of less expensive amenities than can be provided in migrant's present location.

But if these developing areas are rich in amenity, why are they less expensive? One phenomenon is the building boom in and around public lands. Building in and around public lands affords the amenity seekers the values contained within the public land and also limits the number of other seekers that can obtain those same goods. Thus the amenity seekers are taking value indirectly from the environment the public land creates. In such contexts, landscape architects play multiple, sometimes conflicting, roles through design of the recreation areas, public infrastructure (e.g., roads), and private amenity development.

In other cases, land becomes inexpensive because the previous economic system has shifted or even collapsed. The mountainsides of the Appalachian region are not unpopulated. They are populated by those who are unable to follow shifting economic forces that demand highly educated technologists and managers. With high levels of poverty, and concomitant lack of education, health care, etc., the Appalachian landscape is "undervalued" (Glasmeier 2005). In-migration challenges these local populations with increased property prices due to outbidding by wealthy migrants and taxes for the public services they expect. The construction of amenity communities may offer some economic opportunities for the local populations, but because the education, heath care and other systems have not improved, they are less prepared to offer the higher paying services than other in-migrants seeking opportunities. If employed, they operate at the economic margin and, not surprisingly, replicate the cheap franchise highway strip landscapes that Mitchell examines in chapter 1. Of course, the new migrants demand services similar to those they had including police and fire protection, roads, sewers, etc., that lead to increased property, sales, and special district taxes that fall on all residents of the larger community. These increased costs of living drive out those local residents who fail to grasp whatever opportunities they can and thereby build their livelihoods and social capital in ways that Bebbington elucidates in chapter 2.

Even if one does not seek out high natural amenity landscapes, there is certainly a continuing process of producing local amenity landscapes in suburban and urban communities. These communities can and have taken on many forms in the late-20th century, from country club golf course communities to gated, neo-traditional, ecological-green, and cooperative housing communities. Surely these emergent landscapes signal more than just visual preferences or "amenities"! To say so requires that we look beneath the surface – at what is being valued, and how? Why are gated communities valued? Is crime lower in those neighborhoods than in equivalent, but un-gated, communities? Landscape research by Kirk (2004) and others sheds light on owner and public preferences for different *forms* of gated communities, but further empirical (vis-a-vis journalistic) research is needed on their political and economic significance.

Neo-traditional communities are designed to promote community cohesion, but cohesion among whom? A two-bedroom, 1,050 square foot residence in Sea Side, Florida lists for $1.6 million (Seaside 2005). Prairie Crossing, a much-cited conservation development situated on a regional rail transit line in northeastern Illinois conserves water and replaces lawn with prairie, but it is still tied to the automobile and highways for basic shopping and jobs. That is, in many respects it is still a bedroom community, albeit a natively planted one (Thompson 2003). As in the Appalachian example, the rate of landscape change and preparedness of different social groups to engage in it affects who benefits. At Prairie Crossing in 2005, new condominium prices started at $329,000 (Prairie Crossing 2005). Just a few years earlier in the same development, much larger detached homes were available at lower, more affordable prices than the condos, but as evidence of its economic success its property values continue to increase. The challenge then is to produce enough of these communities to meet demand, *and* to ensure the broader economic community is able to buy in at affordable prices and benefit from potential increases in value.

In the short-term Prairie Crossing succeeds in creating a residential landscape that inspires walking within the development – to school, specialty shopping, community events and, to its credit, walking for local landscape pleasure. It succeeds in linking a distant settlement with downtown Chicago via a regional rail link. However, its longer-term, regional-scale, success will also depend upon whether future designers extend these amenities to a wider range of incomes in adjacent site scale developments, and coordinate with regional restructuring of retail, commercial, employment, and transportation systems along the lines envisioned by Metropolis 2020 and others (NIPC 2005; Ranney 2004 [presentation]).

The creation of landscapes of prosperity speaks not only to economic, but also to political forces. Political actors struggle with disaggregated versus centralized forces, as well as local–state–national–international–and–global interactions. Susan Clarke refers to the "garrison state" that may be created under strong centralized political organization when disaster preparedness moves to the forefront of political action. Risks and disasters that range from domestic crime and violence to "natural" hazards (e.g., wildfire, hurricane, and earthquake damages) and international risks (e.g., acts of war or terrorism) are influenced by political forces at all levels. As Clarke argues, the garrison state at the national level "steers" financial resources toward military and related sectors, which it justifies by maintaining public awareness of threat. While the garrison state provides obvious opportunities for landscape architects in the area of security design (see for example, the August 2005 issue of *Landscape Architecture Magazine*), it can also constrain and distort the design of "public" spaces and their "democratic" character. The Mall in Washington, DC is important not only as a space containing national monuments, but also as one of the few public spaces where the population can gather in great numbers to express its collective views. But the very concentration of resources and people can contribute to risk. Urban areas are at greater risk for disaster in part due to the density of infrastructure (institutional, financial, and administrative) contained within them. The jurisdictional nature of government administration restricts the efficiency with which resources can be shifted, but conditions of perceived crisis tend toward greater intergovernmental communication if not cooperation.

The desire for protection from real and perceived hazards also evidences itself in private and quasi-private landscapes. As an extreme case, Helphand (2006) describes sobering, yet inspiring, gardens created in the context of war. As more pervasive phenomena, Clarke cites the gated community with perimeter barriers, private security forces, and public exclusion as one example. Fragmentation of services is not unique to security issues, of course. Provision of open space, communications networks, and tax increment financing all have differential effects on the allocation of resources. These provisions come at a very real financial price, however, and therefore are not available to all, leading to the construction of "premium landscapes." Premium landscapes can be created by the public sector under the best intentions. The cleanup of environmental contamination makes local land more valuable, for example, causing a shift in the economic strata and housing affordability of the locality.

So what are appropriate responses by the landscape architect? Mitchell cites an interview with Martha Schwartz (2004) in which she condemns the ugliness of the American landscape, particularly its urban fringes. "The problem," she states, "is that our notion of the quality of life ends at our front door." "Strip malls pop up where there is a lot of cheap land, for lots of surface parking. It's economics." It is indeed economics. As Mitchell argues, strip malls exist because they are valued sufficiently to exist, that is, they appear to address a problem (including the provision of inexpensive goods easily accessible to the population) for which a solution is desired. An argument against strip malls based solely on their "ugliness" is not likely to carry much power as long as its other functions are being well provided. Even the "ugliness" of the strip mall is easily argued. If we follow the dictums of scenic quality articulated by Thomas Cole (1836) in his essays and embedded in most design curricula that include proportion, scale, color, texture, etc., then it would be difficult to argue that strip malls are "ugly." Beauty and ugliness are not defined soley by the physical properties of the landscape, but also by its contextual properties.

Of course, the financial success of even the mall may be fleeting. Landscape change affects social forces, and vice versa. These changes shift political and economic power – based on changing demands for resources, shifting productivity, and perception of value that may increase or decline through "status" and "stigma" affects. The work of James Wines and SITE presents a case in point. Their designs for showrooms for BEST, Inc. gained widespread recognition in the 1970s for calling attention to the industrial design and cultural character of commercial space. By deconstructing and exposing elements and ironies of these social and physical structures, they creatively explored the role of commercial buildings in suburban environments. Although innovative as environmental design, the shifting economic landscape drove BEST, Inc. to bankruptcy, and at least one of Wine's buildings was reconstructed into a used-furniture dealership before being torn down. In the context of recent hurricanes and other disasters, his purposely eroded, broken, and tilted buildings might be considered more disconcerting than amusing – which could in turn increase their political if not economic salience.

Changing demographics, markets and fashions cause malls to fail, and the abandoned strip mall is a visible reminder of the dynamics of the economic landscape, and not necessarily the failure of malls as a provider of services. In 2000, the National Endowment for Arts, fueled by its "Mayors Institute on Urban Design", and the "Your Town" programs, sponsored a conference on redressing the dead mall. It emphasized a deeper understanding of the political and economic driving forces that created, and subsequently abandoned, malls. Many see existing malls as a new "community" space, but fail to recognize that it is a private enterprise constructed for the exchange of goods and services that can restrict participation and behaviors at the owner's will. The presence of many people does not constitute community if their purpose in gathering is solely satisfying individual goals, rather than collective ones. The lessons from the NEA *Redressing the Mall* program emphasize the use of what Clarke calls "steering resources": community organizations, local boards, and committed proponents who gather the requisite public and private resources needed to transform abandoned commercial space. While visual aspects of redevelopment are often emphasized as the metric of a project's potential, it takes major political and financial resources, and the confidence of those who control it, to actually execute the project.

To put it another way, beauty is *not* only skin-deep. When viewed in the light of an expanded landscape aesthetic, of either the sort that Mitchell or J.B. Jackson espouse, it is difficult to argue that the mall is any less beautiful than a park (and, indeed, may be judged by some as more beautiful than many parks); and when viewed in the light of increasing access to goods and services to a larger number of citizens, the mall may well be judged a beautiful (or even a socially heroic!) work. Early award-winning shopping mall designs in the mid-20th century, such as Lawrence Halprin's Old Orchard Mall in Skokie, Illinois, certainly had these connotations.

Of course, the argument works the other way as well. We may judge a landscape ugly not because it lacks the proper aesthetic properties, but because of negative associations with either low-income or luxuriantly valued properties. If we look at the Appalachian landscape, does it become less attractive knowing that behind the carefully preserved trees is a mountain-top removal coal mine? Or that a family is living there without water because their pipes froze and they cannot afford to have it repaired because the mechanization of the coal mines and the policies of the mining companies have forced them into unemployment or disability? Doesn't living behind a fenced perimeter take just a little of the shine off the roses? Doesn't living outside the fence remove a little of the sense of community? (Helphand 1999).

Conversely, consider the frequent criticisms of nouveau riche developments and their "McMansions" "monster homes," "trophy homes", and so on (Lecesse 2003). Does this suite of criticisms of low- and high-end development regress toward a bourgeois design aesthetic and ideology – as some critics of contemporary land-scape architecture have argued? (Tigerman personal communication, ca.1988).

The argument here is that landscape architecture must make a fuller accounting of its works, one that reflects the significance of landscape in culture and nature. To paraphrase Mitchell, landscape *is* important, but not just for the fairly narrowly construed definitions of aesthetics that operate in both high and mainstream design.

The premium landscapes described by Clarke and the amenity landscapes described by Culbertson are built within a fairly narrow window of characteristics used to create identity (or brand) and marketing for landscape projects. Often the concept of community design centers on a golf course providing value not only for golf enthusiasts but homeowners who value the views into the golf landscape. Even communities designed under the constructs of "New Urbanism" do so within a very constrained design palette of typically "traditional" architecture derived from classic urban federal or rural agrarian styles, centered on small but typically national chain commercial enterprises. Coffee Creek, Indiana, an award winning planned community, has substituted a conservation reserve for the golf course, but it is still reliant on traditionally designed architecture. And, as already discussed, its prospective market of homebuyers is a small segment of the larger public (cf. Design for the Other 90% exhibition, http://www.peoplesdesignaward.org/design_for_the_other_90/; checked 1 June 2007).

Tony Bebbington in chapter 2 provides some clues about opportunities for expanding the constructs of community, and thus expanding the scope of potential design practice. Economic opportunity, or lack of it, is an instrument of freedom (Sen 1999). The inability to make a living in a particular location limits freedom, it limits choice. The 2005 Gulf Coast hurricanes have limited economic opportunities for many of the region's residents, differentially by race and class, while expanding opportunities for the engineering and construction sectors. Likewise, public investment and regulation of private investment creates and restricts opportunity. Can we as landscape architects envision working with communities centered not on retail commercialism but on other forms of livelihood including barter, cooperative ownership, and artisanal production (Hester 2006)? Can we envision clusters of homes that, regardless of exterior style, provide convenient shelter and access to resources for the full breadth of the economic community? If public investment is used to stimulate private investment, the idea is for the private sector to generate enough confidence in the future of the public realm to be willing to commit its resources. This is true for both institutional investors and individual residents, and it is true for both the wealthy and the poor.

Can communities build capital? Capital comes in at least three major forms: natural; financial; and human, social, and cultural (Bebbington 1999). Natural variation in the landscape leads to different opportunities for garnering resources. Whether rich agricultural land, or forested mountains, or areas less vulnerable to certain hazards, communities could be built that reflect those variations. Social capital is built by empowering community – its capabilities, meanings, and material well-being (Bebbington, chapter 2, Figure 4). In addition to front porches, what might the return of community gathering spots – for economic, political, and social exchange – accomplish? How might community-held equity in affordable housing enable a broader range of homeowners to capitalize on rising home values while maintaining access to the type of vibrant community use that builds cultural as well as human and social capital?

Landscapes of Struggle, Investment, and Institutional Change

The choices our communities make, public and private, affect the allocation of resources to and within them, and thereby shape and change the functions of their landscapes in profound ways. In this regard, the landscape is highly political. While landscape architects may see themselves as agents of visual change, they of course are also agents of social, economic, and environmental changes. To view a single work of landscape architecture as an entity into itself is to deny this larger realization. Several examples illuminate this point.

Pullman, Illinois is generally regarded as the first planned industrial community, or company town, in the USA. Built by George Pullman as a place for his workers to live in better physical conditions than were generally available in Chicago, the community provided modern technology such as interior plumbing, gas and water, fire protection, and access to light and air. Economically, Pullman's rationale was to attract a strong and contented labor force, thereby increasing productivity and reducing the risk of strike. The design by architect Solon Beman and landscape architect Nathan Barrett provided for locally produced materials (brick) and community space including lakes, parks, and promenades, along with accessible privately owned markets and other community elements. It included fire resistant building standards and land application of domestic wastewater. The deliberate creation of Pullman outside of the city of Chicago avoided the tax and political issues of the growing city, and ostensibly saved residents from the hazards of uncontrolled city environments. However, the entire enterprise was centrally managed and tightly controlled. While providing generous and healthy living environments, Pullman also deprived its residents of political power (Chicago Historical Society 1999). Ironically, the failure of Pullman to adjust rents in the face of declining wages during the depression of 1893–1894 led to a strike by Pullman employees that was joined by the National Railway Workers, creating a national strike broken by the deployment of Federal troops and the arrest of labor leaders.

Another irony is that the success of the community, from a living perspective, was tempered by complaints about its uniformity, the sameness of the housing, on the one hand, and the distinction in architecture between the working and management classes, on the other. Uniformity and distinction were both associated with authority in this experiment. Pullman differentiated housing according to employee (and thus) class divisions. Single-family detached homes were allocated to executives with English style town homes constructed for managers, and more modest homes for the workers. In other words, the premium landscapes constructed in Pullman were consistent with the arguments by Susan Clarke and others about emergent processes of urban design. In addition, the properties were owned by the company so there was no incentive for employees to invest in the community or build its social capital. On the other hand, Pullman did create extensive and public community spaces and what, at the time, would be considered amenities (e.g., indoor plumbing, gas, and water) for all.

Fast-forward a century to the *Groundswell* exhibition of contemporary landscape architecture at the Museum of Modern Art in New York City in 2005. As part of this exhibition of contemporary landscape architecture, keynote speaker and urban geographer David Harvey touched nerves by suggesting that the greening of abandoned industrial sites is not so much a progressive transformation of degraded sites as it is window dressing for environmentally and socially abusive industries that have exported production and pollution to other regions (Harvey 2005). He asks, "Where is the outrage?" rather than offering the self-congratulatory pat on the back for creating avant garde or pretty sites on what once was ugly. This argument bears detailed examination, and extension of contemporary landscape architecture from the USA and Europe to a truly global political and economic scale. This extension is beginning to happen with the expansion of international design practice in China, but critical discourse on that growth sector in the design industry is also warranted.

For millennia, differences in the landscape have offered differing opportunities for the livelihoods of its inhabitants. To be sure, landscape design modifications and inventions along with trade, transportation, and migration have appeared to level the playing field somewhat, allowing livelihoods to be made where lesser opportunities prevailed before. In fact, we value landscape as a bundle of its physical properties and the modifications made to it. In Illinois, the value of farmland is a bundle of its soil properties and the presence of drainage tile to make it farmable using conventional techniques. Of course, if some modifications add value, others take away value (cf. Berger [2007] on the linkage between landscape development and waste). The extraction of minerals may devalue a property not only because of the absence of additional supplies of the mineral, but because of additional, sometimes unintended consequences of the extraction process. The draining of farmland may improve the value of the land farmed, but contribute to flooding of other lands, potentially reducing opportunity to provide livelihoods elsewhere.

Reaction to the North American dust bowl of the 1930s started first with financial instruments used to guarantee mortgages, support crop prices, and provide the means to preserve the agricultural industry through the disaster. Financial instruments enabled people to stay in agriculture and thus had an effect on the landscape. But to the extent that the dust bowl was caused by human misfeasance in poor agricultural practices, these policies alone were insufficient to recover and prevent future occurrences. The creation of the Soil Conservation Service represented the approach of addressing the physical landscape impacts of the dust bowl by developing strategies and practices to restore productivity and prevent future erosion. Hedgerows, buffer strips, contouring and other practices are physical design elements that certainly shaped the rural landscape.

At an earlier time, during perhaps the peak of agricultural prosperity, the creation of model farms provided guidelines for designing the farm landscape with the intention of having Midwestern farms "fit the peculiar scenery, climate, soil, labor, and other conditions of the prairies, instead of copying literally the manners and materials of other regions" (Miller 1915). The "prairie style" dwelling promoted by Wilhelm Miller and others fused conservation of native vegetation, restoration of scenic values local to the region, and promotion of the social values of civic life and democracy.

To this day, the US Department of Agriculture continues the tradition of providing incentives for conservation of soil, water, and other land resources, e.g., through the Conservation Reserve Program and the Wetlands Reserve Program, which shape landscape architectural practice in suburbanizing as well as rural areas (cf. Nassauer and Wascher, chapter 8 in this volume). Under the Conservation Reserve Program, agricultural producers receive monetary rent payments and cost-sharing for placing erodible or other sensitive lands into easements employing conservation practices such as native plantings, tree cover, riparian buffer strips, etc. (USDA 1997). The Wetland Reserve Program is similar in nature, with the objective of protecting, restoring, or enhancing wetlands on their property (USDA 2004).

With approximately 40% of the US land area in farmland, the impact of farm policy on the landscape is enormous. The USA has about 938 million acres in farmland with about half in croplands. At the same time, approximately 32.7 million acres were enrolled in either the CRP or WRP. Approximately 23% of farmland is enrolled in federal or other crop insurance programs (USDA 2002). Very little of the agricultural landscape is directly affected by physical design efforts, while the effects of a change in price supports for a particular crop, or policy toward an agricultural product (such as ethanol) on the physical form and condition of the landscape can be huge.

The Federal Government has likewise intervened in urban, suburban, and rural housing policy and markets for over 50 years by subsidizing mortgages below private market rates or by reducing the risk to lenders by backing enterprises (such as Fannie-Mac and Freddy-Mac) that provide funding for loans.

> The dominant position of Fannie Mae and Freddie Mac … stems largely from their special relationship to the Federal government, which has contributed to a perception among investors that the government will take any action necessary to prevent either Enterprise from defaulting on its obligations. (US Office of Federal Housing Enterprise Oversight, 2000)

While the US federal government does not directly insure lenders from default on mortgages, it does so through specific policy directions such as through the Veterans Administration loan guarantee and Affordable Housing initiatives that shape the context and scale of residential landscape design.

Technology, predominately information technology, has also affected the housing market by reducing transaction costs of mortgage management (origination, assumption of risk, loan servicing) (Office of Federal Housing Enterprise Oversight 2000). Automation, intercommunications lead to economies of scale and thus consolidation in the marketplace. The internet is increasingly being used to originate home mortgages, reducing labor costs, etc., further. The financial landscape constructed by government institutions is one that is highly regulated to dampen the effects of local or broad disturbances to the marketplace (ebbs and flows in economic sectors, local or regional disasters, etc.) and to maintain stability in the broader trends of a culture.

Globalization, the extension of economic production elements and markets independent of regional or national political boundaries, is clearly growing in the world's economy. Historically, we have thought of economic activity as being localized or regionalized endeavors, e.g., centers of production (agriculture, steel, or distribution) organized according to spatial geographies of proximity and access. Communities plan in order to have the physical resources needed for economic production (available land, access to transportation) as well as the human resources (a trained and available workforce, good schools, affordable housing) ready to meet economic development opportunity.

On the face of it, the decentralization of economic production would seem to call into question almost 100 years of zoning and other efforts when a community may not expect to package a full ensemble of land uses to support a particular industry or economic sector. Some would argue that globalization, supported by information technology, supports a highly spatially fragmented network not dependent on a particular geography (except for production of raw materials). Technology indeed allows spatial expansion of the relationship between economic agents, e.g., think of the impact the invention of the telephone had on communications between, for example, suppliers and customers. A more important driver or regulator of globalization is the financial market, one that may well dominate the effects of any public actors or institutions (Babcock-Lumish and Clark, chapter 7). Cities like Chicago are important as centers of financial exchange, though clearly subordinate to the global centers of London, New York, and Tokyo.

The growth of financial instruments over the last 30 or 40 years and investment in financial resources allows the consolidation of capital and its investment in very large enterprises. Communities are not built house by house or subdivision by subdivision, but in many instances in a "wholesale" manner. The private capital available so largely dwarfs available public investment as to render the public sector to a supporting role, at best, in shaping the landscape. The public works of "stars" such as Robert Moses whose financial resources could shape a city appear to be diminished, if not extinguished.

There are exceptions, however. Portland, Oregon's investment in light rail systems and other mass transit and environmental improvement have led to a demographic shift of densification within the city, while Chicago's greening of the city (both physically and environmentally) is intended to draw investment and improve the well-being of its residents. Urban rents surrounding Chicago's new Millennium Park have skyrocketed. Nonetheless, the magnitude of public financial investment is dwarfed by private resources. In fact, increasingly larger portions of public resources are being allocated away from civic infrastructure and economic development to welfare services. It could be argued that even the efforts of Portland and Chicago are simply localized efforts having more to do with cities trying to develop some competitive advantage in a changing marketplace – but that, in fact, is exactly the kind of situation that provides fertile ground for design practice.

What do these changing markets imply for landscape architecture? One can see at least two sides to this story. With public sector investment in the physical environment on the decline in the face of increasing demands from other sectors, and that investment itself being dwarfed by private investment, one might conclude that opportunities for practice would be on the decline as far as public investment is concerned. One must realize however, that the financial landscape is as variable and differentiated as the physical landscape, and opportunities in the financial market are differentiated by variations in risk. As Babcock-Lumish and Clark point out in chapter 7, modern portfolio practice calls for highly diverse investments, that is, for distributing investments among many opportunities as a way of managing risk. Changes in perception of financial risk can lead to rapid shifts in investments as no investor is wholly vested in those assets. This in- and out-migration has, of course, an analogy in residential decision-making. Neighborhoods that have the perception of value (parks, schools) attract investment while other neighborhoods become stigmatized and see outward migration. A major difference between these situations is that in residential markets, homeowners are vested in the property to a much greater extent (emotionally, as well as financially), and the exchange of assets through buying, selling, and moving between homes makes inertia a much stronger element. But if these transactions happen readily in the residential market, imagine the shifts in financial resources possible when a local investment is just a small fraction of the total portfolio. Ownership of assets may change repeatedly, and frequently, and investments may flow into and out of a particular region with great rapidity.

Outside of the housing market, other financial instruments have been developed including Real Estate Investment Trusts (REITs). REIT's purchase and operate properties using capital assets provided by investors. REIT's open access to the commercial real estate market to average investors in a manner similar to mutual funds, but income is generated as a regulated portion of trust income plus trust price fluctuations. Of course, the management objectives of any given trust's managers will influence their impact on the landscape. Consider the following claims:

> We continue to meet or exceed the growth of our peers. We've accomplished this success with hard work, dedication and vision. We continually seek ways to improve each commercial and neighborhood property for our residents while ensuring strength in sales and occupancy. Desirable locations, quality construction materials, accompanied with care for the environment and the beauty of our property settings help us to set the standard in our industry (IRET accessed 12/20/05).

If people find value in "open space", if developers are increasingly (re)using open space to differentiate market offerings, and if "traditional" development is truly something the market seeks, then the design professions can provide it. But consumers/residents are savvy consumers, and while they may buy into something because it is cleverly marketed; if it doesn't deliver, the market moves on.

Once again, however, the financial landscape is as differentiated as the geographic landscape. Opportunities and risk varies from location to location based on physical, political, or perceptual variation. Rather than leading development in communities, local governments are in the position of attempting to attract development through differentiation.

Thus, a polluted landscape diminishes its value because it limits its productive potential. Remove the pollutant, and the value of that landscape increases. In another example of the direct and indirect connections within the landscape, empirical studies suggest that environmentally degraded sites suppress values beyond the degraded areas themselves (Braden et al. 2004). The authors argue that the real estate market in Waukegan, Illinois is suppressed by even distant pollution in the harbor, that is, areas not directly affected by the pollution still feel the effects due to the perception of risk (physical or financial) associated with the region. These results suggest powerful economic incentives to the community for environmental improvements in the landscape. It does not require a great leap of imagination to believe that other markets in the region are similarly affected.

In the case of Waukegan harbor, it is in the public's financial interests to remediate the harbor pollution in order to realize an increase in property tax revenue from increased valuation. In the case of flood mitigation, increased off-site benefits may provide the mechanism for financial incentives to private developers to incorporate conservation practices. There is still room for win-win situations.

Of course, in our interconnected system, there are potential risks. The degraded environment may provide affordable land for lower income persons, and by improving the conditions, make the land attractive to those who can outbid existing residents, resulting in ecological gentrification.

Communities historically defined in spatial terms of neighborhood, or uniform cultural enclaves have expanded to include other communities (e.g., through trust or practice) enabled in no small part by telecommunications and computing technologies in which individuals are able to create and maintain relationships (business, political, personal) without having to meet someone in a particular space. As has been pointed out numerous times, we still use spatial constructs to navigate through these communities (chat rooms, etc.). While these emerging modes and landscapes of community building are gaining legitimacy (one need only to review on-line purchase habits), many segments of community are resisting this trend. One such community may well be the real estate development market. In casual observation one notes that in development projects, actors (financiers, builders, managers, agents and others) work in close, enduring relation to one another (cf. Babcock-Lumish and Clark, Chapter 7). The community of trust is a risk management strategy developed by historic patterns of success, and quite likely close personal accountability (a commercial aristocracy?). The nature of the community makes it resistant to change as change would increase uncertainty and the perception of risk. Innovation may mainly occur from within, based on that personal trust, and external innovation may be slow in adoption (until well after it has began to prove its value).

The enlarged understanding of the myriad forces driving landscape change would not be complete without further consideration of the role of institutions as a means of initiating, or mediating landscape change. While some change is induced directly through the initiatives or policies of an institution or organization, it is abundantly clear that a large number of initiatives and policies are usually present in the course of landscape transformations. These institutional forces operate at many scales and with varying levels of direct involvement. As we have seen, the growth of the financial institution enables development far beyond the physical reach of the institution by providing highly mobile capital for landscape investment. We also see that investment having a range of spatial interconnections as well. The allocation of water resources in the west, and the seemingly countless institutional instruments that have been constructed to mediate use of water, is but one example.

The very nature of the interconnections among the actors, and actions, indicate the complexity of this situation. The impact of urbanization on hydrologic systems is a well known example. Managing such impacts when they cross property and jurisdictional boundaries frequently encounter manifold barriers to a comprehensive response. Consider the watershed of Blackberry Creek discussed by Johnston and Braden. The stream is affected by land use policies and actions distributed among private and public bodies, spanning several incorporated municipalities, each with its own zoning and storm water regulations (as well as differing objectives), set within the planning and regulatory authority of the county, with administrative and regulatory controls at the state and national level, including Soil and Water Conservation Districts, or EPA Non-Point Source Pollution Standards. And those are just the direct impacts. Add the indirect effects of tax laws, agricultural subsidies, and foreign policy. As Aldo Leopold wrote "The water must be confused by so much advice" (Leopold 1949).

As discussed by Tom Evans, Abigail York, and Elinor Ostrom in chapter 5, a common response to this complexity has been through consolidation of authority or action in the form of centralized or universal policies. Consolidation reduces conflicting regulations (e.g., landscape ordinances or storm water management), promotes equity, provides economies of scale, and reduces variance.

However, it is not clear that this approach always results in the intended outcome. Evans et al. cite several examples where consolidation resulted in poorer service provision than the highly disaggregated predecessor institution. While police service provision may seem somewhat detached from landscape architecture, the lesson is instructive. In response to rising concerns toward adequate provision of police protection in the face of rising crime rates, consolidation of police forces was enacted to reduce duplicity and jurisdictional overlap among agencies. This might make sense if the police were solely responsible (and effective) for maintaining law and order. The reality, however, is that law and order are produced by a community of actors including local citizens, social organizations, and government institutions. Consolidation of police services often had the effect of breaking the bonds between these community members, resulting in less effective police services.

While creating economies of scale might make sense in some contexts, the landscape may not be one of them. It seems clear that landscape change operates on many spatial and temporal scales. The landscape involves individual and institutional actors, is constructed by builders, designers, policy makers, and is built and rebuilt in continuous action. It is affected by local action and by actions taken in distant locales. To suggest a single or simple mechanism for managing landscape change seems ill-informed and counter-effective. These complex interactions indicate that landscapes are produced by communities, not the institutions, but institutional complexity serves an important role mediating the web of transactions leading to landscape change.

Landscapes of Possibility: The Integrative Power of Design

To pursue the visual theme introduced above – How can a socially just, environmentally healthy, economically prosperous landscape be envisioned and pursued? The point of this question is not simply to visualize the form of such a place, but to learn to understand the landscape along a spectrum of dimensions: its history, economics, social networks, demographics, and so on, and to view the work of landscape architects from the perspectives afforded by these dimensions. Satisfaction of core, albeit complex, values is the goal. Decent housing, opportunities for livelihoods, healthy ecosystems, places to assemble and speak in communities. Are these not at the core?

The chapters presented in this book have examined facets of landscape change using a variety of frameworks, and reflecting a rereading of the landscape that focuses not so much on what a landscape looks like as on understanding how it is produced, defined, and recreated in response to changing political, economic, technological, and other forces. This approach recognizes the role that variations in landscape, whether by their inherent nature or by our production efforts, have a reciprocal role in creating political and economic change.

In large part, the practice of landscape architecture appears to have followed the "trickle down" principle. Working with the higher ends of the economic spectrum of society is assumed to allow innovations to work their way through a culture, eventually reaching all. The higher ends of the economic spectrum tend to garner the largest assets and are thus empowered to initiate the most substantial changes in the landscape. At the same time, economic and political groups also pursue distinction, which drives and complicates the diffusion of landscape innovations. It is suggested here, therefore, that pursuit of other models may prove important in sustaining fundamental professional design opportunities and aspirations.

What can we conclude about processes of landscape change? First, it is important to acknowledge that landscapes do not just happen – they are produced, consumed, wasted, conserved, adapted, and transformed. Landscapes are created to address problems of production, distribution, perceived security, lack of amenities, or maintenance of class or other distinctions. Premium landscapes may be a product of innovation as in transit-oriented design, or ecologically sensitive design that includes people, but they may also be a product of differentiation, a partitioning of available resources as well as security and amenities that fosters exclusion.

Second, while it is widely acknowledged that landscapes are politically contested, their political structures, dynamics and reception are less well understood. Differentiation in landscape resources changes the ability of people to pursue livelihoods. The frequent complaint that skateboarding damages parks is a perhaps trivial example of a power contest between largely teenage skateboarders and other largely adult segments of society. Environmental racism and injustice in facility siting is a weighty concern, from the local to global scales. Suburbanization, gentrification, and other processes of co-opting emergent landscapes can constrain the ability of existing residents to continue or improve their own livelihoods.

Third, landscapes are interconnected. They have connections in the environment that lead to upstream–downstream problems that cascade in turn into economic and political consequences. They are connected through social values as when the relative attractiveness of one location removes value from another. They are connected by political action. Allocation of public funds for barge shipping in the Midwestern USA affects the vast agricultural landscape not only in the Midwest, for example, but arguably internationally as well.

Fourth, because human-environment problems change, the viability or value or landscapes also change. Forces that historically have shaped a landscape may diminish, leaving only their traces. In some instances, the landscape may be abandoned, until some other function is identified. In other instances the landscape may be adapted to those changing circumstances.

It is this last notion that perhaps is most illustrative of the landscape of possibility. The landscape architecture profession was deeply influenced (if not transformed) by the environmental movement of the 1960s and 1970s. Curricula were greatly modified while new guiding principles replaced old ones. Opportunities for design practice expanded to include environmental restoration and sustainable design. While we are still learning how to understand the environmental impacts of landscape design, principles of ecology including diversification, redundancy, and systems perspectives have become embedded in our thinking and action. The authors in this book may argue that just as environmental issues affected the profession, and the profession changed to better respond to those issues, so might the profession respond in the future to deeper understanding of the dynamics of political and economic forces for future design.

The landscape architect is not a principal driver of political and economic forces that effect landscape change, nor, by the same token, is the landscape architect separate from the communities shaped by those forces. While the executives of a public pension plan in Oregon may enable the creation of a residential community in the mountains of North Carolina through their investment in an REIT, all are conducted in the context of community – communities of practice and trust. The investors trust in the objectives and performance of the REIT, and the REIT trusts in the security and stability of the investors. The REIT also trusts in the objectives and performance of the local developers, designers, and contractors. The developers trust in the consistency of rules and regulations mediating development options, and local communities trust that the rules and regulations will manage local public/private, upstream/downstream, and temporal interactions. Communication, information, and their effect on the perception of risk mediates the endeavor.

In this light, opportunities for participation are abundant. What is clear is that diverse institutional and professional instruments are needed to manage landscape change. Local knowledge contributing to effective negotiation between local and global forces, participation in state and federal regulatory and incentive programs, participation of communities of practice, and trust all can have profound effects on the shape and nature of the landscape.

The Landscape Futures Initiative of the Landscape Architecture Foundation enabled this collection of perspectives on the role of political and economic forces on landscape change. While of course this is an extremely complex and interconnected subject, a prevailing theme emerges. What we have learned from the conference, and the papers presented in this collection, is that the variety of instruments of landscape change is continuing to increase. Financial institutions may garner the resources for landscape change that make cities (and many nations) capital budgets pale in comparison, but this simply suggests that roles are changing, not the state of affairs. Rather than looking to public agencies to drive capital development, public institutions may reshape their communities through environmental improvement, cultural opportunity, and other physical and intellectual transformations that in turn shape larger economic and political opportunities. While individual resources are increasingly pooled into larger institutional bodies, investment decisions are still being made by a relatively small number of (often local) participants.

The role of the landscape in political processes is underestimated. Access to or separation from landscape resources (including raw materials, environmental quality, or physical risk), affect the livelihoods of people and therefore their empowerment and freedom. Protest is one instrument of change that, in some forms, depends on the public landscape as a forum for expression, but the studies in this volume showed that local institutions (NGOs, community groups, or local government bodies) also provide mechanisms of change through their ability not to drive change but to steer larger institutional drivers of landscape change.

For both the researcher and designer, we see expansive possibilities for enriching the roles of landscape architecture in community formation and vitality. When responding to future landscape change, therefore, landscape architects must generate creative alternatives to emerging questions, such as:

- What purposeful landscape transformations can increase all citizen's abilities to maintain or enrich their livelihoods?
- What alternatives to authentic security are available beyond physical barriers and surveillance techniques?
- What models of community are available beyond Neo-traditional, Golf Course, and Second-home Amenity landscapes?
- What institutions (public, private, quasi-public) can be created to serve as steering resources for the investment of capital resources in sustainable landscape change?
- And in which communities of practice and trust must landscape architects involve themselves and help create in order to influence progressive landscape change that expands opportunity and broadens the range of choice?

The answers to such questions – expressed in the built environment as well as the academy – can demonstrate the integrative power of landscape and landscape architecture in contexts of political and economic change.

References

Bebbington A (1999) Capitals and capabilities: a framework for analysing peasant viability, rural livelihoods and poverty. *World Development* 27(12): 2021–2044

Berger A (2007) *Drosscape: Wasting Land in Urban America*. Princeton Architectural Press, New York

Braden JB, Patunru AA, Chattopadhyay S, and Mays N (2004) Contaminant cleanup in the Waukegan harbor area of concern: homeowner attitudes and economic benefits. *Journal of Great Lakes Research* 30(4): 474–491

Chicago Historical Society (1999) The Pullman Era. www.chicagohs.org/history/pullman.html

Cole Thomas (1836) Essay on American Scenery. *The American Monthly Magazine*. January, 1836

Glasmeier AK (2005) *An Atlas of Poverty in America: One Nation, Pulling Apart, 1960–2003*. The Pennsylvania State University, University Park, PA

Harris D and Ruggles DF (2007) *Sites Unseen: Landscape and Vision*. University of Pittsburgh Press, Pittsburgh, PA

Harvey D (2005) Where is the Outrage? *The Newsletter of the Architectural League of New York*. Summer, pp 4–7

Helphand K (1999) Leaping the property line: observations on recent American garden history. In Conan M (ed) *Perspectives on Garden Histories.*, pp 137–159. Dumbarton Oaks, Washington, DC

Helphand K (2006) *Defiant Gardens: Making Gardens in Wartime*. Trinity University Press, San Antonio, TX

Hester R (2006) *Design for Ecological Democracy*. MIT Press, Cambridge, MA

Hough M (1992) *Out of Place: Restoring Identity to the Regional Landscape*. Yale University Press, New Haven, CT

Hunt JD (2000) *Greater Perfections: The Practice of Garden Theory*. University of Pennsylvania Press, Philadelphia, PA

Investors Real Estate Trust (2005) http://www.iret.com, accessed 12/20/05

Kirk N (2004) Perceptions of Ideal Residential Environments presented in the symposium "Lawn, Gate, House: Construction of the Spirit of Residential Identity" at EDRA35/2004, Albuquerque, New Mexico

Landscape Architecture Foundation (2002) Landscape Futures Initiative http://www.lafoundation. org/Futures.htm, accessed 12/2005

Lecesse M (2003) No shrinking columbine: a trophy house in the Colorado Rockies attempts to blend in while standing out. *Landscape Architecture* 83(11): 84–89

Leopold A (1949) Illinois bus ride. In *A Sand County Almanac*, pp 117–119. Oxford University, New York

Lewis P (1979) Axioms for reading the landscape. Some guides to the American scene. In Meinig D (ed) *The Interpretation of Ordinary Landscapes*, pp 11–32. Oxford University Press, New York

NIPC (Northeastern Illinois Planning Commission) (2005) *Realizing the Vision: 2040 Regional Framework Plan*. NIPC, Chicago, IL

Prairie Crossing (2005) New Condominiums at Prairie Crossing http://www.prairiecrossing.com/pc/site/homes/index.html, accessed 9/5/2005

Ranney G (2004) Chicago Metropolis 2020: An Example of Political and Economic Driving Forces. Presentation at the LAF Places of Power conference. Chicago, IL

Ruggles DF (2000) *Gardens, Landscape and Vision in the Palaces of Islamic Spain*. Penn State University Press, University Park, PA

Seaside Florida (2005) Real Estate Listings http://www.seasidefl.com/realEstateListingsDetails.asp?currentPage=1&salesId=1116, accessed 9/5/2005

Sen A (1999) *Development as Freedom*. Oxford University Press, New York

Schwartz M (2004) Can America Go Public? Interview with Deborah Solomon, *New York Times Magazine*, May 16: 19

Tigerman S (~1988) Personal communication to Wescoat on the bourgeois ethos of contemporary landscape architecture, Chicago, IL

Thompson W (2003) Land matters. In *Landscape Architecture*, October, 2003

USDA Farm Service Agency (1997) *Conservation Reserve Program Fact Sheet*. USDA, Washington, DC

USDA (2002) *2002 Census of Agriculture - Volume 1 Geographic Area Series Census, US - State Data*. US Department of Agriculture, Washington, DC

USDA Natural Resources Conservation Service (2004) *Farm Bill 2002: Wetlands Reserve Program*. WRP Fact Sheet, September, 2004

U.S. Office of Federal Housing Enterprise Oversight (2000) *2000 Report to Congress*. US OFHEO, Washington DC

Watts May (1957) *Reading the Landscape of America*, revised edition. 1975, Macmillan, New York

Wescoat JL Jr, and Wolschke-Bulmahn J (eds) (1996) *Mughal Gardens: Sources, Places, Representations, and Prospects*. Dumbarton Oaks, Washington, DC

Index

The GeoJournal Library

21. V.I. Ilyichev and V.V. Anikiev (eds.): *Oceanic and Anthropogenic Controls of Life in the Pacific Ocean.* 1992
ISBN 0-7923-1854-4
22. A.K. Dutt and F.J. Costa (eds.): *Perspectives on Planning and Urban Development in Belgium.* 1992
ISBN 0-7923-1885-4
23. J. Portugali: *Implicate Relations.* Society and Space in the Israeli-Palestinian Conflict. 1993
ISBN 0-7923-1886-2
24. M.J.C. de Lepper, H.J. Scholten and R.M. Stern (eds.): *The Added Value of Geographical Information Systems in Public and Environmental Health.* 1995
ISBN 0-7923-1887-0
25. J.P. Dorian, P.A. Minakir and V.T. Borisovich (eds.): *CIS Energy and Minerals Development.* Prospects, Problems and Opportunities for International Cooperation. 1993
ISBN 0-7923-2323-8
26. P.P. Wong (ed.): *Tourism vs Environment: The Case for Coastal Areas.* 1993
ISBN 0-7923-2404-8
27. G.B. Benko and U. Strohmayer (eds.): *Geography, History and Social Sciences.* 1995
ISBN 0-7923-2543-5
28. A. Faludi and A. der Valk: *Rule and Order. Dutch Planning Doctrine in the Twentieth Century.* 1994
ISBN 0-7923-2619-9
29. B.C. Hewitson and R.G. Crane (eds.): *Neural Nets: Applications in Geography.* 1994
ISBN 0-7923-2746-2
30. A.K. Dutt, F.J. Costa, S. Aggarwal and A.G. Noble (eds.): *The Asian City: Processes of Development, Characteristics and Planning.* 1994
ISBN 0-7923-3135-4
31. R. Laulajainen and H.A. Stafford: *Corporate Geography. Business Location Principles and Cases.* 1995
ISBN 0-7923-3326-8
32. J. Portugali (ed.): *The Construction of Cognitive Maps.* 1996
ISBN 0-7923-3949-5
33. E. Biagini: *Northern Ireland and Beyond.* Social and Geographical Issues. 1996
ISBN 0-7923-4046-9
34. A.K. Dutt (ed.): *Southeast Asia: A Ten Nation Region.* 1996
ISBN 0-7923-4171-6
35. J. Settele, C. Margules, P. Poschlod and K. Henle (eds.): *Species Survival in Fragmented Landscapes.* 1996
ISBN 0-7923-4239-9
36. M. Yoshino, M. Domrös, A. Douguédroit, J. Paszynski and L.D. Nkemdirim (eds.): *Climates and Societies − A Climatological Perspective.* A Contribution on Global Change and Related Problems Prepared by the Commission on Climatology of the International Geographical Union. 1997
ISBN 0-7923-4324-7
37. D. Borri, A. Khakee and C. Lacirignola (eds.): *Evaluating Theory-Practice and Urban-Rural Interplay in Planning.* 1997
ISBN 0-7923-4326-3
38. J.A.A. Jones, C. Liu, M-K.Woo and H-T. Kung (eds.): *Regional Hydrological Response to Climate Change.* 1996
ISBN 0-7923-4329-8
39. R. Lloyd: *Spatial Cognition.* Geographic Environments. 1997
ISBN 0-7923-4375-1
40. I. Lyons Murphy: *The Danube: A River Basin in Transition.* 1997
ISBN 0-7923-4558-4
41. H.J. Bruins and H. Lithwick (eds.): *The Arid Frontier.* Interactive Management of Environment and Development. 1998
ISBN 0-7923-4227-5
42. G. Lipshitz: *Country on the Move: Migration to and within Israel, 1948−1995.* 1998
ISBN 0-7923-4850-8
43. S. Musterd, W. Ostendorf and M. Breebaart: *Multi-Ethnic Metropolis: Patterns and Policies.* 1998
ISBN 0-7923-4854-0
44. B.K. Maloney (ed.): *Human Activities and the Tropical Rainforest.* Past, Present and Possible Future. 1998
ISBN 0-7923-4858-3

The GeoJournal Library

45. H. van der Wusten (ed.): *The Urban University and its Identity*. Roots, Location, Roles. 1998   ISBN 0-7923-4870-2
46. J. Kalvoda and C.L. Rosenfeld (eds.): *Geomorphological Hazards in High Mountain Areas*. 1998   ISBN 0-7923-4961-X
47. N. Lichfield, A. Barbanente, D. Borri, A. Khakee and A. Prat (eds.): *Evaluation in Planning*. Facing the Challenge of Complexity. 1998   ISBN 0-7923-4870-2
48. A. Buttimer and L. Wallin (eds.): *Nature and Identity in Cross-Cultural Perspective*. 1999   ISBN 0-7923-5651-9
49. A. Vallega: *Fundamentals of Integrated Coastal Management*. 1999
                                                            ISBN 0-7923-5875-9
50. D. Rumley: *The Geopolitics of Australia's Regional Relations*. 1999
                                                            ISBN 0-7923-5916-X
51. H. Stevens: *The Institutional Position of Seaports*. An International Comparison. 1999
                                                            ISBN 0-7923-5979-8
52. H. Lithwick and Y. Gradus (eds.): *Developing Frontier Cities*. Global Perspectives– Regional Contexts. 2000   ISBN 0-7923-6061-3
53. H. Knippenberg and J. Markusse (eds.): *Nationalising and Denationalising European Border Regions, 1800–2000*. Views from Geography and History. 2000
    ISBN 0-7923-6066-4
54. R. Gerber and G.K. Chuan (eds.): *Fieldwork in Geography: Reflections, Perspectives and Actions*. 2000   ISBN 0-7923-6329-9
55. M. Dobry (ed.): *Democratic and Capitalist Transitions in Eastern Europe*. Lessons for the Social Sciences. 2000   ISBN 0-7923-6331-0
56. Y. Murayama: *Japanese Urban System*. 2000   ISBN 0-7923-6600-X
57. D. Zheng, Q. Zhang and S. Wu (eds.): *Mountain Geoecology and Sustainable Development of the Tibetan Plateau*. 2000   ISBN 0-7923-6688-3
58. A.J. Conacher (ed.): *Land Degradation*. Papers selected from Contributions to the Sixth Meeting of the International Geographical Union's Commission on Land Degradation and Desertification, Perth, Western Australia, 20–28 September 1999. 2001
                                                            ISBN 0-7923-6770-7
59. S. Conti and P. Giaccaria: *Local Development and Competitiveness*. 2001
    ISBN 0-7923-6829-0
60. P. Miao (ed.): *Public Places in Asia Pacific Cities*. Current Issues and Strategies. 2001   ISBN 0-7923-7083-X
61. N. Maiellaro (ed.): *Towards Sustainable Buiding*. 2001   ISBN 1-4020-0012-X
62. G.S. Dunbar (ed.): *Geography: Discipline, Profession and Subject since 1870*. An International Survey. 2001   ISBN 1-4020-0019-7
63. J. Stillwell and H.J. Scholten (eds.): *Land Use Simulation for Europe*. 2001
                                                            ISBN 1-4020-0213-0
64. P. Doyle and M.R. Bennett (eds.): *Fields of Battle*. Terrain in Military History. 2002
                                                            ISBN 1-4020-0433-8
65. C.M. Hall and A.M. Williams (eds.): *Tourism and Migration*. NewRelationships between Production and Consumption. 2002   ISBN 1-4020-0454-0
66. I.R. Bowler, C.R. Bryant and C. Cocklin (eds.): *The Sustainability of Rural Systems*. Geographical Interpretations. 2002   ISBN 1-4020-0513-X
67. O. Yiftachel, J. Little, D. Hedgcock and I. Alexander (eds.): *The Power of Planning*. Spaces of Control and Transformation. 2001   ISBN Hb; 1-4020-0533-4
                                                            ISBN Pb; 1-4020-0534-2

The GeoJournal Library

68. K. Hewitt, M.-L. Byrne, M. English and G. Young (eds.): *Landscapes of Transition.* Landform Assemblages and Transformations in Cold Regions. 2002
ISBN 1-4020-0663-2
69. M. Romanos and C. Auffrey (eds.): *Managing Intermediate Size Cities.* Sustainable Development in a Growth Region of Thailand. 2002   ISBN 1-4020-0818-X
70. B. Boots, A. Okabe and R. Thomas (eds.): *Modelling Geographical Systems.* Statistical and Computational Applications. 2003   ISBN 1-4020-0821-X
71. R. Gerber and M. Williams (eds.): *Geography, Culture and Education.* 2002
ISBN 1-4020-0878-3
72. D. Felsenstein, E.W. Schamp and A. Shachar (eds.): *Emerging Nodes in the Global Economy: Frankfurt and Tel Aviv Compared.* 2002   ISBN 1-4020-0924-0
73. R. Gerber (ed.): *International Handbook on Geographical Education.* 2003
ISBN 1-4020-1019-2
74. M. de Jong, K. Lalenis and V. Mamadouh (eds.): *The Theory and Practice of Institutional Transplantation.* Experiences with the Transfer of Policy Institutions. 2002
ISBN 1-4020-1049-4
75. A.K. Dutt, A.G. Noble, G. Venugopal and S. Subbiah (eds.): *Challenges to Asian Urbanization in the 21st Century.* 2003   ISBN 1-4020-1576-3
76. I. Baud, J. Post and C. Furedy (eds.): *Solid Waste Management and Recycling.* Actors, Partnerships and Policies in Hyderabad, India and Nairobi, Kenya. 2004
ISBN 1-4020-1975-0
77. A. Bailly and L.J. Gibson (eds.): *Applied Geography.* A World Perspective. 2004
ISBN 1-4020-2441-X
78. H.D. Smith (ed.): *The Oceans: Key Issues in Marine Affairs.* 2004
ISBN 1-4020-2746-X
79. M. Ramutsindela: *Parks and People in Postcolonial Societies.* Experiences in Southern Africa. 2004   ISBN 1-4020-2542-4
80. R.A. Boschma and R.C. Kloosterman (eds.): *Learning from Clusters.* A Critical Assessment from an Economic-Geographical Perspective. 2005
ISBN 1-4020-3671-X
81. G. Humphrys and M. Williams (eds.): *Presenting and Representing Environments.* 2005   ISBN 1-4020-3813-5
82. D. Rumley, V.L. Forbes and C. Griffin (eds.): *Australia's Arc of Instability.* The Political and Cultural Dynamics of Regional Security. 2006   ISBN 1-4020-3825-9
83. R. Schneider-Sliwa (ed.): *Cities in Transition.* Globalization, Political Change and Urban Development. 2006   ISBN 1-4020-3866-6
84. B.G.V. Robert (ed.): *Dynamic Trip Modelling.* From Shopping Centres to the Internet Series. 2006   ISBN: 1-4020-4345-7
85. L. John and W. Michael (eds.): *Geographical Education in a Changing World.* Past Experience, Current Trends and Future Challenges Series. 2006
ISBN 1-4020-4806-8
86. G.D. Jay and R. Neil (eds.): *Enterprising Worlds.* A Geographic Perspective on Economics, Environments & Ethics Series. 2007   ISBN 1-4020-5225-1
87. Y.K.W. Albert and H.G. Brent (eds.): *Spatial Database Systems.* Design, Implementation and Project Management Series. 2006   ISBN 1-4020-5391-6
88. H.J. Miller (ed.): *Societies and Cities in the Age of Instant Access.* 2007.
ISBN 978-1-4020-5426-6
89. J.L. Wescoat, Jr. and D.M. Johnston (eds.): *Political Economies of Landscape Change.* Places of Integrative Power. 2008   ISBN 978-1-4020-5848-6

The GeoJournal Library

90. E. Koomen, J. Stillwell, A. Bakema and H.J. Scholten (eds.): *Modelling Land-Use Change*. Progress and Applications. 2007   ISBN 978-1-4020-5647-5
91. E.Razin, M.Dijst and C.Vázquez (eds.): *Employment Deconcentration in European Metropolitan Areas*. Market Forces versus Planning Regulations. 2007
ISBN 978-1-4020-5761-8